THE FRENCH CULINARY INST

SALUTE TO

HEALTHY
COOKING

THE FRENCH CULINARY INSTITUTE'S
SALUTE TO
HEALTHY COOKING
from AMERICA'S FOREMOST FRENCH CHEFS

BY ALAIN SAILHAC, JACQUES PÉPIN, ANDRÉ SOLTNER, JACQUES TORRES,
AND THE FACULTY OF THE FRENCH CULINARY INSTITUTE

Food Photography by Maria Robledo

RODALE

Printed in the United States of America
Rodale Inc. makes every effort to use acid-free ∞, recycled paper ♲

Interior Designer: Debra Sfetsios
Cover Designers: Lynn N. Gano, Debra Sfetsios
Cover Photographers: Bodi (Chefs), Maria Robledo (Food)
Interior Photographers: Maria Robledo (Food), Matthew Septimus (French Culinary Institute)
Interior Illustrator: Jacques Pépin

Library of Congress Cataloging-in-Publication Data

The French Culinary Institute's salute to healthy cooking : from
    America's foremost French chefs / food photography by Maria Robledo.
        p.   cm.
    Includes index.
    ISBN 0–87596–440–0 hardcover
    ISBN 1–57954–468–1 paperback
  1. Cookery, French.   I. French Culinary Institute (New York, N.Y.)
    TX719.F796   1998
    641.5944—dc21   97–48758

Distributed to the book trade by St. Martin's Press

2 4 6 8 10 9 7 5 3 1 hardcover
2 4 6 8 10 9 7 5 3 1 paperback

Visit us on the Web at www.rodalestore.com, or call us toll-free at (800) 848-4735.

RODALE
WE INSPIRE AND ENABLE PEOPLE TO IMPROVE
THEIR LIVES AND THE WORLD AROUND THEM

To
JOHN R. CANN
and
DOUGLAS A. P. HAMILTON,
without whom
FCI would
not be where
it is today

In all Rodale cookbooks, our mission is to provide
delicious and nutritious recipes. Our recipes also
meet the standards of the Rodale Test Kitchen for
dependability, ease, practicality, and, most of all, great
taste. To give us your comments, call (800) 848-4735.

CONTENTS

ACKNOWLEDGMENTS

This book could not have been accomplished without the artistry and support of our colleagues at The French Culinary Institute, most particularly, Chefs Dieter Schorner, Victoria Wells, and Susan Lifrieri.

Many thanks to Leah Stewart, assistant to the deans at The French Culinary Institute. Her friendship, loyalty, and skill do not go unnoticed.

Commendations to Laura Pensiero, R.D., graduate of The French Culinary Institute, whose recipe testing and nutritional analyses kept us ever alert to health-conscious dining. Her expertise is much appreciated.

Gratitude to Judith Choate, who shaped our words, thoughts, intentions, and recipes into book form. Her understanding and competence helped ease our way.

Thanks to Julia Stambules of All-Clad for her generous donation of the nonstick cookware used to test the recipes for this book.

Appreciation to all of the students, past, present, and future, of The French Culinary Institute, whose enthusiasm, interest, and courage give us constant inspiration.

And last but certainly not least, much honor and praise to Dorothy Cann Hamilton and Douglas Hamilton, whose valued leadership and trust allow us the opportunity to do what we do at our very best.

—Chefs Alain Sailhac, Jacques Pépin, André Soltner, Jacques Torres

PREFACE

I arrived in the United States on September 12, 1959, and started working at Le Pavillon in New York City the following day.

The kitchen at Le Pavillon was run at that time by the legendary Pierre Franey, who became an older brother figure to me. The restaurant was owned by Henri Soulé and operated by him in the strict, classical manner of a French restaurant. The sauces, the dishes, and the service itself were in the style of the late Escoffier, whose manner of cooking was the French restaurant standard not only before and after World War II but also up until the late 1950s, with some minor variations.

When I look back over the past 38 years and consider what has happened to cooking in the United States, it amazes me. The outstanding quality of the foods available to us now in supermarkets and open markets, the exceptional quality of the wines at our disposal, the flair, style, and quality of today's restaurants, along with the knowledge, interest, and enthusiasm of the general public, place the cooking world now at the antipodes of what it was then.

Having been a part of the changes and a witness to the transformation, I also have changed with the times, as have other people, and the cuisine I prepared in my apprenticeship and, later on, in Paris is quite distant and unrelated to what I do now.

Yet, for many, many years, French or continental restaurants, the name often given to French restaurants in the United States, continued to use an old style of cooking, with thick sauces blanketing the food, and called it French cooking. Partly because of this, real French cooking sometimes has been misunderstood by the American public at large.

In the past few years, people have developed an interest in health and have sought the "lighter side" of cooking. Mediterranean cooking, which usually translates as "Italian cooking" to Americans, has become more popular, and many people are insisting that "this is the end of French cooking; French cooking is dead!" In fact, that is not an inaccurate statement, but the "French cooking" people are alluding to, that which was prevalent in the first half of the twentieth century, has been dead—or at least greatly modified—for a lot longer in France than in the United States.

The top restaurants in the United States—Daniel, Le Cirque, and Jean-Georges in New York City; Jean-Louis Palladin's Napa in Las Vegas; Citrus in Los Angeles; Chez Panisse and Fleur de Lys in San Francisco—are all serving a modified, modern, and exciting French cuisine. This cuisine has evolved and changed while retaining its classic techniques and proper foundation. It has, particularly in the United States, developed in the past few years into a light, diversified, interesting, and complex cuisine using more vegetables and shorter cooking times and placing a greater emphasis on seasonability and freshness.

Some of the confusion related to French cooking arises because of its multifaceted and complex nature. There definitely are different types of cuisine in France.

The cuisine of the farm, which is never written down but verbalized from parent to child, is limited in scope and entirely dependent upon ingredients grown in a particular area. It does not travel and is quite simple, yet it is difficult to partake of in some ways because the farmer will automatically extend and "fuss" over a meal if a guest has been invited to share his table.

Cuisine *ménagère*, or "home cooking," has to be simple, fast, not too expensive, and diversified to please the family. Preparing it is not an easy task, and it tends to encompass food that is simple, straightforward, and familiar, like a roast, a stew, or a pan-fried fish with salad and a vegetable.

Cuisine *bourgeoise* reached its apex at the end of the nineteenth century and during the first 40 years of the twentieth century. After the French

Revolution, the great bourgeoisie, who had become rich, tried to emulate the nobility and devise a cuisine of its own. That cuisine, extolled in Proust, Balzac, Maupassant, and Flaubert, among others, is perhaps the greatest cuisine in France. It is still regional, depending on seasonal ingredients in a specific area of France, but with some of the sophistication and complexity of the professional chef's kitchen.

The cuisine of the professional chef, up until the appearance of nouvelle cuisine in the 1970s, was the cuisine of Escoffier. Chefs still make use of it to a more or less greater extent. This cuisine of the professional chef is more learned, more focused, and follows stricter rules. It has a structure formulated in a body of rules to which everyone must adhere. There must be a consensus in the kitchen when reference is made to food names—like a *brunoise* or a *mirepoix*—or when talking about certain procedures of cooking, from braising to poaching.

Unlike the other cuisines, the cuisine of the professional chef travels, because it is based on the academic knowledge of the chef. Ingredients are transformed, adapted, and combined to fit a style or to meet certain requirements. Through his knowledge of the basics and his whims, the chef creates, modifies, accommodates, or adjusts ingredients to fit the moment and the style. It is this professional cuisine that is best known outside of France, thanks to the travels of several of the great chefs of France's three-star restaurants, like Bocuse, Vergé, and Troisgros.

It is this cuisine of the professional that represents "French cuisine" in the minds of most Americans. Yet, although this starred cuisine is certainly a part of it, Michelin bestows its one-, two-, or three-star ratings on only about 500 restaurants out of the 130,000 in the whole of France. This is a minute percentage of the total number of restaurants in France, but unfortunately, the richer, pricier, more esoteric, starred cuisine is too often thought to be the standard and the norm of the French kitchen.

The goal of The French Culinary Institute (FCI), as a learning institution, is to preserve the classicism and the technical body of knowledge that is the base of French cuisine, and this is what we strive to do. The student is exposed to more than 200 "competencies," which are distinct techniques, procedures, or processes of handling food. These competencies are the same as those I learned during my apprenticeship, but they can be interpreted in a more modern recipe.

For example, I learned the proper way of poaching an egg, just as today's student does. Years ago, however, that poached egg may have been placed in a puff pastry shell, coated with a rich cream sauce finished with butter, and garnished with deep-fried croquettes of chicken puree and cream for the classic dish called *Oeufs Pochés Brimont*. Nowadays, the poached egg may be coated with a thin layer of crystal-clear aspic and garnished with a julienne of fresh vegetables. The basic principles and techniques remain, but they are demonstrated in a modern, lighter way.

In this book, the chefs at The French Culinary Institute have taken the lightening of recipes and the lowering of calories one step further. The more than 150 recipes have been carefully chosen and arranged in menus that follow the seasons and are favorable to your waistline and general health.

The Consommé with Miniature Vegetables is classic, lean, and full-flavored but contemporary with the addition of tiny balls of turnips, carrots, and peas. The Eggplant Terrine with Roasted Vegetables is made of eight different vegetables and herbs and is served with a light Tomato Vinaigrette. The fragrant Red Snapper in Parchment Paper employs the age-old technique of papillote (paper casing) and is flavored with shallots, thyme, lemon, mushrooms, and tomatoes but contains a minimum amount of butter and olive oil. Even desserts like the Meringue Shells with Marinated Strawberries are delicate, light, flavorful, and fat-free. These recipes are perfect expressions of a modern cooking philosophy that wants to keep the body fit and healthy and the savory senses satisfied.

We take advantage of a greater diversity of ingredients, many of which were unknown a quarter century ago—from Asian vegetables and new types of herbs to never-before-used grains and beans, and organically grown fish, shellfish, poultry, and meat. These products are made into dishes that suit the lifestyles of people today: a lighter cuisine with smaller portions, reduced cooking times, more diversity and originality, all attractively presented on plates or platters.

These recipes are a statement that defines a philosophy in tune with today's eclectic and demanding cook as well as with today's health concerns; they are a symbiosis between the desirable and the necessary.

Happy cooking!

—Jacques Pépin
Dean of Special Programs
The French Culinary Institute

INTRODUCTION

I always knew that the French were serious about food, but it was in my first correspondence with the director of Ferrandi, France's premier cooking school, that I found out how seriously healthy and passionately qualitative about ingredients they were. In the very first letters that we exchanged about the grand plan of bringing Ferrandi to New York City, Monsieur Rémande wanted to know who would be responsible for buying the vegetables!

Like many baby boomers, I got my first taste of Europe during my college years. While attending a British university, I dreamt constantly of the great food across the Channel. On holidays, I would bus and ferry my way to Calais and literally eat my way down to Paris. I marveled at how much good food there was to be had in the smallest bistro, made from the simplest ingredients in the tiniest of towns. I often questioned why we didn't have this in America. Surely we have the raw ingredients: world-class beef, abundant fresh- and saltwater fish, and renowned soil for farming fruits and vegetables.

The seed for The French Culinary Institute (FCI) was planted in 1980 when I, along with other educators, was invited on an official tour of the top vocational schools in Europe, one of which was Le Centre des Formations Technologique de Métier d'Alimentation de Chambre de Commerce et de l'Industrie de Paris—known among friends as Ferrandi. I was so taken with that school and the food I ate in its restaurant that I knew it would truly be a great endeavor to start a similar program in the United States.

The answer to the questions I had asked myself about food in America suddenly became clear. What we needed was formal training for chefs. As an educator, I would be challenged to bring the same schooling of French chefs to America. In 1984, I started a joint project with Ferrandi in which its exact curriculum was translated and adapted for American students. Antoine Shaeffers, a very talented chef instructor from the Ferrandi staff, and I opened the doors of The French Culinary Institute in March of 1984. Antoine was followed by Christian Foucher, a fellow chef instructor of Ferrandi, who served as principal chef of FCI until 1989. Since then, many talented teachers and gifted students have brought the school to national prominence, not the least of whom are Jacques Pépin, Alain Sailhac, André Soltner, Jacques Torres, Dieter Schorner, Daniel Leader, and Roger Fessaguet.

Jacques Pépin was the first of our deans to join the school. In 1989, it was time to install a permanent staff of chefs based in America. The Chamber of Commerce and Ferrandi were very proud of the quality of student we were producing in New York, but the logistics of keeping a Ferrandi staff member as the principal instructor were getting difficult. Thank God for Jacques Pépin! Jacques shared our goal of wanting to teach Americans the French method of technique along with quality and discipline. Jacques was also an experienced teacher, having already taught and inspired many American chefs with his monumental works, *La Technique* and *La Méthode*. As dean of special programs, Jacques is with us one week a month. His national commitments and TV appearances keep him circling the nation and the globe the other weeks of the year.

Chef Pépin has brought the school his Zen-like mastery of technique as well as a personal warmth with his professionalism that is an inspiring example to our students. But by 1989, The French Culinary Institute was growing and needed a strong and inspiring presence every day. Enter Alain Sailhac.

At The French Culinary Institute, our students' final exams are judged by a panel of prominent New York chefs. One of the most prominent to visit us was Alain Sailhac, the chef of Le Cirque. Le Cirque not only was considered by many to be one of the top restaurants in America but also was a training ground for legendary American chefs...David Bouley, Rick Moonen, Terrance Brennan, to name a few who have emerged from that kitchen. I always chided Alain back then that *he* really ran the best culinary school. So when the time came to look for the executive dean of the school, Alain was not only the obvious choice but also a real coup if we were to proceed on our quest to be the best cooking school in America.

The growth of the school under the leadership of Chef Alain has been dramatic. His vast knowledge of all aspects of the restaurant world has helped the school to add programming in pastry and bread baking. With his leadership, we have been able to attract the best chefs in the profession to join the faculty: Jacques Torres, Dieter Schorner, Daniel Leader, and the extraordinary André Soltner.

The first time I met André Soltner, I stepped on his foot in an elevator. I was mortified when I realized who he was. I was accompanying the head chef and director of Ferrandi to a monthly meeting of the New York French chefs at the Vatel Club, where we were to explain that we were opening a culinary school based directly on the Ferrandi curriculum. Little did André Soltner or I have any idea that 14 years later we would be working together. In fact, Chef André was incredulous back then when he heard that our course of study was only six months long. Today, he shakes his head and says, "Incredible, but it works." Chef André came to us when he retired from his legendary Lutèce restaurant. Twice, his retirement made the front page of the *New York Times*. Never did I think that I could approach him to teach at FCI.

One day in 1995, my good friend Thomas Kelly, associate professor at Cornell University in Ithaca, New York, called to tell me of Cornell's interest in attracting Chef Soltner to its hallowed halls but that it had been rumored that he was interested in joining our chefs at FCI. I was in shock. I called Chef Soltner immediately and invited him to lunch with Alain, Jacques, and me. After an intensive tour of the school, we sat down to what was to be a serious business lunch. At the moment we sat, Jacques leaned across the table and said, "André, before anyone says anything, both Alain and I want you to know that we really want you to come and teach here." André sat back and smiled. Jacques leaned over again and added, "because we feel that someone older than the two of us should teach here." Laughter broke out and continued for the next two hours. At the end of the momentous meal, André said to me, "Dorothy, I don't know what you want me to teach, but if these two guys can be this happy here, so can I." I don't know if I have ever received a greater compliment in my life.

The school continued to progress and expand. Jacques Torres, while remaining at Le Cirque, taught occasional classes at FCI during 1993. I was so taken with his natural teaching ability that I knew one day, when the time was right, Jacques could create the most dynamic pastry arts school in the country. Thankfully, we did not have to wait too long. Le Cirque was taking a sabbatical to create Le Cirque 2000, and Chef Torres had time to write a curriculum, design a state-of-the-art pastry kitchen and classrooms, and hire a stellar teaching staff chaired by one of the most beloved and respected pastry chefs in the country, Dieter Schorner.

Jacques Torres teaches classes twice a month and oversees all curriculum refinements, but most of all, he is the visionary and soul of our pastry department, which keeps our students on the cutting edge of the professional pastry world.

Every day, I reflect on how lucky I am to be surrounded by such masters. They continue, through their hard work and modesty, to teach me and the students what professionalism is all about.

The philosophy of The French Culinary Institute can be summed up simply in the words "Quality, Discipline, and Reality." Our students are trained to be good workers, respectful of the kitchen. Our curriculum is classical but contemporary in its conception. Our method is total immersion. In just six months, we graduate cooks who are ready to enter the country's best restaurants, in both pastry and culinary positions. Most recently, we have introduced a six-week intensive bread-baking curriculum under the direction of Daniel Leader, master baker and author of the award-winning book *Bread Alone*.

I am very proud that The French Culinary Institute now has the opportunity to bring to the public our passion for French cuisine. We truly believe it to be one of the healthiest, most satisfying cuisines in the world, and I am a living example. As a child, I was brought up on traditional American fare (and portion sizes) as well as Czechoslovakian dumplings. Needless to say, I was fat as a kid. But my experience with French food in college opened my eyes not only to good food but also to a healthy way of eating. If you truly eat the French way—balanced meals, no snacking, small portions of meat, lots of fresh vegetables and fruit—you no longer wonder how French women eat so well and manage to keep their figures.

L'École, the restaurant of The French Culinary Institute, exemplifies this. A typical meal could include roasted eggplant and red pepper terrine, pan-roasted fillet of sea bass sautéed with cucumbers, and beef with artichokes, potatoes, and tomatoes. We were honored this year with a 23/30 rating from *Zagat's Restaurant Survey*, which also noted that "Plenty of pros could learn from the students.... It's no wonder L'École is more popular than ever."

For once, perhaps we have found the magic pill. You don't have to spend six months at the school to enjoy French cooking techniques and lifestyle. If you follow the menus and the philosophy of this book, you will not only lose weight but also thoroughly enjoy the process.

Bon appétit!

Dorothy Cann Hamilton
Chairman and Founder
The French Culinary Institute
New York, New York

THE FRENCH DIET—
A PARADOX WITH BENEFITS
FOR AMERICANS

WHAT COMES TO MIND WHEN YOU THINK OF FRENCH FOOD?

CHEESE, CROISSANTS, AND FOIE GRAS, FOR SURE. PASTRIES,

SOUFFLÉS, AND DUCK À L'ORANGE, NO DOUBT. BUTTER, CREAM,

AND EGGS, BY ALL MEANS. GOOD HEALTH? GET REAL.

WELL, WE ARE GETTING REAL. AND REALITY SHOWS THAT, DE-

SPITE THE APPARENT PITFALLS OF THE FRENCH WAY OF EATING,

THESE EUROPEANS HAVE MUCH LESS HEART DISEASE THAN

AMERICANS. IT'S A PARADOX THAT HAS HEALTH EDUCATORS ON

THIS SIDE OF THE ATLANTIC SITTING UP AND TAKING NOTICE.

ON THE SURFACE, THE FRENCH DIET DOES HAVE ITS DRAW-

BACKS. OVERALL, THE FRENCH EAT NEARLY FOUR TIMES AS

MUCH BUTTER AND ALMOST THREE TIMES AS MUCH LARD AS

AMERICANS. THE GREAT MAJORITY OF FRENCH PEOPLE VIO-

LATE THE U.S. GOVERNMENT DIET-FOR-A-HEALTHY-HEART

GUIDELINES THAT CALL FOR CONSUMING LESS THAN 30 PER-

CENT OF CALORIES FROM FAT AND LESS THAN 10 PERCENT OF

CALORIES FROM SATURATED FAT. SPECIFICALLY, 86 PERCENT OF

1

French adults get more than 30 percent of their calories from fat, and an astonishing 96 percent obtain more than 10 percent of their calories from saturated fat (most French eat about 14 to 15 percent of calories as saturated fat).

It's no surprise, then, that average French blood cholesterol and blood pressure levels are higher than Americans'. The average Frenchman's cholesterol is 218 to 252 (depending on the area of France from which he hails), compared with 209 in the United States. Frenchwomen's cholesterol levels mirror the men's.

What's very surprising, however, is that the French have a much lower rate of death due to heart disease than Americans. Astonishingly, they are 2½ times less likely to die of heart disease than their trans-Atlantic neighbors. Calorie intake doesn't explain away the difference, since the French eat about the same amount of calories as Americans do.

It is indeed a paradox, as both the scientific and lay communities have come to call this unexpected outcome of the French way of eating. "Just on the basis of higher cholesterol levels and blood pressure readings, the death rate from heart disease in France should be much higher," says Michael H. Criqui, M.D., professor of family and preventive medicine at the University of California, San Diego. Dr. Criqui became intrigued by the French paradox because of his interest in how alcohol affects health. And although you might think that "health" and "alcohol" don't belong in the same sentence, wine consumption seems to play at least some role in explaining this health phenomenon.

But first things first. Before we delve into the possible explanations for the French paradox, let's examine the French way of eating.

An Experience to Savor

"Eating is like making love," says Chef Alain Sailhac, provost and senior dean of culinary studies at The French Culinary Institute. "In

France, we put our whole bodies and minds into experiencing good food and wine." Chef Sailhac, who came to this country from Millau, a city in the south of France, explains that the French don't eat just to fill their bellies or because it's time to eat but to enjoy the experience. "We savor both the food and the company," says Chef Sailhac.

The company is indeed an integral part of the meal. "Almost nowhere in France do you see people standing up to eat a meal on the run as so many Americans do." The French sit and enjoy the meal and the company. Most people, he explains, take an hour or even two for lunch. Similarly, families sit together—sans television—for an hour or more for dinner.

While there's no data to prove it, Chef Sailhac believes that one of the reasons that the French enjoy a lower rate of death from heart attack is the stress-relieving benefit of a lengthy, enjoyable, and satisfying mealtime. "French mealtimes give everyone a chance to relax and unwind," he says.

THE MEDITERRANEAN CONNECTION

Cheese, croissants, and foie gras aside, the French eat the same Mediterranean diet that their southerly neighbors do. While they consume a variety of red meats, the meat is more of a garnish than the focus of the meal. Frequently, says Chef Sailhac, meat is incorporated into a vegetable-intense dish such as a stew.

And therein may lie one of the secrets of the French paradox (and the Mediterranean diet). The French eat bushel-baskets more fruits and vegetables than Americans do. Throughout France, people consume an abundance of fresh fruits and vegetables with every meal. "Shopping for fresh produce is an important part of almost every day," says Chef Sailhac. People choose fresh produce every day and then build a meal around those items.

Breakfast, for example, is often fresh fruit and whole-grain, good-tasting bread with fruit preserves or honey (rather than butter). "Other meals begin with a vegetable focus," says Dorothy Cann Hamilton, president and founder of The French Culinary Institute. "The first course, for example, is generally a vegetable soup, another vegetable dish, or a beet or lentil salad." The third course (which follows meat, fish, or poultry) is always a salad, with plenty of fresh greens. And dessert tends to swirl around fruit—black cherries or figs, for example, with some white cheese.

As a result of their focus on fruits and vegetables, the French typically eat more than five servings of fruits and vegetables daily. In contrast, Americans average just three.

It doesn't stop there. Generous quantities of olive oil are a staple of the French Mediterranean diet. Plenty of whole grains and legumes are characteristic of the French way of eating, as are several fish meals each week. Herbs, too, define French cooking and provide fat-free flavor. Thyme, oregano, rosemary, onions, chives, shallots, and garlic announce their distinctive presence in meals throughout the day. In addition, a glass or two of wine accompanies most evening meals.

"Several aspects of the French diet could explain the French paradox," says Edwin Frankel, Ph.D., adjunct professor of food science and technology at the University of California at Davis. Experts believe that some of these aspects are wine, the high consumption of fruits and vegetables, dietary diversity, generous portions of olive oil (in place of other types of fat), and the frequent inclusion of fish in the weekly diet. Although not as easy to prove, the relaxation factor of French meals may also play a role.

A Glass of Wine a Day Keeps the Doctor Away?

The French paradox's connection to wine consumption was first described by French heart disease researcher Serge Renaud, Ph.D., in 1992. He comes from the southwest of France, home of foie gras and *confit de canard* (duck preserves). At the time, he focused his attention on the routine

SHOULD YOU DRINK ALCOHOL?

If you don't drink now, don't start just to decrease your risk of heart disease. "Research confirms that one to two drinks a day for men and one drink a day for women may help reduce the risk of heart disease," says Michael H. Criqui, M.D., professor of family and preventive medicine at the University of California, San Diego. This amount of alcohol is called light-to-moderate drinking, with each drink defined as 12 ounces of beer, 5 ounces of wine, or 1½ ounces of hard liquor. (Women should note, however, that even this level of alcohol consumption may slightly increase breast cancer risk.) Dr. Criqui defines moderate drinking as two drinks or less a day for men and one drink or less for women. He defines light drinking as less than one drink a day.

"But there's also indisputable evidence that any amount over this quickly offsets the benefits," says Dr. Criqui, who explains that if the U.S. Food and Drug Administration were asked today to approve alcohol as a drug for lowering heart disease risk, they would not grant approval. "The risks are far greater than the benefits."

Men imbibing three or more drinks a day actually increase the risk of developing heart problems, including fatal heart rhythm abnormalities and heart failure.

In addition, the risks of alcohol-associated accidents, addiction, and liver disease quickly mount. Cancer and hemorrhagic (bleeding) strokes are also much higher in people who consume more than light-to-moderate amounts of alcohol.

The best advice about alcohol consumption relates to current habits.

- People who do not drink should not start.
- Those who consume light-to-moderate amounts of alcohol can feel safe in continuing their current pattern of intake.
- Heavy drinkers should reduce their intake of alcohol to the light-to-moderate level.

consumption of two glasses of red wine daily as the most likely explanation for the French paradox.

The mechanism, Dr. Renaud proposed, centered on wine's effect on blood platelets. For starters, alcohol makes platelets less sticky, which means that they're less likely to clump together. That begins to take on significance when you realize that just one teaspoon of blood contains more than a million of these disk-shaped platelets. While the body depends on them to seal wounds and stop bleeding, overactive platelet clumping can produce tiny blood clots. In turn, these tiny clots can stymie blood flow within critical arteries that supply blood to the heart. The eventual result is a heart attack. The immediate trigger of most heart attacks, in fact, is overzealous platelet clumping.

The evidence, says Dr. Renaud, went beyond the test tube. Preliminary studies showed that blood from people in Var, a city in southern France, had much less platelet clumping than blood from people in Girvan, a city in southwest Scotland. While alcohol consumption averaged 45 grams per day in Var, it was only 20 grams per day in Girvan.

Alcohol also raises the levels of "good" cholesterol, or HDL cholesterol. HDL cholesterol somehow snares excess cholesterol in the bloodstream and helps escort it out of the body via the liver. Alcohol seems to enhance this process.

"Studies do confirm that alcohol consumption can help decrease heart disease rates," Dr. Criqui says. "But they also point out that alcohol abuse decreases longevity. The trouble is, it's very easy to cross the line from responsible alcohol use to irresponsible alcohol use and addiction." That's why he and other heart disease experts don't recommend that you start drinking to prevent heart disease.

HOT DIETARY SUPERSTARS

Fortunately, though, the alcohol in wine may not totally explain the French paradox. The answer could lie with some of those important dietary substances called phytochemicals—and possibly even more traditional nutrients—abundant in fruits and vegetables.

Phytochemicals are simply plant compounds that, almost since the beginning of life on Earth, have given plants protection from viruses, harsh weather, and the insults of handling. Scientists have recently discovered that phytochemicals may offer health benefits to people who eat the plant foods containing them. Wine is high in phytochemicals, but so are the fruits and vegetables that are so integral to the French diet—and so important a part of the menus in this book.

"When we first heard about the French paradox, my colleagues and I wondered if flavonoids, the phytochemicals that are particularly high in red wine, could be at least partly responsible for the protection against heart disease," says Dr. Frankel. It makes sense, he says, that something besides alcohol accounts for the beneficial effect of red wine. "Research suggests that something besides alcohol in wine, especially red wine, is significantly superior to alcohol provided by other beverages, such as beer or whiskey. It seems that phenolic antioxidants may be conferring this benefit." Phenolics are a family of phytochemicals that include flavonoids. In the hierarchy of phytochemicals, flavonoids are one class of substances under the larger "phenolic compound" umbrella.

Researchers around the world subsequently found that the red wine solids stripped of their alcohol content were able to stop platelet clumping. They also found that these nonalcoholic substances prevent cholesterol from depositing on arterial walls and blocking them.

Further evidence for the heart-protective power of the nonalcohol component of red wines comes from the laboratory of flavonoid researcher John Folts, Ph.D., professor of medicine and head of the coronary thrombosis research lab at the University of Wisconsin School of Medicine in Madison. In his experiments, pure alcohol stopped platelet clumping, but only when blood alcohol reached 0.2 (that's *double* the legal limit for intox-

OTHER BENEFITS OF THE FRENCH DIET

A diet that leans heavily on flavonoid-rich foods like fruits and vegetables helps more than just your heart. Those undesirable free radicals that wreak other havoc can also damage DNA, the blueprint by which cells reproduce themselves. The consequences of this damage can lead to cancer.

Mounting evidence points to the cancer-protection power of flavonoids. In addition to disarming free radicals, flavonoids seem to take the punch out of carcinogens by detoxifying them. Flavonoids also block the access of carcinogens to cells, often by attaching themselves to carcinogens. This makes the carcinogens too big and bulky to enter cells. Flavonoids appear to reduce DNA damage. They may also interfere with the binding of hormones to cells, thus inhibiting growth of hormone-dependent cancer cells, such as breast, ovarian, endometrial, and prostate cancers.

Flavonoids, especially one type called quercetin, also seem to have infection-fighting ability. Microbiology professor Joseph V. Formica, Ph.D., of Virginia Commonwealth University's School of Medicine in Richmond, says that it makes sense that flavonoids seem to have infection-fighting ability in humans, as that's what they do in plants. "Louis Pasteur puzzled over the infection-fighting ability of wine, believing that its ability to squelch infections is far greater than can be accounted for by its meager 12 percent alcohol content," says Dr. Formica. There had to be something else in wine that accounted for the ability. "Flavonoids may explain the difference."

Quercetin seems to be particularly effective against enveloped viruses, or viruses protected by a covering. "Quercetin apparently works to stop viral infections by interfering with the virus's reproductive machinery," explains Dr. Formica. "In order for a virus to produce a full-blown infection, it must reproduce itself repeatedly. Quercetin, however, apparently attaches itself to the virus's DNA, which prevents the virus from multiplying."

ication of 0.1). "That's a whopping bunch of alcohol," cautions Dr. Folts. Red wine did the job when blood alcohol was a modest 0.03—presumably because it also contains flavonoids.

Fortunately, for those who prefer not to imbibe, purple grape juice is also an excellent source of flavonoids. In one experiment, people who drank a 5-ounce glass of purple grape juice every morning and evening for a week significantly reduced the tendency of their blood to form potentially dangerous clots. Other studies have shown that three 5-ounce cups of tea have equal flavonoid power. What's not as effective is red grape juice. And white grape juice and purple grape "drink"—which does not contain pure grape juice—are not very effective at all.

A RADICAL THEORY

Here's how flavonoids may work to stave off heart disease. Among their many biological actions, flavonoids are powerful antioxidants. While every living thing needs oxygen to exist, the process of using oxygen creates by-products that are toxic. These by-products are called free radicals. They are unstable, high-energy particles that ricochet wildly from cell to cell trying to stabilize themselves. As they gad about madly, though, they leave a trail of damage.

When it comes to heart disease, free radicals exert several damaging actions. They modify the body's undesirable LDL cholesterol through oxidation. Oxidation is the same kind of reaction that makes vegetable oils rancid—the oil gains oxygen molecules and decomposes. Oxidized LDL is far more likely to swell and then lodge in and block arteries. Free radicals also alter platelet function, causing them to clump together inappropriately, which also contributes to the artery-clogging process.

"Although the body has its own system of scavenging free radicals, it needs help from the outside," says Dr. Frankel. "There is considerable ev-

WHERE THE FLAVONOIDS ARE

A close look at flavonoids reveals that wine isn't the best source of these beneficial compounds.

- The absolute *best sources*: onions, kale, green beans, broccoli, endive, celery, cranberries, and citrus fruit (the peel and white pulp).
- Foods with *medium levels* of flavonoids: red wine, tea, lettuce, tomatoes, red peppers, fava beans, strawberries, apples, grapes, grape juice, and tomato juice.
- Items with *low levels*: cabbage, carrots, mushrooms, peas, spinach, peaches, white wine, coffee, and orange juice.

Since dietary diversity is one key to heart health, you'd be well-advised to emulate the French and eat generous amounts of all these foods.

idence that flavonoids and other phytochemicals in fruits and vegetables serve as powerful antioxidants." And that means that they can stop platelets from clumping and LDL from oxidizing and depositing on arterial walls. Flavonoids and related compounds may also turn down the volume on other naturally occurring substances in the body that contribute to the artery-clogging process. Finally, flavonoids reduce the inflammation in blood vessels that contributes to artery clogging.

The flavonoids in red wine come from the pigment that lends the red color to grape skins. (This also explains why red wine is more heart-protective than white wine. When grapes are crushed to make white wine, the flavonoid-rich grape skins and seeds—called the must—are removed early in the process. For red wine, however, the must is removed much later, giving more time for flavonoids to be drawn into the wine.) There are at least three major types of flavonoids in red grapes, plus another type of phytochemical called anthocyanin and at least two other types of phenolic compounds.

Fortunately, the same flavonoids and other phenolic compounds found in grapes are abundantly present in many fruits and vegetables. "That means that not just red wine but the vast array of fruits and vegetables enjoyed by the French contribute to protecting them from heart attacks," says Dr. Frankel.

And there's plenty of evidence from around the world that lends support to the flavonoid theory of heart attack protection. A Dutch study of 800 older men found that those who ate the most flavonoids (the amount in four cups of tea, one apple, and a quarter cup of onions a day) had only one-third the risk of dying of heart attacks as men who ate the least.

A subsequent study that looked at flavonoid intake in seven different countries found that the higher the flavonoid intake, the lower the rate of death from heart disease. Flavonoid intake accounted for an 8 percent difference in deaths from heart disease between those who ate more flavonoids and those who ate the least. In another study, Finnish researchers found that people with very low intakes of flavonoids during a 25-year period had higher risks of heart disease.

CAROTENE AND FRIENDS

Heart attack protection goes beyond the flavonoids in fruits and vegetables. Produce is loaded with several other beneficial phytochemicals. Dark green leafy vegetables and red-orange vegetables and fruits are known for their high carotenoid content. While studies of carotene supplements have proved disappointing in terms of their ability to prevent cancer and heart disease, trials of carotenoids obtained from real food have produced very encouraging results.

One of these studies, the Lipid Research Clinics Coronary Primary Prevention Trial, studied nearly 4,000 middle-aged men with high blood cholesterol levels over a period of 13 years. Half the participants were given a cholesterol-lowering drug and the other half a placebo (a sugar pill). Researchers also tracked dietary carotenoid intake among the half receiving the placebo. Investigators found that men with the highest blood levels of carotenoids (which meant that they had the highest intake of carotenoid-rich food) were 36 percent less likely to get heart disease.

Another huge study produced similar results. Studying almost 90,000 healthy female nurses, researchers found that women who ate the most beta-carotene as fruits and vegetables had a 22 percent lower risk of heart disease than women who ate the least.

How does all this relate to what's on your plate? It means that colorful foods like sweet potatoes, red bell peppers, spinach, kale, cantaloupe, apricots, and peaches should jazz up every meal.

Another phytochemical, tocotrienols, may offer more heart attack protection. Abundant in some oils and grains, tocotrienols seem capable of stopping the oxidation of LDL cholesterol. They may also turn down the body's own production of cholesterol.

Garlic and other vegetables in the allium family (such as onions and shallots) are endowed with a different class of phytochemicals called organosulfur compounds. They may provide additional help by turning down the amount of cholesterol produced by the liver. Dr. Folts has also shown that garlic can stop platelet clumping by reducing platelet stickiness.

Asparagus and legumes (Mediterranean people eat a lot of legumes, such as lentils and other dried beans and peas) contain yet another group of phytochemicals, saponins. Among their talents, saponins are thought to bind up cholesterol from the intestinal tract and usher it out of the body unabsorbed. They probably do the same with bile acids, thereby preventing them from being transformed into cholesterol.

VARIETY IS MORE THAN THE SPICE OF LIFE

"The greater number of different foods that the French eat might also explain the French paradox," says nutrition researcher Susan Ahlstrom Henderson, R.D., health sciences research associate in the School of Public Health at the University of Michigan in Ann Arbor, who has explored explanations for the French paradox. "Just by virtue of the fact that they shop daily for what is fresh, the French end up eating a much wider variety of food, especially of fruits and vegetables."

For a typical French shopper, that might mean tomatoes and curly lettuce are at their best one day, while greens peak the following day, and eggplant looks good on the third. Americans, on the other hand, tend to eat the same fruits and vegetables over and over again. That may be because they shop less often. It may also signify less adventuresome palates. "The French also choose a wider variety of each fruit or vegetable," says Henderson. For example, they might choose yellow, orange, and red tomatoes—instead of just the traditional red."

Such variety—dietary diversity, as nutrition experts call this style of eating—offers an incredible advantage, says Henderson. "Eating so many different fruits and vegetables means not only getting a lot more phytochemicals but also getting a wider variety of them. And research has shown that that's important in fighting cancer, heart disease, and other health troubles." Yellow tomatoes, says Henderson, may have different phytochemicals than orange or red ones. Similarly, different varieties of salad greens also have distinctive phytochemicals. As you increase the variety of foods you eat, you increase your chances of getting more phytochemicals. "Looking at the whole French diet in terms of dietary diversity may provide a new insight into the French paradox," says Henderson.

<u>OLIVE OIL: LIQUID GOLD FOR THE HEART</u>

Like other Mediterranean people, the French consume much of their fat as olive oil. "It's very intriguing that people throughout the Mediterranean lead quite unhealthy lives—smoking heavily, not exercising, and having poor access to medical care—but that they live longer than Americans," says Dimitrios Trichopoulos, M.D., Ph.D., professor of epidemiology and cancer prevention at Harvard School of Public Health. "They have to be doing something right, and olive oil seems to play a critical role."

It was the Greeks—who, according to Dr. Trichopoulos, consume olive oil as they do oxygen—who gave us the first clue that olive oil may play some role in reducing the chance of having a heart attack. Although the Greeks have a diet fairly high in fat—which accounts for 40 percent of their calories—they have an exceptionally low rate of heart disease.

Olive oil has at least two attributes to lower heart disease risk: the type of fat it contains and a rich supply of its own phytochemicals.

Although olive oil has roughly the same amount of fat calories as butter and any other type of fat, it is a better type of fat. Olive oil is nearly three-quarters *monounsaturated* fat. Butter, on the other hand, is 62 percent saturated fat.

You can virtually visualize how each of these fats affects the body. Saturated fat is solid at room temperature (think of what butter or the cooling juices on a platter of roast beef look like). Both polyunsaturated and monounsaturated fats are liquid at room temperature (think of a bottle of corn or olive oil). You can envision arteries getting clogged by the hard white residue that is so representative of saturated fat. Researchers know that saturated fat raises blood levels of undesirable LDL cholesterol. When substituted for saturated fats, monounsaturated fat raises HDL cholesterol—that's the type of good cholesterol that helps keep fatty sludge from depositing in arteries—while polyunsaturated fats seem capable of lowering both HDL and LDL cholesterol. They apparently do so by turning up the volume on the body's cholesterol-removal machinery.

Olive oil has at least one more thing going for it. Nature richly endowed olive oil with at least two phytochemicals that have been identified for their protective role against heart disease (and possibly cancer). Like the flavonoids in red wine, olive oil phytochemicals fall under that same phenolic compound umbrella and work in the same fashion to fight heart disease. Namely, they are thought to protect LDLs from the dangerous oxidation.

What kind of olive oil should you reach for? Do as the French do: Use extra-virgin olive oil. While all olive oils are created equal when it comes to the monounsaturated fat content, extra-virgin has the most phenolic compounds. Extra-virgin olive oil is made from the first pressing of perfectly ripe olives. The first pressing leaves in the polyphenols and doesn't produce the bitter acid taste that some later pressings have. It is the rich polyphenol content that gives extra-virgin olive oil its gentle but rich fruity taste.

A FINE KETTLE OF FISH

If you think that there's something fishy about the French diet, you're right. The French eat fish several times a week. And that simple di-

THE FRENCH DIET—A PARADOX WITH BENEFITS FOR AMERICANS

etary difference could help explain—in more ways than one—the lower rate of heart attacks in France. Research is compelling, consistent, and persistent that fish-eaters are less likely to die of heart disease than those who completely avoid the denizens of the deep.

Fish may help lower heart attack risk by at least two means. First, there's a special type of polyunsaturated fatty acid in fish called omega-3's. This special type of "body fat" helps fish survive in the cold waters in which they live; it's also thought to confer some of the health benefits that fish-eaters realize. Here's how: Omega-3's seem to keep the body's immune system from working overtime. Specifically, they put the brakes on the body's production of prostaglandins, leukotrienes, and thromboxanes. While the body needs some of these chemicals to function normally, too-high concentrations can encourage platelets to clump overtime. Omega-3's are thought to prevent this overzealous clumping.

Fish oil also may keep HDL cholesterol levels healthfully high, especially in women. In fact, eating fish may keep HDL cholesterol from dropping as it's known to do on a low-fat diet.

Fish oil apparently exerts yet another effect on the heart. It is thought to help the heart beat in a steady, healthy rhythm. Although you don't realize it, your heart beats an average of 72 times each minute, or more than 100,000 times every day. Although your heart may occasionally "skip a beat" or race momentarily, it tends to beat evenly, thanks to the heart's sophisticated electrical conducting system.

Sometimes, though, the electrical system goes awry, causing the heart to beat unevenly. This is called arrhythmia. While some arrhythmias are perfectly harmless, others are dangerous and can cause the heart to stop beating altogether (cardiac arrest). There is increasing evidence that the omega-3's in fish may guard against dangerous arrhythmias, somehow fortifying heart muscle against unstable beats. In a study at the University of

Washington in Seattle, people who ate enough fish to get 5.5 grams of omega-3 fatty acids in a month—just one 3-ounce serving of salmon or any other fatty fish weekly—had only half the risk of cardiac arrest of people who ate no omega-3's.

Considering how many types of fish there are and how delicious seafood in general is, working fish into your weekly menus should present no challenge at all. Use the following divinely delectable menus from the chefs at The French Culinary Institute to serve up healthy helpings of all the foods that make French food good for your heart—and your soul.

FRENCH COOKING—
EASY, ACCESSIBLE, DELICIOUS, AND HEALTHY

FRENCH FOOD IS MUCH MORE THAN THE HAUTE CUISINE

OF THE FOUR-STAR RESTAURANT. THOSE RICH SAUCES,

FAT-LADEN MEATS, LUXURIOUS FOIE GRAS, AND EXTRA-

ORDINARY DESSERTS ALL HAVE THEIR COUNTERPARTS IN

THE SENSIBLE MEALS SERVED DAILY IN EVERY FRENCH

HOUSEHOLD.

THE FOUR-STAR CHEFS WHO LEAD THE FRENCH CULINARY IN-

STITUTE (FCI) EACH HAVE A FOOT IN BOTH DOMAINS. ALL

TRAINED IN THE TRADITIONAL FRENCH APPRENTICE SYSTEM,

WITH A FORMIDABLE BASE IN CLASSICAL FRENCH TECHNIQUE.

YET THEY REMAINED FIRMLY ENTRENCHED IN THE REGIONAL

FAMILY MEALS OF THEIR CHILDHOODS.

CHEF ALAIN SAILHAC IS FROM MILLAU, IN THE HEART OF THE

CÉVENNES. CHEF JACQUES PÉPIN WAS BORN IN BOURG-EN-

BRESSE NEAR LYON, THE GASTRONOMIC CAPITAL OF FRANCE.

CHEF ANDRÉ SOLTNER COMES FROM THANN IN ALSACE-

LORRAINE. CHEF JACQUES TORRES, THE YOUNGEST OF THESE

grand masters, came to the United States from Bandol in southern Provence.

The history and tradition of the French kitchen, both classic and home, are well-represented by these four chefs. Each brings both of these disciplines as well as years of experience to the classroom and to the development of contemporary French menus.

Chef Alain Sailhac is senior dean of studies. He's one of the culinary world's most prominent chefs, gaining four stars at Le Cygne and three stars at Le Cirque, both in New York City. As a Master Chef of France, Alain personifies the spirit of the contemporary French kitchen.

He began his career at age 14, bicycling miles at dawn to perform his kitchen duties: cleaning the floor and shoveling coals for the hot oven fires. As he worked his way up the professional ladder, he honed his skills in restaurants and hotels all around the world, culminating in his star status at New York's Le Cirque, the '21' Club, and the Plaza Hotel.

Looking for a challenge to top off his career and for the opportunity to pass along his hard-earned knowledge, Chef Sailhac became dean, and official mentor to the chefs of future generations, at The French Culinary Institute in 1990. From his early career in the south of France to the haute cuisine of New York, Alain Sailhac has spent the better part of his life defining the standards by which the world's greatest chefs have been measured.

Chef Jacques Pépin is FCI's dean of special programs. In addition, he's a master chef, television personality, food columnist, cookbook author, and cooking instructor to America's home cooks. Chef Pépin first experienced life in the kitchen at his parents' restaurant, Le Pélican. At 13, he began his formal apprenticeship at the distinguished Grand Hotel de L'Europe in his hometown of Bourg-en-Bresse. The great hotels of Paris served as his next training ground, from which he went on to become personal chef to three French heads of state, including Charles de Gaulle.

In his early years in the United States, Jacques worked as director of development for the Howard Johnson Company. He then pioneered in the development of new concepts in French restaurants while gaining his master of arts degree in eighteenth-century French literature from Columbia University in New York City. Chef Pépin is recognized as one the foremost interpreters of French cooking for the American television audience. His many cookbooks and magazine articles have made classic French cooking accessible and easy for even the most inexperienced cook.

Chef André Soltner is master chef and senior lecturer for the Institute. For more than 30 years, he was the chef-proprietor of New York's four-star Lutèce Restaurant. In the early 1960s, he set the tone for the restaurant explosion that was to come. Never swaying from his commitment to a classic French menu, Chef Soltner gained thousands of loyal customers and hundreds of awards and

accolades. Among the many trophies he holds are the Grande Médaille d'Or, Meilleur Ouvrier de France Culinaire, Académie Culinaire de France, and the James Beard Foundation's Lifetime Achievement Award.

For years, Chef Soltner has served as mentor and guide to America's young chefs. His experience in, enthusiasm for, and deep understanding of the cuisine of France has, in turn, very well served America's entry into international haute cuisine.

Jacques Torres is dean of pastry arts. Currently chef-pâtissier at New York's four-star Le Cirque 2000 restaurant, Chef Torres is considered by many to be the world's patriarch of modern patisserie. This is, in part, because at age 26 he was awarded the coveted Meilleur

Ouvrier de France Pâtissier by the French government. This prestigious award, honoring France's finest craftspeople, acknowledged Chef Torres's mastery of his art at the youngest age in the award's history.

Chef Torres began his career as a bakery apprentice at age 14. Discovered at 18 by Michelin two-star chef Jacques Maximin, he was encouraged to refine his skills and develop his sense of artistic creativity as pastry chef at the Hotel Negresco in Nice. A sense of adventure and a desire to broaden his experience led him to America and to the Ritz-Carlton Hotel Group. He has since received many honors, including the James Beard Foundation's Pastry Chef of the Year and membership in the Académie Culinaire de France.

Although known for the sense of humor and charm portrayed by his intricate desserts, Jacques Torres is never more serious as when approaching their creation. The combination of his expertise and his attitude has led to unique and superlative creations in the kitchen.

Redefining French Cooking

Together, these four chefs have developed this compendium for healthy French cooking. Their recipes redefine the use of fats, particularly saturated fats, as well as high-cholesterol foods and over-the-top desserts.

They've combined the traditional French home cook's eye toward economy, sensible portions at the table, moderate consumption of all foods, and pleasurable mealtimes into a well-rounded excursion into healthful French cooking. With their vast knowledge of ingredients, flavors, and textures—and how they interact in the pot and on the plate—the chefs have created menus with savory character and satisfying goodness.

The menus, developed with seasonal availability in mind, are preceded by a chapter that introduces you to fundamental techniques, equipment, and ingredients for cooking French meals healthfully. This is not a diet book, but it is a book that will help you eat very well in the French manner.

Taking tips from their years in restaurant kitchens and their own desire to eat healthier diets, the chefs have combined their skills to create this book. Here are just a few of the suggestions they offer to redefine French cooking for the new American kitchen.

- Cook with nonstick cookware.
- Skim off the fat in stocks, broths, sauces, and gravies.
- Trim all excess fat from meats and poultry.
- Use low-fat products in place of traditional high-fat ingredients.
- Remove skin from poultry.
- Use nonstick cooking spray in place of fat or use olive oil and butter very sparingly in combination with nonstick cookware.
- Replace pâte brisée and other high-fat pastry with phyllo dough.
- Use low-fat, low-cholesterol game in place of beef.
- Substitute nonfat dairy products for their fattier counterparts.
- Use herbs, aromatic vegetables, and other low-fat flavorings and condiments as seasonings in place of oils, butter, and excessive salt.

MASTERING THE BASICS

THE CLASSIC FRENCH KITCHEN IS A HIGHLY CONTROLLED AND WELL-DISCIPLINED SETTING. IT IS, IN PART, THIS ATMOSPHERE THAT ALLOWS THE CHEF HIS CREATIVITY. THE TECHNIQUES AND COOKING EQUIPMENT ARE EASILY TRANSLATED TO THE HOME KITCHEN AND WILL AFFORD YOU, THE HOME COOK, THE SAME EFFICIENCY AND DEXTERITY.

THE FOREMOST RULE IN ANY PROFESSIONAL KITCHEN IS CLEANLINESS, FOLLOWED BY A WELL-ORDERED, SYSTEMATIC WORK ROUTINE. OF COURSE, ALL OF THIS IS EASIER WITH A KITCHEN CREW, BUT WE BELIEVE THAT YOU WILL BE SURPRISED AT HOW EASILY THIS FORMAT CAN TRANSFORM YOUR WORKPLACE. FOLLOWING ARE SOME SUGGESTIONS.

  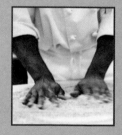

1. Prepare your work area as it has been universally done for generations in the professional kitchen. This area consists of a cutting board placed on a damp kitchen towel or paper towel to keep it from slipping, with knives and equipment arranged to the right of the board and bowls above it. When peeling vegetables, work with unprepared items on the left and place prepared items in a bowl to the right. Always catch the peelings in a bowl and, at all times, keep the work area neat.

2. Prepare your ingredients in the French technique known as *mise en place* (literally, "putting in place"), and you will have a jump start on both preparation and cleanup. Every element of your recipe should be cleaned, cut into the required size, and measured or whatever else might be called for. The items should be placed in individual bowls or on plates or trays before you begin to cook. This not only provides you with all ingredients close at hand and ready to go but also helps familiarize you with the recipe.

3. Clear the countertops and other preparation and cooking areas of all extraneous material.

4. Wear an apron with the strings tied in the front. Tuck a clean kitchen towel into the strings to easily wipe your hands and countertop.

5. Have two or three wet cloths on the countertop to make continuous cleanup easy.

6. Fill the sink with hot, soapy water so that you can wash utensils as you cook. Alternately, have the dishwasher emptied and ready to receive utensils as they are dirtied. When using the dishwasher, just make sure that you will not need the utensils before the cycle is complete.

7. Have cooling racks and serving pieces selected and within reach before needed.

OUTFITTING THE KITCHEN

Although you will not require the *batterie de cuisine* of the restaurant kitchen, there are a few pieces of equipment that will make healthy French cooking a breeze. When purchasing new items for your kitchen, we recommend that you acquire the best that your pocketbook can supply. Even though this may cost more at the outset, the longevity and stability of the utensils will reward you in the long run.

We recommend that you have, at the minimum:

- 2 nonstick sauté pans: 10″ and 6″ or 8″, with at least 1 lid
- 2 nonstick saucepans: 2 quarts and 3 quarts, with lids
- 1 saucepan with a steamer insert, 1 collapsible steaming basket that will fit into a 3-quart saucepan, or 1 inexpensive bamboo steamer
- 1 rondeau (a large round, shallow pan with two handles and a lid, used for searing, braising, and stewing): 4 quarts
- 1 heavy-duty stockpot

- 1 or 2 nonstick baking sheets
- 1 nonstick baking pan: 13″ × 9″
- 1 large nonstick roasting pan, with rack and lid
- 1 casserole: 2 quarts
- 1 nonstick tart pan with removable bottom: 9″
- 6 or 8 nonstick molds or ramekins (not only for desserts but also as *mise en place* containers): 4 or 6 ounces

- 1 chef's knife: 8″, 10″, or 12″, according to comfort when the knife is balanced in your hand
- 1 paring knife
- 1 serrated knife, for bread and tomatoes

- ✤ 1 steel for sharpening knives, or an electric sharpener
- ✤ 1 block, magnet bar, or other safe, convenient method for storing knives
- ✤ 1 upright container (such as a flowerpot or ceramic crock) to hold small, constantly used implements in an easy-to-reach area, such as near the stove

- ✤ 1 slotted spoon
- ✤ 1 skimmer
- ✤ 2 whisks: 1 balloon and 1 sauce
- ✤ 1 rubber spatula
- ✤ 1 plastic spatula made specifically for nonstick cookware
- ✤ 2 or 3 wooden spoons of varying sizes, with 1 having a long handle
- ✤ 2 ladles: 2 ounces and 4 ounces
- ✤ 1 cooking fork (long handle, long tines)
- ✤ 2 tongs: 1 medium and 1 large

- ✤ Set of metal or plastic measuring cups for dry measure
- ✤ Set of glass measuring cups with lips for liquid measure
- ✤ Set of measuring spoons
- ✤ Scale for measuring grams and ounces

- ✤ Heavy-duty electric mixer
- ✤ Heavy-duty food processor
- ✤ Heavy-duty blender
- ✤ Handheld immersion blender

- ✤ Chinois or china cap (a fine-mesh conical sieve for fine straining)
- ✤ Colander

- Food mill
- Round mesh strainer with handle or pasta strainer
- Traditional stainless steel mandoline or the less expensive plastic vegetable slicer

- Set of stainless-steel work bowls, ranging in size from 1 cup to 6–8 quarts
- Hardwood cutting board, at least 16″ × 12″
- Box grater
- Salad spinner
- Pastry bag with a few basic tips
- Rolling pin
- Instant-read thermometer
- Candy thermometer

- Cloth dish towels
- Pot holders
- Oven mitt
- Paper towels

If this seems like kitchen overkill, it is not. You will use much of this equipment daily. And when cooking for more than one or two people, you will find yourself wishing for more pots and pans (and hands).

We suggest that all of your cookware be nonstick simply because it helps save calories and fat by requiring very little or no oil for successful cooking. At the French Culinary Institute, we have had great success with All-Clad cookware, but there are other brands that offer excellent features as well. When storing nonstick cookware, place a kitchen towel or a triple layer of paper towels between pans to prevent scratching that would mar the cooking surface.

When roasting, whether using a nonstick pan or a conventional pan, line it with aluminum foil prior to filling, then place the meat or poultry on a rack. This not only speeds cleanup but also keeps the meat or poultry away from the fat that will accumulate in the pan.

In addition to basic equipment, the healthy French kitchen should have a well-stocked pantry. Among the items with a prominent place on the shelf, you should find:

- Fine-quality dried herbs (as well as fresh, when available)
- Whole peppercorns in a pepper mill
- Coarse and sea salt
- Olive and other oils, particularly canola and safflower
- An assortment of vinegars
- Flours
- Sugars
- Leavening agents
- Canned tomatoes
- Rices and other grains

Your freezer should always contain a supply of homemade stocks, stored in easy-to-use 1-cup containers, and butter (to keep it fresh for the occasional use).

INDISPENSABLE TECHNIQUES

Once you have the equipment and the well-stocked pantry, a few basic kitchen techniques will speed you on your way to healthy cooking in the French manner.

All vegetables should be well-washed in a sink filled with cold water. Rinse by agitating the water with your hands, repeating the process until the water is clear and clean. Properly washed, dried, and stored, fresh products will stay fresh for longer periods than when poorly handled. The new resealable plastic bags made specifically for storing produce are particularly useful storage aids.

In the French kitchen, there are also classic methods of shaping and cutting vegetables. This is done to give a particular form for uniform cooking and to improve aesthetic presentation. These are among the most commonly used.

Brunoise: Vegetables cut into minute cubes, approximately ⅛″ or less square.

Chiffonade: Leafy vegetables cut into thin strips by rolling a stack of three or four leaves into a cigar shape and then cutting them crosswise into fine julienne.

Ciseler: To finely chop onions, shallots, and garlic. This method produces a fine, tiny dice and doesn't force the juices out as regular chopping would. To cut an onion in this manner, first wash and peel it. Then cut it in half through the root end. Place each half, cut side down, with the root end to the left (if you're right-handed). Make fine vertical slices, then make horizontal cuts, both extending almost all the way to the root. Finally, slice parallel to the root. The pieces should fall in an even dice. For other vegetables, you may need to trim off round edges to obtain flat surfaces so that an even dice can be cut. Save trimmed pieces for soups or stocks.

Cocotte: Vegetables trimmed into oval shapes about 2″ long.

Concasser: Herb sprigs or tomatoes coarsely chopped with a chef's knife.

Émincer: To slice vegetables, usually crosswise, very thinly.

Hacher: Finely minced small bunches of herb sprigs to be used as flavoring or garnish.

Jardinière: Vegetables cut into thin squared sticks, usually about 2″ long and less than 1/16″ thick.

Julienne: Vegetables cut into thin, uniform matchsticks, usually about 2″ long and ⅛″ to ⅒″ thick.

Macédoine: Vegetable squares cut from jardinière sticks.

Mirepoix: Vegetables—classically, carrots, onions, and celery—cut into unshaped chunks, no more than ⅟₁₆″ in size.

Paysanne: Vegetables cut into cubes or triangles, often from jardinière sticks.

Tourner: Vegetables trimmed into small, faceted, uniform shapes, usually oval or olive-shaped. Different sizes have different descriptive names depending upon their lengths.

You can, as professional chefs do, prepare vegetables in two ways. Those *à l'anglaise* are cooked in advance until just tender, then refreshed in cold water and reheated with seasonings at serving time. Vegetables *à l'étuvé* are cooked and served immediately. The former allows you extra time during the final stages of meal preparation.

Blanching vegetables is done to set color and flavor, firm the flesh, or loosen skin for ease of removal. This is accomplished by placing prepared vegetables in rapidly boiling salted water for a brief period, usually no more than 30 seconds. Quickly drain them and immediately plunge them into ice or very cold water to halt the cooking process.

The **roasting of vegetables** is often done to enhance their flavor by allowing the sugars to caramelize without the addition of excessive fats. Root vegetables, garlic, and tomatoes are frequently roasted.

Citrus peel is frequently zested to use as a flavoring in all types of dishes. The pungent aroma adds enormous savor without the addition of calories or fat. Use a zester, small paring knife, or vegetable peeler to remove only a thin layer of oily colored rind from any citrus fruit. Cut the rind into very thin strips or chop it into a very fine dice. To grate zest, remove only the colored outer rind using the smallest grid of a box grater.

One of the most important and health-aware techniques is to cool hot foods in an **ice-water bath**. This technique halts the cooking process and speeds cooling in order to prevent the formation of bacteria. Foods cooled in this manner are easily skimmed free of fat particles and are frequently then chilled further with refrigeration or freezing. Place the container of hot food into a larger receptacle (a plugged sink works well) filled with enough ice and cold water to come about two-thirds up the sides of the hot container. Stir the contents from time to time and add ice, as necessary, to the outer container to speed cooling.

As you venture forth into the realm of healthy French cooking, you will find that the tenets of The French Culinary Institute—*Qualité, Discipline, et Réalité*—will come alive in your kitchen. Quality in the meals that you will learn to prepare, discipline in your organized home kitchen, and the reality of the deeply flavored, health-conscious diet you will discover.

Some of the recipes are not listed as they would be for the "professional" chef. For example, recipes do not call for peeling and trimming carrots, as that is understood for the home cook.

BASIC RECIPES

The recipes in this section are often used as components of other recipes throughout the book. Many of them are also used as flavorings for simple sautéed dishes; as sauces for grilled meat, poultry, or fish; or as dressings for salads or vegetables.

Brown Veal Stock, Brown Chicken Stock, and White Chicken Stock are truly French kitchen basics that you should always have on hand, preferably frozen in 1-cup amounts. Acquaint yourself with these few recipes. They will help you healthfully cook dishes that are filled with the essence of fine French cooking.

BROWN VEAL STOCK
(*Fond Brun*)

Brown veal stock, a core ingredient for many of our recipes, is a freezer must-have. We suggest doubling, or even tripling, this recipe and freezing the stock in easy-to-use 1-cup containers.

5	pounds veal bones
1	large carrot, chopped
1	medium onion, chopped
5	quarts water
¾	cup chopped plum tomatoes
¼	cup tomato paste
1	clove garlic, minced
3	sprigs fresh flat-leaf parsley
2	sprigs fresh thyme

Preheat the oven to 400°F.

Rinse the bones and remove all fat and blood. Using a cleaver, chop the bones into small pieces and evenly spread them in a heavy roasting pan. Place in the oven and roast for about 10 minutes, or until the bones begin to brown.

Add the carrots and onions. Stir to combine. Continue to roast for 15 minutes, or until the vegetables are lightly browned. Remove from the oven and, using a slotted spoon, transfer the bones and vegetables to a large stockpot.

Place the roasting pan over high heat and add 1 quart of the water. Bring to a boil and deglaze the pan, stirring constantly with a wooden spoon.

Pour the deglazing liquid over the bones and vegetables. Add the remaining 4 quarts water. Bring to a boil over high heat. Reduce the heat to medium-low and skim the foam off the top. Add the tomatoes, tomato paste, garlic, parsley, and thyme. Gently simmer for about 6 hours, frequently skimming foam off the top.

Remove from the heat and strain through a fine sieve into a nonreactive container. Place the container in an ice-water bath (page 33) and let cool.

Cover and refrigerate for at least 8 hours. Remove and discard the layer of fat that has solidified on top. Cover and store in the refrigerator for up to 3 days. Or pour into 1-cup containers, cover, label, date, and freeze for up to 6 months.

YIELD: 5 CUPS

PER CUP

46 CALORIES
1.4 G. TOTAL FAT
0.5 G. SATURATED FAT
12 MG. CHOLESTEROL

CONSOMMÉ
(*Consommé*)

The clarity of this traditional French soup is achieved by the "raft," which forms on the top of the simmering broth, holds onto all particles and impurities that attach themselves to it. Consommé is best served just barely warm in a simple, beautifully clear Burgundy glass. However, small soup cups with handles also make a lovely presentation. You may want to add herbs—thyme, rosemary, and tarragon are traditional choices—to boost the flavor with a slight herbal essence.

12	ounces lean ground chicken
12	ounces lean ground beef
8	ounces very ripe plum tomatoes, cored and chopped
2	ribs celery, sliced
1	large carrot, cut into brunoise (page 31)
1	medium leek, white part only, well-washed and sliced
4	sprigs fresh flat-leaf parsley
3	large egg whites
3	quarts White Chicken Stock (page 37)

In a heavy stockpot, combine the chicken, beef, tomatoes, celery, carrots, leeks, parsley, and egg whites. Using 2 wooden spoons, grind the ingredients together.

Add the stock. Slowly bring to a simmer over medium-low heat. Stir frequently until all the ingredients come to the surface and form a "raft." After the raft forms, do not stir again. Slowly simmer for 1 hour.

Line a fine sieve with cheesecloth and place in a nonreactive container set in an ice-water bath (page 33).

Using a ladle, very gently scoop out and discard the center of the raft until you can see the liquid. Carefully ladle the liquid, 1 scoop at a time, into the sieve. Take care not to disturb the remaining raft.

After the consommé has been strained, do not agitate it. Let cool, then cover and refrigerate for at least 8 hours. Carefully remove and discard any fat that has solidified on top.

Cover and store in the refrigerator for up to 3 days. Or pour into 1-cup containers, cover, label, date, and freeze for up to 3 months.

YIELD: 6 CUPS

PER CUP

55 CALORIES
0.5 G. TOTAL FAT
0.1 G. SATURATED FAT
1 MG. CHOLESTEROL

BROWN CHICKEN STOCK
(*Fond Brun de Volaille*)

To make a rich stock, roast the bones and vegetables before cooking them in liquid. This produces intense flavor without any added calories or fat.

4   pounds chicken bones or carcasses
2   large carrots, sliced
2   large ribs celery, sliced
1   leek, white part only, well-washed and sliced
6   quarts water
2   sprigs fresh flat-leaf parsley
1   tablespoon dried thyme
1   bay leaf
1   very ripe plum tomato, cored and chopped

Preheat the oven to 450°F. Rinse the chicken bones, removing any bloody parts. Using a cleaver, cut the bones into small pieces and evenly spread them in a heavy roasting pan. Place in the oven and roast for 5 minutes. Using a wooden spoon, stir the bones and then roast for an additional 10 minutes. Drain off all the fat.

Stir the carrots, celery, and leeks into the pan and return the pan to the oven. Roast for 10 minutes, or until the bones are nicely browned but not burned. Transfer the bones and vegetables to a fine sieve and let the fat drain off.

Place the roasting pan over high heat and add 1 quart of the water. Bring to a boil and deglaze the pan, stirring constantly with a wooden spoon.

Transfer the roasted bones and vegetables to a large stockpot. Add the remaining 5 quarts water. Add the deglazing water from the roasting pan.

Tie the parsley, thyme, and bay leaf in a small piece of cheesecloth and add to the pot. Stir in the tomatoes and bring to a boil. Reduce the heat to medium-low and simmer for 3 hours, or until a rich stock has formed.

Remove from the heat and strain through a fine sieve into a nonreactive container. Place the container in an ice-water bath (page 33) and let cool.

Cover and refrigerate for at least 8 hours. Remove and discard the layer of fat that has solidified on top. Cover and store in the refrigerator for up to 3 days. Or pour into 1-cup containers, cover, label, date, and freeze for up to 6 months.

YIELD: 4 CUPS

PER CUP

41 CALORIES
1.5 G. TOTAL FAT
0.3 G. SATURATED FAT
12 MG. CHOLESTEROL

WHITE CHICKEN STOCK
(*Fond Blanc de Volaille*)

If you have a very large stockpot, it is a good idea to triple this recipe so that you will have a convenient store of this much-used stock in the freezer. This de-fatted, unsalted stock can be used to healthfully enrich all manner of soups, stews, and sauces.

8	pounds chicken bones or carcasses, all skin and fat removed
10	cups water
2	large ribs celery, sliced
1	large carrot, sliced
1	leek, white part only, well-washed and sliced
4	sprigs fresh flat-leaf parsley
1	tablespoon dried thyme
2	bay leaves

Place the chicken bones in a container large enough to hold them. Cover with ice water and soak for 3 hours, refreshing the ice as needed. This will pull out all of the blood and other impurities that can cause the stock to cloud. Using a slotted spoon, remove the bones from the soaking water; take care not to disturb the impurities deposited on the bottom of the container. Discard the ice water.

Place the bones in a large stockpot. Add the water. Bring to a boil over high heat, skimming off any foam from the top. Reduce the heat to medium-low. Add the celery, carrots, and leeks.

Tie the parsley, thyme, and bay leaves in a small piece of cheesecloth and add to the pot. Cook at a very low simmer for 4 hours.

Remove from the heat and slowly strain through a fine sieve, taking care that the particles at the bottom do not mix into the stock. Pour into a nonreactive container. Place the container in an ice-water bath (page 33) and let cool.

Cover and refrigerate for at least 8 hours. Remove and discard any fat that has solidified on top.

Cover and store in the refrigerator for up to 3 days. Or pour into 1-cup containers, cover, label, date, and freeze for up to 6 months.

YIELD: 4 CUPS

PER CUP

35 CALORIES
1.5 G. TOTAL FAT
0.4 G. SATURATED FAT
11 MG. CHOLESTEROL

SMART WHITE CHICKEN STOCK
(*Fond de Volaille Pratique*)

What's smart about this stock is that you eat the chicken and vegetables that produce its wonderful aroma and flavor. You can also serve the stock as a clear soup and the chicken and vegetables as a separate main course. And, of course, the stock can be used in place of any other chicken stock.

1	pound skinless chicken breasts
10	ounces skinless chicken legs
3	quarts water
	Coarse salt
1½	pounds carrots
4	leeks, white part only, well-washed and trimmed
1	large rib celery, peeled to remove all strings and cut into 4 pieces
4	sprigs fresh flat-leaf parsley
1	teaspoon dried thyme
2	bay leaves
	Dijon mustard (optional)

In a rondeau or large heavy-bottomed casserole, combine the chicken breasts, chicken legs, and water. Season with the salt. Slowly bring to a boil over medium heat. Simmer for 20 minutes.

Add the carrots, leeks, and celery. Tie the parsley, thyme, and bay leaves in a small piece of cheesecloth and add to the pot. Cover the pot with a layer of foil into which you have poked about 8 holes and simmer for 1 hour.

If serving immediately, remove from the heat and serve directly from the pot at the table. Pull the chicken pieces apart and divide among shallow soup bowls. Place equal portions of the vegetables in the bowls and ladle broth over the top. Serve with a touch of mustard (if using) and additional salt, if desired.

If using as a stock, remove from the heat and strain through a fine sieve into a nonreactive container. Reserve the chicken and vegetables for another use. Place the container in an ice-water bath (page 33) and cool.

Cover and refrigerate for at least 8 hours. Remove and discard the layer of fat that has solidified on top. Cover and store in the refrigerator for up to 3 days. Or pour into 1-cup containers, cover, label, date, and freeze for up to 6 months.

YIELD: 8 CUPS

PER 2 CUPS

363 CALORIES
11 G. TOTAL FAT
3 G. SATURATED FAT
170 MG. CHOLESTEROL

GRILLED VEGETABLE STOCK
(*Fond de Légumes Grillés*)

This stock is multipurpose. It is a great soup base, a low-fat deglazing liquid, a highly flavorful and healthy poaching essence for fish, and even a basting sauce for lamb and pork. It's so flavorful that a little goes a long way. You can combine any vegetables that you like—grilled tomato, eggplant, and garlic is a favorite Provençal combination. Even a combination of vegetable scraps will work. A teaspoon or so of chopped fresh herbs such as tarragon or parsley will add even more savor with no additional calories.

6   ounces button mushrooms, brushed clean
3   medium red bell peppers, seeded and quartered
1   large white onion, quartered with root intact
1   teaspoon olive oil
1   cup water

Preheat the grill.

Brush the mushrooms, peppers, and onions with the oil. Place on the grill and grill, turning once, for 4 minutes, or until the vegetables are nicely marked but not charred.

Transfer to a large saucepan and add the water. Bring to a simmer over medium heat. Cover and cook at a low simmer for 45 minutes.

Strain through a fine sieve into a heatproof bowl, using a spatula to gently push on the vegetables to extract as much of the flavorful liquid as possible.

Cover and store in the refrigerator for up to 2 days. Or pour into a 1-cup container, cover, label, date, and freeze for up to 6 months.

YIELD: 1 CUP

PER CUP

129 CALORIES
12 G. TOTAL FAT
1.6 G. SATURATED FAT
0 MG. CHOLESTEROL

MUSHROOM STOCK
(*Fond de Champignons*)

An ideal low-fat, profoundly flavorful liquid for deglazing fish, chicken, pork, or vegetable sautés. Just before serving, you might stir in a bit of chopped fresh chervil for a subtle hint of freshness. Other herbs will overpower the gentle fragrance of the button mushrooms.

1   pound button mushrooms, brushed clean
2   cups White Chicken Stock (page 37)

In a large heavy saucepan, combine the mushrooms and stock. Bring to a boil over high heat. Reduce the heat to medium-low and simmer for 30 minutes.

Remove from the heat and, using a slotted spoon, remove and discard the mushrooms. Carefully and slowly strain the stock through a fine sieve, using only about three-quarters of the liquid and allowing the remaining liquid to hold the mushroom particles at the bottom of the pan.

Cover and store in the refrigerator for up to 3 days. Or pour into 1-cup containers, cover, label, date, and freeze for up to 6 months.

YIELD: 2 CUPS

PER CUP

24 CALORIES
0.2 G. TOTAL FAT
0 G. SATURATED FAT
0 MG. CHOLESTEROL

FISH STOCK
(*Fumet de Poisson*)

Fish stock (also called fumet) is a clear, rich broth that's a very useful kitchen basic. We suggest that you triple this recipe and freeze the extra. Be certain that the fish skeletons are well-cleaned of gills and of any impurities around the head, or the stock will be cloudy. Snapper and sole make the finest fumets. Fattier fish, such as salmon, should be avoided.

2   pounds fish skeletons, well-cleaned with gills removed
1   leek, white part with a bit of green attached, well-washed and chopped
1   bay leaf
2   quarts water

If the skeletons are large, crack them into small pieces with a chef's knife. Place in a heavy stockpot. Add the leeks, bay leaf, and water. Bring to a boil over high heat. Reduce the heat to medium-low and simmer, uncovered, for 30 minutes.

Remove from the heat and strain through a fine sieve into a nonreactive container. Place the container in an ice-water bath (page 33) and let cool.

Cover and refrigerate for at least 8 hours. Remove and discard any fat that has solidified on top.

Cover and store in the refrigerator for up to 2 days. Or pour into 1-cup containers, cover, label, date, and freeze for up to 6 months.

YIELD: 4 CUPS

PER CUP

36 CALORIES
0.4 G. TOTAL FAT
0.2 G. SATURATED FAT
16 MG. CHOLESTEROL

CARROT ESSENCE
(*Fond de Carottes*)

You can create a well-seasoned essence using almost any vegetable. However, for vegetables that absorb liquid quickly, such as fennel, use 3 cups of water. The nutrient value will vary only slightly for most vegetable essences.

1	pound carrots, chopped
1½	cups water

In a large heavy saucepan, combine the carrots and water. Bring to a boil over high heat. Reduce the heat to medium-low and simmer for 45 minutes.

Remove from the heat. Use a slotted spoon to remove and discard the carrots. Carefully and slowly strain the stock through a fine sieve.

Cover and store in the refrigerator for up to 2 days.

YIELD: ½ CUP

PER ½ CUP

5 CALORIES
0 G. TOTAL FAT
0 G. SATURATED FAT
0 MG. CHOLESTEROL

41

CELERY ESSENCE
(*Fond de Céleri*)

The bite of fresh ginger contributes an aromatic zest to the otherwise bland flavor of celery. This is particularly nice when the essence is used with grilled fish or chicken.

1 bunch celery, chopped
1½ cups water
1 tablespoon chopped fresh ginger

In a large heavy saucepan, combine the celery, water, and ginger. Bring to a boil over high heat. Reduce the heat to medium-low and simmer for 45 minutes.

Remove from the heat. Use a slotted spoon to remove and discard the celery and ginger. Carefully and slowly strain the stock through a fine sieve.

Cover and store in the refrigerator for up to 2 days.

YIELD: ½ CUP

PER ½ CUP

2 CALORIES
0 G. TOTAL FAT
0 G. SATURATED FAT
0 MG. CHOLESTEROL

COURT-BOUILLON
(*Court-Bouillon*)

Court-bouillon is a poaching liquid for chicken and fish. (If you use it to poach fish, add the juice of 2 lemons or 3 tablespoons of a favorite vinegar—except balsamic.) But you can also serve it as a broth with the poaching vegetables, which is known as à la nage, *and our nutritional profile includes the vegetables. When serving the bouillon as a broth, use a slotted spoon to remove the coriander seeds, parsley, bay leaf, and thyme.*

2 large carrots, very thinly sliced
1 large onion, very thinly sliced
1 teaspoon coriander seeds
4 sprigs fresh flat-leaf parsley
1 bay leaf
1 sprig fresh thyme
4 cups water
1 cup white wine
  Coarse salt and freshly cracked black pepper

In a large saucepan, combine the carrots, onions, coriander seeds, parsley, bay leaf, and thyme. Stir in the water and wine. Bring to a boil over high heat. Season with the salt and pepper. Boil for 10 minutes. Remove and discard the bay leaf and thyme sprig.

Serve or cover and store in the refrigerator for up to 3 days. Or pour into 1-cup containers, cover, label, date, and freeze for up to 6 months.

YIELD: 5 CUPS   PER CUP

61 CALORIES
0.2 G. TOTAL FAT
0 G. SATURATED FAT
0 MG. CHOLESTEROL

ESSENCE OF SAUTÉED RED PEPPERS, ONIONS, AND GARLIC
(Fond de Poivrons Rouges, Oignons, et Ail Sautés)

This very aromatic essence can be used as a base for vinaigrettes or soups, as a deglazing liquid for a fish or chicken sauté, or as a poaching juice for fish or chicken.

1   teaspoon olive oil
1   clove garlic, minced
2   medium red bell peppers, seeded and finely chopped
1   medium onion, sliced
2   cups water

In a large nonstick sauté pan, warm the oil over medium heat. Add the garlic and sauté for 2 minutes, or until just golden. Stir in the peppers and onions and cook slowly for 3 minutes. Do not brown. Add the water and bring to a simmer. Cover and cook at a low simmer for 45 minutes.

Remove from the heat and strain through a fine sieve into a heatproof bowl, using a spatula to gently push on the vegetables to extract as much of the flavorful liquid as possible.

Serve or cover and store in the refrigerator for up to 2 days. Or pour into 1-cup containers, cover, label, date, and freeze for up to 6 months.

YIELD: 2 CUPS   PER ½ CUP

16 CALORIES
1.2 G. TOTAL FAT
0.2 G. SATURATED FAT
0 MG. CHOLESTEROL

43

Low-Fat Béchamel Sauce
(*Sauce Béchamel Minceur*)

Béchamel sauce is one of the basic white sauces of the classic French repertoire. It is traditionally made by whisking hot whole milk into a butter and flour roux. This is our low-fat version. Use as a sauce for vegetables or as directed in specific recipes.

1½	tablespoons cornstarch
1½	cups 1% low-fat milk
2	whole cloves
½	small onion
1	bay leaf
	Salt and freshly ground white pepper

Place the cornstarch in a small heavy nonstick saucepan. Whisk in ½ cup of the milk until smooth. Whisk in the remaining 1 cup milk. Stick the cloves into the onion and add to the saucepan. Add the bay leaf.

Cook over low heat, stirring frequently, for 12 minutes, or until the mixture is very hot and well-infused with the onion and bay leaf. Raise the heat to medium and simmer, stirring constantly, for 5 minutes, or until the sauce has thickened. Season with the salt and pepper.

Remove from the heat and push through a fine sieve into a clean container.

YIELD: 1½ CUPS

PER ½ CUP

60 CALORIES
0.8 G. TOTAL FAT
0.6 G. SATURATED FAT
4 MG. CHOLESTEROL

Mushroom Sauce
(*Sauce aux Champignons*)

This earthy, low-calorie, low-fat sauce is a perfect accent for grilled vegetables or for a light entrée of grilled chicken or fish mixed with fresh field greens.

3	ounces button mushrooms, brushed clean
1	teaspoon olive oil
½	cup White Chicken Stock (page 37)
1	tablespoon fresh lemon juice
	Salt and freshly ground black pepper

Preheat the oven to 450°F.

Brush the mushrooms with the oil and place on a nonstick baking sheet. Place in the oven and roast for 10 minutes. Stir so that the browned sides are on top. Return to the oven and roast for 5 minutes, or until golden brown.

Transfer the mushrooms to a blender or a food processor fitted with the metal blade. Add the stock and lemon juice. Process until smooth. Season with the salt and pepper.

Serve or cover and store in the refrigerator for up to 2 days.

YIELD: 1¼ CUPS

PER ½ CUP

38 CALORIES
2.4 G. TOTAL FAT
0.4 G. SATURATED FAT
0 MG. CHOLESTEROL

CLASSICAL TOMATO SAUCE
(Sauce Tomate Classique)

This sauce, a staple of Chef Alain Sailhac's childhood, combines some of the aromatic foods of his native Provence—tomato, garlic, and thyme. It has a multitude of uses as a sauce: for grilled, broiled, or sautéed fish; for fish or white-meat sausages; or for any grilled white meat. It can also be used as a base for more complex dishes or as a seasoning for pasta or grilled vegetables. The final cooking period blends the tomatoes and stock and permits the sauce to stay fresh-tasting for a longer storage period. The recipe may easily be tripled, with any excess frozen for future use.

1 tablespoon olive oil
1 small onion, chopped
1 clove garlic, minced
4 very ripe plum tomatoes, peeled, cored, seeded, and quartered
2 sprigs fresh thyme, leaves only
1 cup White Chicken Stock (page 37) or water
   Salt and freshly ground black pepper

Warm the oil in a medium sauté pan over low heat. Add the onions and allow to cook slowly for 5 minutes. Do not brown. Stir in the garlic and cook for 1 minute. Stir in the tomatoes and thyme. Cook for 5 minutes.

(continued)

45

Transfer to a blender or a food processor fitted with the metal blade. Add the stock or water and process until smooth. Pour into a medium saucepan. Season with the salt and pepper. Cover and cook over medium heat, stirring occasionally, for 10 minutes.

Serve or cover and store in the refrigerator for up to 3 days. Or pour into 1-cup containers, cover, label, date, and freeze for up to 6 months.

YIELD: 2 CUPS

PER ½ CUP

50 CALORIES
4 G. TOTAL FAT
0.6 G. SATURATED FAT
3 MG. CHOLESTEROL

ROASTED RED PEPPER AND TOMATO SAUCE
(*Sauce Tomate aux Poivrons Rouges*)

This is a great base for a fresh vegetable or bean soup. To use as a sauce for grilled or broiled fish, add a teaspoon of red wine vinegar for an acidic accent to the delicate fish. It is perfect, as is, as a sauce for meat or pasta.

1 teaspoon olive oil
1 clove garlic, minced
2 medium red bell peppers, roasted, peeled, seeded, and chopped
3 very ripe plum tomatoes, peeled, cored, seeded, and quartered
1 teaspoon fresh thyme leaves
Salt and freshly ground black pepper
1 cup White Chicken Stock (page 37) or water

Lightly brush a large nonstick sauté pan with ½ teaspoon of the oil. Place over medium heat and add the garlic. Sauté for 1 minute. Stir in the red peppers. Reduce the heat to medium-low and cook for 5 minutes.

While the peppers are cooking, lightly brush a small nonstick sauté pan with the remaining ½ teaspoon oil. Add the tomatoes and thyme. "Toast" the tomatoes over medium heat for 5 minutes, or until they are just lightly browned. Add to the pan with the peppers.

Season with the salt and black pepper. Cover and cook for 5 minutes. Stir in the stock or water and simmer for 10 minutes.

Remove from the heat and allow to cool slightly. Pour into a blender or a food processor fitted with the metal blade. Process until smooth.

Serve at room temperature or reheat. Store in the refrigerator for up to 4 days. Or pour into 1-cup containers, cover, label, date, and freeze for up to 6 months.

YIELD: 2 CUPS

PER ½ CUP

41 CALORIES
1.8 G. TOTAL FAT
0.3 G. SATURATED FAT
0 MG. CHOLESTEROL

SPINACH AND WATERCRESS SAUCE
(*Sauce de Cresson aux Épinards*)

This is a superb sauce for grilled or broiled seafood or grilled veal, chicken, pork, or vegetables. Its rich thickness masks the fact that it is virtually nonfat.

1	teaspoon olive oil
5	ounces fresh spinach leaves, washed and stems removed
1½	ounces watercress, stems removed
1	cup chopped fresh flat-leaf parsley
	Salt and freshly ground black pepper
1	small all-purpose potato, cooked, peeled, and cubed
1	cup White Chicken Stock (page 37) or water

Brush a large nonstick sauté pan with the oil. Place over medium heat and add the spinach, watercress, and parsley. Season with the salt and pepper. Cook, stirring frequently, for 2 minutes, or until the greens are wilted.

Place the potato and stock or water in a blender or a food processor fitted with the metal blade. Process until smooth. Pour into the pan. Cover and cook for 8 minutes. Remove from the heat and allow to cool slightly.

Transfer to the blender or food processor. Process until smooth. Season with the salt and pepper. If the sauce is too thick, add more water, 1 tablespoon at a time, until the desired consistency is achieved.

Serve at room temperature or reheat. Store in the refrigerator for up to 4 days. Or pour into 1-cup containers, cover, label, date, and freeze for up to 6 months.

YIELD: 2 CUPS

PER ½ CUP

36 CALORIES
2 G. TOTAL FAT
0 G. SATURATED FAT
0 MG. CHOLESTEROL

PUMPKIN AND PEAR SAUCE
(*Sauce aux Potirons et Poires*)

Pumpkins and pears are two favorites of the fall harvest. A pinch of ginger, either fresh or powdered, adds a refreshing dimension to their delicate flavors. As a sauce, this combination offers a nice balance to roast turkey or chicken. For an interesting soup, puree the sauce with cooked rice (you may need additional liquid) and garnish with toasted pumpkin seeds.

1	tablespoon olive oil
¼	cup chopped onions
6	ounces peeled and chopped pumpkin
1	large pear, peeled, cored, and chopped
1	tablespoon minced fresh ginger
1½	cups water
	Salt and freshly ground black pepper

In a medium nonstick saucepan, warm the oil over low heat. Add the onions and cook slowly for 7 minutes. Do not brown. Stir in the pumpkin and cook for 3 minutes.

Add the pears and ginger. Cook for 5 minutes. Add the water. Season with the salt and pepper.

Raise the heat and bring to a simmer. Cover and simmer for 10 minutes. Remove from the heat and allow to cool for a few minutes.

Transfer to a blender or a food processor fitted with the metal blade. Process until smooth.

Serve or cover and store in the refrigerator for up to 4 days.

YIELD: 2 CUPS

PER ½ CUP

72 CALORIES
4 G. TOTAL FAT
0.5 G. SATURATED FAT
0 MG. CHOLESTEROL

CITRUS SAUCE
(*Sauce aux Agrumes*)

An easy-to-make, very light sauce for grilled or broiled fish or shellfish, grilled pork tenderloins, or grilled or broiled poultry. It would also make a delightful dressing for a fruit salad.

2	oranges
2	grapefruit
	Juice of 1 lime

¼ teaspoon curry powder
1 very ripe medium banana, cubed
Salt and freshly ground black pepper

Using a paring knife, remove the skin and outer membranes from the oranges and grapefruit. Cut out each section from the membranes, catching any juice in a small bowl. Squeeze the juice from the membranes into the bowl. Strain and reserve the juice.

In a medium nonstick saucepan, combine the orange sections (with juice), grapefruit sections (with juice), lime juice, and curry powder. Bring to a simmer over medium heat. Stir in the bananas and season with the salt and pepper. Cover and simmer for 7 minutes.

Allow to cool slightly. Transfer to a blender or a food processor fitted with the metal blade. Process until smooth.

Serve or cover and store in the refrigerator for up to 4 days.

YIELD: 1½ CUPS

PER ½ CUP

156 CALORIES
0.6 G. TOTAL FAT
0 G. SATURATED FAT
0 MG. CHOLESTEROL

FIG AND PLUM CHUTNEY
(*"Chutney" avec Figues et Prunes*)

This chutney is a marvelous condiment for pork, veal, venison, and guinea hen.

½ teaspoon olive oil
2 very ripe large figs, cut into wedges
2 very ripe large plums, pitted and cut into small wedges
4 teaspoons sherry vinegar
Salt and freshly ground black pepper

Warm a small nonstick saucepan over medium heat. Brush the pan with the oil. Add the figs and plums and sauté for 10 minutes, or until the natural sugars have caramelized. Add the vinegar and stir to deglaze the pan. Cook for 1 minute. Season with the salt and pepper.

Serve or cover and store in the refrigerator for up to 4 days.

YIELD: 1 CUP

PER ¼ CUP

42 CALORIES
0.8 G. TOTAL FAT
0.1 G. SATURATED FAT
0 MG. CHOLESTEROL

TOMATO VINAIGRETTE
(*Vinaigrette aux Tomates*)

You can make this vinaigrette even more flavorful by adding 1 teaspoon of chopped fresh herbs such as basil, parsley, or thyme. It is a healthy and very tasty sauce for grilled vegetables or fish. Or use as a base for a slice of vegetable terrine. It can also serve as a colorful dressing for pungent salad greens like watercress or arugula.

2   medium very ripe plum tomatoes, peeled, cored, seeded, and chopped
2   cloves garlic, minced
4   teaspoons fresh lemon juice
2   teaspoons olive oil
Salt and freshly ground black pepper

Place the tomatoes, garlic, lemon juice, and oil in a blender or a food processor fitted with the metal blade. Process until very smooth. Season with the salt and pepper.

Serve or cover and store in the refrigerator for up to 2 days.

YIELD: 1 CUP

PER 1/4 CUP

30 CALORIES
2.4 G. TOTAL FAT
0.3 G. SATURATED FAT
0 MG. CHOLESTEROL

BEET VINAIGRETTE
(*Vinaigrette aux Betteraves*)

This beautiful, deliciously healthy sauce makes a colorful background for steamed or grilled fish or dresses a simple chilled vegetable salad such as mushroom, zucchini, artichoke, or cauliflower with finesse. It is especially good because the intense sweetness of the beets can liven up an otherwise bland vegetable dish. You can substitute fresh orange juice for the stock, if desired. For a change of taste, a few chopped capers or cornichons (tart pickles) or a bit of citrus zest will add a new dimension to the beets.

3   ounces beets, cooked, peeled, and chopped
½   cup White Chicken Stock (page 37)
1   teaspoon olive oil
1   teaspoon red wine vinegar
Salt and freshly ground black pepper

In a blender or a food processor fitted with the metal blade, combine the beets, stock, oil, and vinegar. Process until very smooth. Season with the salt and pepper.

Serve or cover and store in the refrigerator for up to 2 days.

YIELD: 1 CUP

PER ¼ CUP

22 CALORIES
1 G. TOTAL FAT
0.2 G. SATURATED FAT
0 MG. CHOLESTEROL

GREEN VINAIGRETTE
(*Vinaigrette aux Herbes Vertes*)

This sauce must be served immediately or it will darken and lose its intense freshness. It is a particularly fine accompaniment for fish or meat carpaccio or smoked fish.

8	ounces fresh spinach, washed and stems removed
2	tablespoons water
¼	cup Celery Essence (page 42)
2	tablespoons White Chicken Stock (page 37)
1	tablespoon white wine vinegar
1½	teaspoons olive oil
2	tablespoons chopped fresh flat-leaf parsley leaves
1	large sprig fresh oregano, leaves only
1	sprig fresh thyme, leaves only
1	leaf fresh sage
	Salt and freshly ground black pepper

Combine the spinach and water in a large saucepan. Cover and allow to steam over medium heat for 3 minutes, or until wilted. Remove from the heat and drain through a fine sieve, reserving 2 tablespoons of the liquid.

Transfer the spinach and reserved liquid to a blender or a food processor fitted with the metal blade. Add the celery essence, stock, vinegar, oil, parsley, oregano, thyme, and sage. Process until very smooth. Season with the salt and pepper. Serve immediately.

YIELD: 2 CUPS

PER ¼ CUP

13 CALORIES
0.7 G. TOTAL FAT
0.1 G. SATURATED FAT
0 MG. CHOLESTEROL

VEGETABLE VINAIGRETTE
(*Vinaigrette aux Légumes*)

This refreshing but zesty vinaigrette must be used the day it is made or it will become discolored and bitter.

2   very ripe plum tomatoes, cored and chopped
1   cucumber, peeled and chopped
    Juice of 1 lemon
1   teaspoon Worcestershire sauce
½   teaspoon Tabasco sauce
1½ teaspoons chopped fresh flat-leaf parsley
    Salt and freshly ground black pepper

Place the tomatoes and cucumbers in a blender or a food processor fitted with the metal blade. Process until smooth. Pour through a very fine sieve into a small bowl, pressing with the back of a spoon to strain off all of the liquid; discard any remaining solids.

Whisk in the lemon juice, Worcestershire sauce, and Tabasco sauce. Add the parsley. Season with the salt and pepper. Serve immediately.

YIELD: 1 CUP

PER ¼ CUP
19 CALORIES
0.2 G. TOTAL FAT
0 G. SATURATED FAT
0 MG. CHOLESTEROL

CITRUS VINAIGRETTE
(*Vinaigrette aux Agrumes*)

This simple vinaigrette is at its best used as a deglazing liquid for a chicken, pork, or veal sauté or as a sauce for grilled or baked fish. When serving with baked fish, combine the vinaigrette with the juices released from the fish as it bakes and spoon over the fish before serving.

2   large oranges, peeled and sectioned (juice reserved)
2   teaspoons fresh lemon juice
1   tablespoon olive oil

In a blender or a food processor fitted with the metal blade, combine the orange sections (with juice), lemon juice, and oil. Process until smooth.

Transfer to a small saucepan. Cook over medium-high heat for 5 minutes, or until reduced to 1 cup.

Serve or cover and store in the refrigerator for up to 3 days.

YIELD: 1 CUP

PER ¼ CUP

61 CALORIES
2.3 G. TOTAL FAT
0.5 G. SATURATED FAT
0 MG. CHOLESTEROL

TROPICAL VINAIGRETTE
(*Vinaigrette aux Fruits Tropicaux*)

Tropical breezes will waft over a whole roasted fish or pork loin when you combine this vinaigrette with the defatted pan juices. For a nice bite, stir in some chopped cilantro just before serving.

1   whole very ripe mango, peeled and seeded
½   cup chopped fresh pineapple
2   teaspoons minced jalapeño peppers (wear plastic gloves when handling)
1   cup Citrus Vinaigrette (opposite page)
2   teaspoons fresh lemon juice

In a blender or a food processor fitted with the metal blade, combine the mango, pineapple, peppers, vinaigrette, and lemon juice. Process until very smooth.

Serve or cover and store in the refrigerator for up to 2 days.

YIELD: 1⅔ CUPS

PER ⅓ CUP

72 CALORIES
1.5 G. TOTAL FAT
0.3 G. SATURATED FAT
0 MG. CHOLESTEROL

STRAWBERRY VINAIGRETTE
(*Vinaigrette aux Fraises*)

This bright red, sweet sauce is a glorious, low-fat accompaniment to roast duck or other birds or as a deglazing liquid for venison or other game sautés. Always give a sprinkle of freshly ground black pepper before serving to pique the taste buds for the sweetness to come.

	Zest of 1 lemon
1	cup water
6	fresh strawberries, hulled
1	teaspoon fresh lemon juice
1	teaspoon olive oil
	Salt and freshly ground black pepper

Combine the lemon zest and ½ cup of the water in a small saucepan. Bring to a boil over high heat. Reduce the heat to medium-low and simmer for 5 minutes. Drain through a fine sieve.

Place the strawberries and zest in a blender or a food processor fitted with the metal blade. Add the lemon juice, oil, and the remaining ½ cup water. Process until very smooth. Season with the salt and pepper.

Serve or cover and store in the refrigerator for up to 2 days.

YIELD: 1 CUP

PER ¼ CUP

17 CALORIES
1.2 G. TOTAL FAT
0.2 G. SATURATED FAT
0 MG. CHOLESTEROL

BASIC PASTRY
(*Pâtisserie*)

This sweet dough is used for making dessert tarts. It has such a small amount of fat that the plastic wrap is necessary to help hold the dough together as it is shaped. If you use the traditional floured surface, the low-fat dough will lose much of its moisture.

1	cup all-purpose flour
2	teaspoons sugar
½	teaspoon baking powder
	Pinch of salt

¼   cup 1% low-fat cottage cheese
1   tablespoon canola oil
2   tablespoons water

Place the flour, sugar, baking powder, and salt in a food processor fitted with the plastic blade. Pulse briefly to combine. With the motor running, add the cottage cheese and oil. Quickly add the water and pulse until just combined. The dough will be crumbly but moist.

Remove the dough from the processor bowl and, using your hands, gently pat the dough together to form a disk shape. Wrap the dough in plastic wrap and refrigerate for 30 minutes, or until well-chilled.

YIELD: ENOUGH TO MAKE
4 INDIVIDUAL TARTS

PER TART SHELL

162 CALORIES
4 G. TOTAL FAT
0.4 G. SATURATED FAT
0 MG. CHOLESTEROL

SAVORY PASTRY
(*Petits Fours Salés*)

This low-fat pastry is an excellent base for aromatic fillings in entrées, appe-tizers, or hors d'oeuvres. It is not recommended for desserts.

1   cup all-purpose flour
¼   teaspoon salt
1   large egg
1   tablespoon canola oil
1   tablespoon olive oil
1   tablespoon water

Place the flour and salt in a food processor fitted with the plastic blade. Pulse briefly to combine. With the motor running, add the egg, canola oil, olive oil, and water. Pulse until just combined. The dough will be crumbly but moist.

Remove the dough from the processor bowl and, using your hands, gently pat the dough together to from a disk shape. Wrap the dough in plastic wrap and refrigerate for 30 minutes, or until well-chilled.

YIELD: ENOUGH TO MAKE
4 INDIVIDUAL TARTS

PER TART SHELL

192 CALORIES
8.4 G. TOTAL FAT
1 G. SATURATED FAT
53 MG. CHOLESTEROL

Vanilla Pastry Cream
(*Crème Pâtissière à la Vanille*)

This light pastry cream is delicious as a dessert filling or sauce. To make chocolate pastry cream, simply grate 1 ounce of semisweet chocolate into the hot mixture and stir to combine.

2	tablespoons cornstarch
1	cup 1% low-fat milk
½	vanilla bean, split lengthwise
1	large egg
1	large egg yolk
3	tablespoons sugar

Place the cornstarch in a small nonstick saucepan. Whisk in ¼ cup of the milk until smooth. Whisk in the remaining ¾ cup milk. Scrape the seeds from the vanilla bean into the saucepan, then add the bean. Bring the mixture to a boil over medium heat, stirring constantly. Reduce the heat to low and cook for 1 minute. Remove from the heat.

In a small bowl, beat together the egg, egg yolk, and sugar. Beating constantly, add a small amount of the milk mixture to the egg mixture to temper it. Beating constantly, add the egg mixture to the milk mixture in the saucepan.

Cook over low heat, stirring constantly, for 1 minute, or until the mixture has thickened. Strain through a very fine sieve into a clean bowl.

Use the sauce warm or chilled. Store, tightly covered, in the refrigerator for up to 2 days.

YIELD: 1¼ CUPS

PER ¼ CUP

70 CALORIES
2 G. TOTAL FAT
0.7 G. SATURATED FAT
67 MG. CHOLESTEROL

FRENCH CUSTARD SAUCE
(*Crème Anglaise*)

*This low-fat version of the classic French dessert sauce can be used as a base
for plain cakes and tarts or as a sauce for fresh or poached fruit.*

2	tablespoons all-purpose flour
1¾	cups 1% low-fat milk
½	vanilla bean, split lengthwise
2	large eggs
¼	cup plus 1 tablespoon sugar

Place the flour in a medium nonstick saucepan. Slowly whisk in ½ cup of the
milk until smooth. Whisk in the remaining 1¼ cups milk. Scrape the seeds from the
vanilla bean into the saucepan, then add the bean. Bring the mixture to a boil over
medium heat, stirring constantly. Reduce the heat to low and cook for 1 minute. Remove from the heat.

In a small bowl, whisk together the eggs and sugar. Beating constantly, add a
small amount of the milk mixture to the egg mixture to temper it. Beating constantly,
add the egg mixture to the milk mixture in the saucepan.

Cook over low heat, stirring constantly, for 5 minutes, or until the mixture has
thickened. Strain through a very fine sieve into a clean bowl.

Use the sauce warm or chilled. Store, tightly covered, in the refrigerator for up
to 2 days.

YIELD: 2 CUPS

PER ¼ CUP

78 CALORIES
2 G. TOTAL FAT
0.7 G. SATURATED FAT
55 MG. CHOLESTEROL

SPRING MENUS

AH, SPRING. WHEN A YOUNG MAN'S FANCY TURNS TO LOVE, AND EVERY FRENCHMAN CAN THINK ONLY OF THE TENDER STALKS OF ASPARAGUS THAT WILL BE PEEKING THROUGH THE EARTH. THE RITES OF THE FRENCH SPRING PRODUCE MANY OF THE SAME SUCCULENT TREASURES THAT AMERICANS LOOK FORWARD TO AFTER A LONG, BARREN WINTER. IN FRANCE, NOT JUST GREEN ASPARAGUS APPEAR IN THE MARKETPLACE BUT ALSO FAT STALKS OF WHITE AND PURPLE, ALONG WITH *FRAISES DES BOIS*, THOSE TINY, SWEET WILD STRAWBERRIES FOUND ONLY IN THE WOODS. AS IN AMERICA, BRIGHT GREEN SUGARY PETITE PEAS, BABY ARTICHOKES, PERKY WATERCRESS, CRUNCHY RADISHES, THE FIRST INVIGORATING GREENS— CHARD, CHICORY, SORREL, AND SPINACH—AND THE ELUSIVE AND EXPENSIVE MORELS AND OTHER WILD MUSHROOMS ALL FIND A PLACE ON THE TABLE. MEALS ARE SOMEWHAT LIGHT- ENED AS WE REQUIRE LESS SUSTENANCE TO PREPARE OUR- SELVES FOR THE INDOLENT DAYS OF THE SUMMER TO COME.

ASPARAGUS SOUP

BREAST OF CHICKEN WITH FENNEL

STRAWBERRIES MARINATED IN PORT

PER SERVING

612 CALORIES

19 G. TOTAL FAT (28% OF CALORIES)

6 G. SATURATED FAT

172 MG. CHOLESTEROL

ASPARAGUS SOUP
(Soupe d'Asperges)

For a more intense green color, cook half of the asparagus stalks until very tender in the same water in which you blanch the tips. Add the pieces to the soup at the point you are making the puree. This soup is also very tasty served chilled with a dollop of nonfat sour cream in the center.

1½	pounds asparagus
2	teaspoons olive oil
½	medium onion, chopped
1	small all-purpose potato, peeled and cubed
5	cups White Chicken Stock (page 37)
	Salt and freshly ground black pepper
8	leaves fresh basil, cut into chiffonade (page 31)

Trim the tough bottoms from the asparagus stalks. Cut off the tips and set aside. Cut the remaining stalks into ½″ pieces.

Bring a medium saucepan of water to a boil over high heat and add a pinch of salt. Add the asparagus tips and cook for 30 seconds. Drain and set aside.

Warm the oil in a large saucepan over medium heat. Add the onions and allow them to cook very slowly for 10 minutes. Do not brown. Stir in the potatoes and the asparagus stalks. Add the stock and bring to a boil. Season with the salt and pepper.

ASPARAGUS SOUP

Reduce the heat to medium-low and simmer for 20 minutes, or until the vegetables are very tender. Remove from the heat and allow to cool slightly.

Transfer to a blender or a food processor fitted with the metal blade. Process until smooth.

Strain through a fine sieve into a clean saucepan. Bring to a simmer over medium heat. Simmer for 2 minutes, or until just heated through.

Divide among 4 soup bowls. Lay the asparagus tips on top and sprinkle with the basil. Serve immediately.

YIELD: 4 SERVINGS

PER SERVING

141 CALORIES
5 G. TOTAL FAT
0.9 G. SATURATED FAT
14 MG. CHOLESTEROL

BREAST OF CHICKEN WITH FENNEL
(Blanc de Poulet au Fenouil)

The pure, natural flavors of the dish speak for themselves. The fragrance sings of spring, and the healthful composition is a dieter's delight. You can replace the fennel essence with either Mushroom Stock (page 40) or White Chicken Stock (page 37).

2	large bulbs fennel
2	teaspoons olive oil
1	large onion, chopped
	Salt and freshly ground black pepper
6	ounces button mushrooms, brushed clean and halved or quartered
2	cloves garlic, minced
4	boneless, skinless chicken breasts (5 ounces each)
2	red bell peppers, roasted, peeled, seeded, and diced
½	cup fennel essence (see note)
1	tablespoon sherry vinegar
4	sprigs fresh fennel

Remove any hard or discolored outer layers from the fennel bulbs. Trim the root ends and feathery tops. Cut the bulbs in half lengthwise, then cut crosswise into ½" slices.

Warm 1 teaspoon of the oil in a large heavy-bottomed nonstick saucepan over medium-low heat. Add the onions and allow them to cook very slowly for 10 minutes, or until they are just beginning to color. Add the fennel and season with the salt and black pepper. Reduce the heat to low to allow the vegetables to steam slightly and to prevent excessive browning. Cook, stirring occasionally, for 8 minutes, or until the onions and fennel are tender and nicely browned but still crunchy.

Add the mushrooms. Cover and cook for 5 minutes. Stir in the garlic and re-move from the heat.

Season the chicken breasts with the salt and black pepper. Brush a large non-stick sauté pan with the remaining 1 teaspoon oil. Place over medium heat and place the chicken in the pan in a single layer. Cook for 8 minutes, or until nicely browned. Turn the pieces and cook for 3 minutes. Top with half of the roasted peppers. Cook for 5 minutes, or until the breasts are golden brown. Transfer the chicken and peppers to a plate. Cover with foil to keep warm.

Place the sauté pan over medium-high heat. Add ¼ cup of the fennel essence and stir with a wooden spoon to deglaze the pan. Pour into the saucepan with the fennel. Place the saucepan over medium heat and add the remaining ¼ cup fennel essence. Cook, stirring with the wooden spoon, for 1 minute, or just until the saucepan is deglazed.

Add the chicken and pepper mixture. Stir in the vinegar. Cover and cook for 5 minutes.

Place equal portions of the vegetables in the center of each of 4 warm dinner plates. Place a chicken breast in the center of the vegetables and sprinkle with the remaining roasted peppers. Garnish with the fennel sprigs.

Chef's Note: To make fennel essence, see the recipe for Carrot Essence (page 41) and make the adjustments suggested.

YIELD: 4 SERVINGS

PER SERVING

307 CALORIES
7.7 G. TOTAL FAT
1.8 G. SATURATED FAT
119 MG. CHOLESTEROL

STRAWBERRIES MARINATED IN PORT
(*Fraises Marinées au Porto*)

We used real vanilla ice cream in the nutritional analysis for this recipe. You could, of course, substitute nonfat vanilla yogurt or low-fat ice cream for even less fat.

2	cups hulled and quartered fresh strawberries
½	cup port
2	tablespoons fresh orange juice
1	teaspoon sugar
½	teaspoon grated orange zest
2	cups French vanilla ice cream
4	sprigs fresh mint

Place the strawberries in a large shallow glass bowl.

In a small bowl, whisk together the port, orange juice, sugar, and orange zest. Pour over the strawberries. Toss to combine. Cover and refrigerate for 2 hours, stirring occasionally.

Divide the ice cream among 4 wine goblets. Pour the strawberries over the top. Garnish with the mint.

YIELD: 4 SERVINGS

PER SERVING

164 CALORIES
6 G. TOTAL FAT
3.2 G. SATURATED FAT
39 MG. CHOLESTEROL

VEGETABLE TERRINE

SADDLE OF RABBIT WITH GARLIC

STRAWBERRY-RHUBARB SOUP

<u>PER SERVING</u>

683 CALORIES

13 G. TOTAL FAT (17% OF CALORIES)

3 G. SATURATED FAT

129 MG. CHOLESTEROL

VEGETABLE TERRINE
(*Confit de Légumes en Terrine*)

This is one of André Soltner's signature dishes. At Lutèce, it was often served warm as an appetizer garnished with a few grilled shrimp or, frequently, as a side dish to a simple entrée.

2	large leeks, white part with a little green
	Salt
3	large very ripe tomatoes
¼	cup water
4	shallots
4	cloves garlic
1	teaspoon sugar
2	teaspoons olive oil
5	ounces domestic or wild mushrooms, brushed clean and halved if large
1	tablespoon fresh lemon juice
2	small eggplants, cut lengthwise into ¾″ slices
2	medium zucchini, cut lengthwise into ¾″ slices
2	red bell peppers, roasted, peeled, seeded, and cut lengthwise into ¾″ slices
	Freshly ground black pepper
	Pinch of cayenne pepper

3   tablespoons minced fresh oregano
¾   cup Vegetable Vinaigrette (page 52)
4   sprigs fresh flat-leaf parsley

Split the leeks in half lengthwise, leaving the root ends intact. Wash thoroughly under cold running water. Place the leeks in a medium saucepan and add cold water to cover by about 1". Add a pinch of salt. Bring to a boil over high heat. Reduce the heat to medium-low and simmer for 8 minutes, or until just tender. Drain well. Cut off the root ends and pull the leeks apart. Set aside on a few layers of paper towels to absorb any remaining moisture.

Cut the core from the stem end of the tomatoes. Bring a large saucepan of water to a boil over high heat. Add the tomatoes. Cook for 30 seconds. Drain and rinse under cold running water, pushing off the skins. Cut in half crosswise and squeeze out and dis-card the juice and seeds. Press the tomato halves flat and set aside on paper towels to drain.

In a large heavy-bottomed sauté pan, combine the water, shallots, garlic, sugar, 1 teaspoon of the oil, and 1 teaspoon salt. Bring to a boil over medium-high heat. Re-duce the heat to medium-low and simmer, shaking the pan frequently, for 10 minutes, or until the shallots and garlic are tender and nicely glazed. Remove from the pan and set aside.

Return the pan to the heat and add the mushrooms. Stir in the lemon juice and season with salt. Cook over medium-high heat, stirring frequently, for 5 minutes, or until the mushrooms are tender. Using a slotted spoon, remove the mushrooms from the pan and set aside.

Preheat the oven to 375°F.

Use the remaining 1 teaspoon oil to brush each side of the eggplant, zucchini, and roasted peppers. Place the slices in a single layer on a nonstick baking sheet and season with salt, black pepper, and cayenne. Roast for 15 minutes. Using tongs, care-fully turn the slices and season with salt, black pepper, and cayenne. Roast for 15 min-utes. Remove from the oven and reduce the temperature to 325°F.

Line a 9" × 5" loaf pan with parchment paper. (If necessary, lightly coat the pan with nonstick spray to hold the paper in place.)

Place 2 of the outer eggplant slices having the most skin in the bottom of the pan, skin side down. Using half of the remaining eggplant, make a generous layer over the bottom slices. Using half of the zucchini, make a layer over the eggplant. Sprinkle with 1½ teaspoons of the oregano. Season with salt and black pepper.

Using half of the roasted peppers, make a layer over the zucchini. Place 2 of the tomato halves over the peppers. Sprinkle with the shallots and garlic. Top with all of the leeks.

Place the remaining roasted peppers over the leeks. Sprinkle with the re-maining 1½ teaspoons oregano. Season with salt and black pepper. Arrange the

(continued)

remaining tomatoes over the peppers. Top with the remaining zucchini. Add the remaining eggplant, placing 2 skin-covered slices on top, skin side up. Press down the edges to seal the seams.

Cover the pan with foil, sealing the edges closed. Place the loaf pan in a roasting pan. Add cold water to come halfway up the sides of the loaf pan.

Bake for 40 minutes. Remove from the oven and place on a wire rack to cool, leaving the foil in place. When cool, set a slightly smaller pan on top of the terrine. Place some weights (such as filled jars) in the pan to compress the vegetables together in the terrine. Refrigerate for at least 8 hours.

Unmold the terrine and cut into 8 slices. Place a pool of the vinaigrette on each of 4 chilled salad plates. Place 1 slice of terrine on each plate; slightly wedge another slice into it. Drizzle with additional vinaigrette and garnish with the parsley.

YIELD: 4 SERVINGS

PER SERVING

186 CALORIES
5 G. TOTAL FAT
0.6 G. SATURATED FAT
0 MG. CHOLESTEROL

SADDLE OF RABBIT WITH GARLIC
(Râble de Lapin Rôti à l'Ail)

This beautiful dish complements the refreshing spring weather. It is colorful, light, and a welcome change from the winter doldrums. Complex flavors are achieved with little fat, making a healthy yet very French meal.

26 large cloves garlic, unpeeled
1 teaspoon peanut oil
2 rabbit saddles (10 ounces each), well-tied with
 butcher's twine to form 2 small tight roasts
 Salt and freshly ground black pepper
½ cup dry white wine
½ cup Brown Veal Stock (page 34)
1 sprig fresh thyme
1 teaspoon Dijon mustard
24 baby carrots, well-scrubbed with a little stem attached
½ cup water
1 teaspoon unsalted butter
 Sugar

SADDLE OF RABBIT WITH GARLIC

Preheat the oven to 375°F.

Place the garlic in a small saucepan and add cold water to cover by 1″. Bring to a simmer over medium-high heat and cook for 5 minutes. Remove from the heat and drain well. Peel 16 cloves and set them aside. Separately reserve the remaining unpeeled cloves.

Place the oil in an ovenproof nonstick sauté pan large enough to hold the rabbit. Warm over medium heat. Season the rabbit with the salt and pepper and place in the hot pan. Brown all sides. Add the unpeeled garlic and place in the oven. Roast for 15 minutes, or until an instant-read thermometer inserted in the center registers 160°F.

While the rabbit is roasting, combine the carrots, water, ½ teaspoon of the butter and ½ teaspoon sugar in a medium sauté pan. Season with salt and pepper. Cover and cook over medium heat for 7 minutes. Remove the cover and continue cooking, occasionally shaking the pan and swirling the carrots in the liquid, for 3 minutes, or until all of the liquid has evaporated and the carrots are tender and nicely glazed. (If the liquid evaporates before the carrots have cooked, add 1 tablespoon water at a time to the pan.)

Remove the rabbit from the oven. Transfer to a warm plate. Lightly cover with foil to keep warm.

Place the sauté pan with the unpeeled garlic over medium heat. Stir in the wine, stock, and thyme. Raise the heat to medium-high and bring to a boil. Reduce the heat to medium and simmer for 6 minutes, or until the liquid is reduced by one-half. Pour the pan juices through a fine sieve into a small saucepan, pushing to extract all of the liquid. Whisk in the mustard. Taste and adjust the seasoning. Cover and keep warm.

In a small sauté pan, combine the peeled garlic, a pinch of sugar, and the remaining ½ teaspoon butter. Season with salt and pepper. Sauté over medium heat for 5 minutes, or until nicely glazed.

Slice each rabbit saddle into 8 equal slices. Place 4 slices on each of 4 warm dinner plates, forming a square. Slice each caramelized garlic clove into 3 wedges and fan a clove out on each slice of rabbit. Arrange the carrots between the rabbit slices and drizzle the sauce over all.

YIELD: 4 SERVINGS

PER SERVING

355 CALORIES
7 G. TOTAL FAT
2 G. SATURATED FAT
126 MG. CHOLESTEROL

STRAWBERRY-RHUBARB SOUP
(*Soupe aux Fraises et Rhubarbe*)

This refreshing dessert is very low in fat. If you can't (or don't want to) eat butter, add a little water to the rhubarb as you sauté it. This will lessen the flavor a bit, but the soup will still be delicious.

1	teaspoon unsalted butter
3	stalks rhubarb, peeled and cut into 1½″ chunks
2	cups hulled and sliced fresh strawberries
½	cup fresh orange juice
¼	cup sugar
¾	cup nonfat vanilla yogurt
4	leaves fresh mint

Melt the butter in a medium nonstick sauté pan over medium-high heat. Add the rhubarb and sauté for 1 minute. Reduce the heat to medium. Cover and cook for 7 minutes, or until the rhubarb is tender and has released all of its liquid. Remove from the heat. Uncover and allow to cool slightly.

Transfer to a blender or a food processor fitted with the metal blade. Add the strawberries, orange juice, sugar, and ½ cup of the yogurt. Process until smooth. Pour into a medium bowl. Cover and refrigerate for at least 1 hour, or until the soup is well-chilled.

Pour the chilled soup into 4 small glass bowls. Place 1 tablespoon of the remaining yogurt in the center of each bowl. Stick a mint leaf into the yogurt.

YIELD: 4 SERVINGS

PER SERVING

142 CALORIES
1 G. TOTAL FAT
0.6 G. SATURATED FAT
3 MG. CHOLESTEROL

MUSSEL SALAD WITH GREEN BEANS

FILET MIGNON ON A STRING

EXOTIC FRUIT SOUP WITH A SUGAR GRID

<u>PER SERVING</u>

704 CALORIES

15 G. TOTAL FAT (19% OF CALORIES)

5 G. SATURATED FAT

123 MG. CHOLESTEROL

MUSSEL SALAD WITH GREEN BEANS
(Salade de Moules et Haricots Verts)

Low in fat and cholesterol, this salad could easily be a luncheon main course or a light supper for two. You can double the recipe for heartier portions.

1	pound haricots verts or small green beans, trimmed and cut into 1½″ pieces
	Salt
1½	pounds fresh mussels
2	teaspoons unsalted butter
3	medium shallots, minced
¼	cup dry white wine
1	large ripe tomato, peeled, cored, seeded, and diced
1	cup Vegetable Vinaigrette (page 52)
	Freshly ground black pepper
½	hothouse (or English) cucumber, sliced paper-thin (see note)
1	tablespoon chopped fresh flat-leaf parsley

MUSSEL SALAD WITH GREEN BEANS

Place the haricots verts or beans in a medium saucepan and add cold water to cover by about 1″. Add a pinch of salt. Bring to a boil over medium-high heat. Reduce the heat to medium-low and simmer for 5 minutes, or until the beans are very tender. Drain well. To stop the cooking, immediately plunge the beans into a bowl of ice water.

Drain well and place in a medium bowl.

Squeeze each mussel in the palm of your hand and discard any whose shells open. Scrub the remaining mussels to remove grit; cut off the beards. Wash in 3 changes of cold water. Set aside.

Melt the butter in a large saucepan over medium heat. Add half of the shallots and sauté for 3 minutes, without browning. Add the mussels and wine and raise the heat to medium-high. Cover and cook for 3 minutes, or until the mussels open. Discard any mussels that do not open. Remove from the heat. Carefully lift the mussels from their shells, removing the small, tough membrane (the lip) from each one.

Add the mussels to the bowl with the beans. Add the tomatoes, vinaigrette, and the remaining shallots. Season with the pepper. Toss to combine. Taste and adjust the seasoning.

Arrange the cucumbers around the edge of each of 4 chilled salad plates. Place equal portions of the mussel salad in the center. Sprinkle the parsley over the top.

If desired, leave the mussels in their shells and serve as above.

Chef's Note: It is best to use a mandoline (see page 29) to make paper-thin cucumber slices.

YIELD: 4 SERVINGS

PER SERVING

117 CALORIES
3 G. TOTAL FAT
1 G. SATURATED FAT
29 MG. CHOLESTEROL

FILET MIGNON ON A STRING
(Filet de Boeuf à la Ficelle)

This deliciously light way to prepare beef gets its unusual name from the cooking method. A string tied around each filet helps it keep its shape, and the long tail of the string is secured to the pot handle for easy removal of the meat from the poaching liquid. The lean filets are very tender and the delicate vegetable garnish very tasty.

1½   cups diced carrots
1½   cups diced turnips
½   cup diced celery

2   cloves garlic
1   leek, white part with a little green, well-washed and
        thinly sliced crosswise
1   sprig fresh thyme
6   cups water
     Salt and freshly ground black pepper
4   filet mignons (4 ounces each, 1½" thick), trimmed of
        all fat
2   tablespoons freshly grated horseradish

In a large saucepan, combine the carrots, turnips, celery, garlic, leeks, thyme, and water. Season with the salt and pepper. Bring to a boil over medium-high heat. Reduce the heat to medium-low and simmer gently for 35 minutes.

Carefully mold each filet into an even pucklike shape. Using butcher's twine, neatly make a tie around the outside of each filet, leaving about an 18" (depending on the depth of your pan) tail of twine. Soak the string tails in cold water for a few minutes.

Lower the filets into the simmering broth and tie the string tails to the handle of the saucepan, taking care that they do not get near the heat. For medium-rare, simmer for 10 minutes. Remove from the heat and lift the filets from the pan by pulling on the string. Place on a warm platter and allow to stand for 3 minutes. Carefully cut off the string.

Place a filet in the center of each of 4 warm dinner plates. Using a slotted spoon, remove the vegetables from the broth and place equal portions around the filets. Sprinkle the horseradish over the meat and vegetables. Add 1 to 2 tablespoons of broth to each plate.

YIELD: 4 SERVINGS

PER SERVING

310 CALORIES
12 G. TOTAL FAT
4 G. SATURATED FAT
94 MG. CHOLESTEROL

Exotic Fruit Soup with a Sugar Grid

(Soupe de Fruits Exotiques Couverte d'un Dôme en Sucre)

Once you get the knack of making these sugar grids, you can turn all sorts of low-fat, low-cal desserts into masterpieces with this bit of fancy garnish. The grids may be made days in advance, but they must be stored, separated, in a very dry spot.

4	cups plus 1 tablespoon water
1½	cups sugar
	Grated zest of 2 limes
	Juice of 2 limes
1	vanilla bean, split lengthwise
2	tablespoons light corn syrup
1	papaya, peeled, seeded, and cut into ¼" dice
1	banana, peeled and cut into ¼" dice

In a medium saucepan, combine 4 cups of the water and 1 cup of the sugar. Add the lime zest and lime juice. Scrape the seeds from the vanilla bean into the saucepan, then add the bean. Bring to a boil over medium heat. Remove from the heat and strain into a large bowl. Set aside to cool. Cover and refrigerate for 1 hour, or until well-chilled.

Rinse out the saucepan and add the remaining 1 tablespoon water, the remaining ½ cup sugar, and the corn syrup. Cook over medium heat, stirring frequently, for 15 minutes, or until the mixture reaches 165°F on a candy thermometer. Remove from the heat and pour into a heatproof glass bowl. Allow the syrup to cool for 7 minutes, or until it begins to just thicken slightly.

Coat a large piece of parchment paper with nonstick spray. Working quickly, dip a dinner fork into the hot syrup. Carefully drizzle the dripping syrup back and forth, then crosswise, over one-quarter of the paper, making a grid slightly larger than the diameter of the soup bowls you will be using. You will have to repeatedly dip the fork into the syrup to make each grid. Continue making grids until you have 4 of equal size.

Pour equal portions of the chilled lime base in each of 4 chilled soup bowls. Stir in equal portions of the papayas and bananas. Place a sugar grid over the top of each bowl.

YIELD: 4 SERVINGS

PER SERVING

277 CALORIES
0 G. TOTAL FAT
0 G. SATURATED FAT
0 MG. CHOLESTEROL

WATERCRESS, CHICORY, AND RADISH SALAD WITH BEET VINAIGRETTE

WINE-STEAMED SALMON

MERINGUE SHELLS WITH MARINATED STRAWBERRIES

PER SERVING

447 CALORIES

11 G. TOTAL FAT (23% OF CALORIES)

2 G. SATURATED FAT

73 MG. CHOLESTEROL

WATERCRESS, CHICORY, AND RADISH SALAD WITH BEET VINAIGRETTE
(Salade de Cresson, Chicorée, et Radis à la Vinaigrette aux Betteraves)

This very low fat salad also makes a terrific base for grilled chicken breast or pork tenderloins. You can, of course, use any vinaigrette, but the beet adds an interesting color play.

1	chicory heart, torn into pieces
2	medium red radishes, thinly sliced
4	cups tightly packed watercress, tough stems removed
¼	cup Beet Vinaigrette (page 50)
	Salt and freshly ground black pepper

Reserve a handful of the chicory and about a quarter of the radishes.

In a medium bowl, combine the watercress, the remaining chicory, and the remaining radishes. Add the vinaigrette and toss to coat. Season with the salt and pepper.

Place equal portions on each of 4 salad plates. Scatter the reserved chicory and radishes over the top.

YIELD: 4 SERVINGS

PER SERVING

40 CALORIES
2 G. TOTAL FAT
0.3 G. SATURATED FAT
0 MG. CHOLESTEROL

75

WINE-STEAMED SALMON
(Saumon à la Vapeur de vin blanc sur Salade de Concombres)

Steaming fish in wine preserves its flavor while gently cooking the fish. Try this method for other fish fillets as well.

1¼   pounds salmon fillet, skin and bones removed
      Salt and freshly ground black pepper
2   tablespoons dry white wine
2   bay leaves
2   tablespoons chopped fresh dill
2   medium cucumbers, peeled and halved lengthwise, seeded, and cut into ¼" slices
2   tablespoons Citrus Vinaigrette (page 52)
1   tablespoon nonfat plain yogurt
4   sprigs fresh dill

Divide the salmon into 4 equal portions. Season lightly with the salt and pepper. Place the fish in a nonstick sauté pan just large enough to hold the fish. Add the wine, bay leaves, chopped dill, and enough water to come ⅛" up the side of the fish. Cover with a tight-fitting lid. Bring to a boil and steam on medium heat for 5 minutes. Turn off the heat and let sit, covered, for 4 minutes, or until the fish flakes easily when tested with a fork. Using a wide spatula, gently remove the fish to a plate.

Meanwhile, combine the cucumbers, vinaigrette, and yogurt in a small bowl. Toss to combine. Taste and adjust the seasoning. Place equal portions of the cucumber mixture in the center of each of 4 chilled salad plates.

Place 1 salmon fillet on top of the cucumber mixture and garnish with the dill sprigs.

YIELD: 4 SERVINGS

PER SERVING

227 CALORIES
8.9 G. TOTAL FAT
1.4 G. SATURATED FAT
73 MG. CHOLESTEROL

MERINGUE SHELLS WITH MARINATED STRAWBERRIES (PAGE 78)

MERINGUE SHELLS WITH MARINATED STRAWBERRIES
(Fraises Marinées dans les Puits d'Amour)

Both the meringues and the strawberries can be made in advance, so this is a great nonfat dessert for company. The meringues can be made up to a week in advance but must be stored airtight or they will soften and lose their shape. If desired, this recipe may be doubled.

2	large egg whites
½	teaspoon fresh lemon juice
½	cup sugar
	Strawberries Marinated in Port (page 63)
4	sprigs fresh mint

Preheat the oven to 200°F.

Place the egg whites and lemon juice in a large bowl. Beat with an electric mixer on medium speed until soft peaks form. Gradually add the sugar and beat on high speed until the whites are shiny and stiff.

Fit a pastry bag with a fluted tip. Fill the bag with the egg-white mixture. Onto a nonstick baking sheet, carefully squeeze out four 3″-diameter circles by forming a spiral, working from the inside out, to form the meringue base. Carefully pipe a line around the exterior edge of the circles to form a basket effect.

Bake the meringues for 3 hours, or until they are very dry and a dark cream color. Remove from the oven and cool on the baking sheet.

Place a meringue shell on each of 4 dessert plates. Prepare the strawberries marinated in port, eliminating the ice cream and mint. Fill the center of each shell with the strawberries. Garnish with the mint.

YIELD: 4 SERVINGS

PER SERVING

180 CALORIES
0.3 G. TOTAL FAT
0 G. SATURATED FAT
0 MG. CHOLESTEROL

GREEN BEAN SOUP

LAMB CHOPS WITH SPRING VEGETABLES

MANGO TART TATIN

PER SERVING

666 CALORIES

23 G. TOTAL FAT (31% OF CALORIES)

7 G. SATURATED FAT

89 MG. CHOLESTEROL

GREEN BEAN SOUP
(Soupe aux Haricots Verts)

In France, haricots verts are very slim green beans. They're sometimes available in America, so use them if you can find them. If not, use the youngest, crispest beans available to capture the flavors of spring. If you like, you can replace 2 cups of the water with White Chicken Stock (page 37).

1	teaspoon unsalted butter
1	teaspoon canola oil
2	leeks, white part only, well-washed and thinly sliced crosswise
2	ribs celery, chopped
5–6	cups water
12	ounces haricots verts or small green beans, trimmed and cut into 1″ pieces
	Salt and freshly ground black pepper

Warm the butter and oil in a medium saucepan over medium heat. Add the leeks and celery. Sauté for 10 minutes, or until the vegetables are soft. Add 5 cups of the water. Bring to a boil over medium-high heat. Reduce the heat to medium-low and simmer for 20 minutes. Add the haricots verts or beans and cook for 10 minutes, or until the vegetables are very tender.

(continued)

Remove from the heat and allow to cool slightly. Pour into a blender or a food processor fitted with the metal blade. Process until smooth. (If the soup is too thick, add ¼ cup water at a time until the desired consistency is reached.)

Strain through a medium-fine sieve into a clean saucepan. Reheat briefly over medium heat. Season with the salt and pepper.

Pour equal portions into each of 4 shallow soup bowls.

YIELD: 4 SERVINGS

PER SERVING

85 CALORIES
2 G. TOTAL FAT
0.7 G. SATURATED FAT
3 MG. CHOLESTEROL

LAMB CHOPS WITH SPRING VEGETABLES
(Côtes d'Agneau aux Petits Légumes Printaniers)

This simple lamb dish is intensely flavorful. It's a great way to add lamb to your health-conscious diet.

- 1 medium very ripe tomato
- 1 teaspoon olive oil
- 4 lamb chops (4 ounces each), trimmed of all fat
  Salt and freshly ground black pepper
- 1 cup cubed button mushrooms
- 1 small onion, cut into ¼″ dice
- 1 small carrot, cut into ¼″ dice
- 1 small zucchini, cut into ¼″ dice
- 1 rib celery, cut into ¼″ dice
- 1 cup White Chicken Stock (page 37)
- 1 sprig fresh thyme

Cut the core from the stem end of the tomato. Bring a medium saucepan of water to a boil over high heat. Add the tomato. Cook for 10 seconds. Drain and rinse under cold running water, pushing off the skin. Cut in half crosswise and squeeze out and discard the juice and seeds. Cut the pulp into ¼″ cubes and set aside.

Warm the oil in a large nonstick sauté pan over medium heat. Season the lamb chops with the salt and pepper. Add to the pan and cook for 2 minutes per side. Transfer to a warm plate. Loosely cover the chops with foil to keep them warm.

Pour off all but approximately 1 teaspoon of the fat from the pan. Return the pan to medium heat. Add the mushrooms, onions, carrots, zucchini, and celery. Sauté for 7 minutes. Add the stock, thyme, and the reserved tomatoes. Raise the heat to medium-high and bring to a boil. Reduce the heat to medium-low, cover, and simmer for 7 minutes. Add the reserved chops, cover, and simmer for 3 minutes. Taste and adjust the seasoning.

Place a chop in the center of each of 4 warm dinner plates. Pour an equal portion of the vegetables with their juices over each chop.

YIELD: 4 SERVINGS

PER SERVING

276 CALORIES
15 G. TOTAL FAT
4 G. SATURATED FAT
80 MG. CHOLESTEROL

MANGO TARTE TATIN (PAGE 82)

Mango Tarte Tatin
(Tarte aux Mangues Façon Demoiselles Tatin)

This tart could be made with any soft, ripe fruit with minimal change in calorie or fat. So if you can't find ripe mangoes, use whatever else is available. In a pinch, you could even use canned peaches or apricots.

> Basic Pastry (page 54)
> 2 teaspoons unsalted butter
> ¼ cup sugar
> 1 tablespoon Grand Marnier liqueur
> 2 ripe mangoes, peeled, seeded, and cut lengthwise into thin slices
> ¼ cup nonfat vanilla frozen yogurt (optional)

Prepare the dough and let it rest for 20 minutes.

Preheat the oven to 375°F.

Using ½ teaspoon of butter per pan, coat the inside of each of four (4″ to 5″) tart pans.

Place the sugar in a small nonstick sauté pan. Cook over medium heat, stirring frequently, for 4 minutes, or until the sugar has caramelized to a rich brown color. Carefully stir in the Grand Marnier. Divide among the tart pans.

Place the mangoes over the sugar in each tart pan, slightly overlapping the slices, to make a neat, tight fit.

On a lightly floured board, roll out the pastry dough to approximately ¼″ thick. Cut out 4 pieces large enough to fit over the tart pans. Place over the mangoes, neatly cutting off any excess dough. Gently crimp the dough edge around the pans.

Place the tarts on a baking sheet. Bake for 15 to 18 minutes, or until the fruit is bubbly and the dough is lightly browned and baked through. Remove from the oven and carefully invert each tart onto a warm dessert plate, allowing the juices to run down the tart and onto the plate. Garnish with the frozen yogurt (if using).

YIELD: 4 SERVINGS

PER SERVING

305 CALORIES
6 G. TOTAL FAT
2 G. SATURATED FAT
6 MG. CHOLESTEROL

Baby Artichokes in Vegetable Broth

Poached Lobster with Saffron Sabayon

Crispy Napoleon with Fresh Fruit

<u>PER SERVING</u>

442 CALORIES

10 G. TOTAL FAT (20% OF CALORIES)

3 G. SATURATED FAT

167 MG. CHOLESTEROL

Baby Artichokes in Vegetable Broth
(Petits Artichauts à la Nage de Légumes)

When this classic French dish was served by Chef André Soltner at his esteemed restaurant Lutèce, shrimp or fish fillets were often poached in the broth. This would be an easy addition for the home cook and could quickly turn this light but filling soup into a main-course meal.

2	tablespoons fresh lemon juice
16	fresh baby artichokes
2	teaspoons olive oil
3	ribs celery, thinly sliced crosswise
2	small onions, thinly sliced crosswise
2	medium carrots, thinly sliced crosswise
2	medium tomatoes, peeled, cored, seeded, and cut into ¼″ dice
3	cloves garlic, thinly sliced crosswise
2	sprigs fresh thyme
1	small bay leaf
	Salt
1½	cups water
1	cup dry white wine
8	saffron threads

BABY ARTICHOKES IN VEGETABLE BROTH (PAGE 83)

Fill a large bowl with cold water. Add the lemon juice and set aside.

Remove 1 or 2 layers, depending on the bruising, of the outer leaves from each artichoke. With a sharp knife, cut off the stem end and about ½″ of the top. Cut each artichoke in half lengthwise; if there is a choke visible (the fuzzy interior part), scoop it out with a spoon and discard. Place the artichokes in the bowl of lemon water to prevent them from turning brown.

Warm the oil in a large nonstick sauté pan over medium heat. Add the celery, onions, and carrots. Cook for 2 minutes without browning.

Drain the artichokes well, squeezing each half in the palm of your hand to remove any excess water. Add to the pan. Stir in the tomatoes, garlic, thyme, and bay leaf. Season with the salt. Mix well. Stir in the water, wine, and saffron.

Raise the heat to medium-high and bring to a boil. Reduce the heat to medium-low, cover, and simmer for 12 minutes, or until the artichokes are tender when the bottoms are pierced with a small knife. Remove from the heat and allow to cool to lukewarm. Remove and discard the bay leaf.

Ladle equal portions into 4 shallow soup bowls.

YIELD: 4 SERVINGS

PER SERVING

135 CALORIES
3 G TOTAL FAT
0.4 G. SATURATED FAT
0 MG. CHOLESTEROL

POACHED LOBSTER WITH SAFFRON SABAYON
(Homard à la Nage au Sabayon Safrané)

This is a luxurious addition to your low-fat repertoire. Fresh lobster, available in most supermarkets, is low in fat and should be a definite part of your health-conscious diet.

	Court-Bouillon (page 42)
2	cups water
1	cup dry white wine
2	fresh lobsters (1½–2 pounds each)
2	large egg yolks
½	teaspoon saffron powder
	Salt and freshly ground white pepper
¼	cup low-fat sour cream

Prepare the court-bouillon in a large stockpot. Add the water and wine. Bring to a boil over medium heat; maintain a rolling boil for 5 minutes. Add the lobsters and return to a boil. Reduce the heat and simmer for 12 minutes. Remove from the heat and cover loosely to keep warm.

Place the egg yolks in the top half of a double boiler. Whisking constantly, add 2 tablespoons of the warm lobster liquid. Stir in the saffron. Place over gently simmering water. Whisk constantly for 6 minutes, or until the mixture is the consistency of heavy cream; check frequently to see that the water is not boiling. (If the mixture is thickening too quickly, occasionally lift the top of the double boiler to lessen the heat.) Remove from the heat and season with the salt and pepper. Whisk in the sour cream and set aside.

Remove the lobsters from the pot and, with a sharp chef's knife, split them in half lengthwise. Remove and discard the stomach (the small bag behind the eyes) and the intestinal vein.

Place a lobster half on each of 4 warm plates. Using a slotted spoon, remove the vegetables from the poaching liquid and arrange equal portions over the lobster halves. Drizzle the saffron sauce over the lobsters.

YIELD: 4 SERVINGS

PER SERVING

196 CALORIES
3 G. TOTAL FAT
0.8 G. SATURATED FAT
159 MG. CHOLESTEROL

CRISPY NAPOLEON WITH FRESH FRUIT
(Mille-Feuille Croquante avec Fruits de Saison)

Phyllo dough bakes very quickly, so be careful not to overbake it. When arranging the napoleon, keep in mind that the dessert looks more dramatic with some height. Whatever fruit you decide to use, make sure that it is very ripe and sweet; peel, trim, and slice it into attractive pieces.

2	sheets phyllo dough
1	tablespoon unsalted butter, melted
¼	cup confectioners' sugar
1	pint berries
¼	cup nonfat vanilla yogurt

Preheat the oven to 350°F.

Cover a baking sheet with parchment. Place 1 piece of the phyllo on the baking sheet; keep the remaining sheet of phyllo covered with a damp paper towel. Using a pastry brush, lightly coat the phyllo with half of the butter, making sure to cover the dough completely, especially the edges.

Place the confectioners' sugar in a sifter and sift about half of it over the phyllo. Place the second piece of phyllo on top of the first. Butter this sheet with the remaining butter and dust it with the confectioners' sugar.

Using the tip of a very sharp knife, cut the phyllo lengthwise into 3 equal strips. Then cut crosswise into 4 equal strips, so that you have 12 squares of equal size. Cover the phyllo with a sheet of parchment paper. Weight the paper down with an upside-down wire rack or two.

Bake for 15 minutes, or until golden. Remove the wire racks and paper. Set aside to cool.

When ready to serve, place a phyllo square in the center of each of 4 dessert plates. Place some of the fruit on each square and spread some of the yogurt over the fruit. Repeat to use 4 more squares, most of the fruit, and all of the yogurt. Top with the remaining squares. Garnish the plates with the remaining fruit. If desired, dust with confectioners' sugar.

YIELD: 4 SERVINGS

PER SERVING

111 CALORIES
4 G. TOTAL FAT
2 G. SATURATED FAT
8 MG. CHOLESTEROL

SPRING NOODLES

BRAISED POMPANO WITH JULIENNE OF VEGETABLES

LEMON MOUSSE

<u>PER SERVING</u>

740 CALORIES

22 G. TOTAL FAT (27% OF CALORIES)

8 G. SATURATED FAT

111 MG. CHOLESTEROL

SPRING NOODLES
(*Nouilles Printanières*)

Low in calories and fat, this colorful appetizer is very filling. The recipe can easily be doubled for a main course, where a little sprinkle of freshly grated cheese would be a welcome addition.

1	tablespoon olive oil
2	small shallots, thinly sliced
6	ounces button mushrooms, brushed clean and halved or quartered
	Salt and freshly ground black pepper
1	small zucchini, cut in half lengthwise and sliced crosswise into ¼″ pieces
4	ounces haricots verts or small green beans, trimmed and cut into 2″ pieces
1	red bell pepper, roasted, peeled, seeded, and cut into ¼″ dice
½	cup fresh baby peas or thawed frozen petite peas
1	tablespoon chopped fresh tarragon
8	ounces dry egg noodles

Warm the oil in a large nonstick sauté pan over medium-low heat. Add the shallots and allow them to cook slowly for 5 minutes. Do not brown. Raise the heat to medium and stir in the mushrooms. Sauté for 3 minutes. Season with the salt and black pepper. Cook, stirring frequently, for 5 minutes, or until the mushrooms have released all of their liquid.

Add the zucchini and sauté for 5 minutes. Add the haricots verts or beans, red peppers, and peas. Sauté for 2 minutes. Stir in the tarragon.

Cook the noodles in a large pot of boiling water according to the package directions. Drain well and place in a large bowl. Add the vegetables and toss to combine.

Place equal portions in each of 4 shallow soup bowls.

YIELD: 4 SERVINGS

PER SERVING

144 CALORIES
3 G. TOTAL FAT
0.5 G. SATURATED FAT
25 MG. CHOLESTEROL

BRAISED POMPANO WITH JULIENNE OF VEGETABLES
(Pompano Braisé à la Julienne de Légumes)

This method of roasting fish creates a very moist, aromatic fillet. You can roast any firm-fleshed fish in this manner and serve it with just the pan juices and a wedge of lemon.

1	teaspoon canola oil
1½	teaspoons unsalted butter, softened
2	carrots, cut into julienne (page 32)
2	ribs celery, cut into julienne (page 32)
2	leeks, white parts only, well-washed and cut into julienne (page 32)
	Salt and freshly ground white pepper
2	tablespoons minced shallots
4	pompano fillets (6 ounces each)
1	cup dry white wine
½	cup White Chicken Stock (page 37) or water
	Low-Fat Béchamel Sauce (page 44)
	Juice of ½ lemon
1	tablespoon chopped fresh flat-leaf parsley

Combine the oil and 1 teaspoon of the butter in a large nonstick sauté pan. Place over medium-high heat. Add the carrots, celery, and leeks. Sauté for 4 minutes, or until the vegetables are just barely tender. Season with the salt and pepper.

(continued)

BRAISED POMPANO WITH JULIENNE OF VEGETABLES (PAGE 89)

Preheat the oven to 325°F.

Using the remaining ½ teaspoon butter, lightly brush the bottom of an oven-proof pan large enough to hold the fish fillets in a single layer. Sprinkle the shallots over the bottom. Season both sides of the fish with the salt and pepper. Place the fillets on top of the shallots. Add the wine and stock or water.

Place over high heat until the liquid is almost boiling. Cover the pan and place in the oven. Bake for 15 minutes, or until the fillets have cooked through; test with the point of a sharp knife.

Using a slotted spoon, lift the fillets from the pan. Strain the pan juices through a fine sieve into a medium nonstick saucepan. Return the fillets to the pan and cover to keep warm.

Strain the béchamel sauce into a saucepan. Cook over medium heat, whisking constantly, for 5 minutes, or until the sauce has thickened. Whisk in the lemon juice. Season with salt and pepper. Fold in the reserved vegetables and bring to a simmer. Cook for 2 minutes.

Place a fillet in the center of each of 4 warm plates. Pour equal portions of the sauce and vegetables over the fish and around the plate. Sprinkle with the parsley.

YIELD: 4 SERVINGS

PER SERVING

416 CALORIES
17 G. FAT
6 G. SATURATED FAT
78 MG. CHOLESTEROL

LEMON MOUSSE
(Mousse au Citron)

This light, refreshing dessert can be made up to 2 days ahead of use. Just make sure that it is well-covered so it does not absorb other food odors.

¾	cup nonfat vanilla yogurt
⅓	cup nonfat sweetened condensed milk
	Zest of 1 lemon
¼	cup fresh lemon juice
¼	cup plus 1 tablespoon water
¼	cup plus 1 tablespoon sugar
2	large egg whites
⅛	teaspoon cream of tartar
1	teaspoon unflavored gelatin
4	sprigs fresh mint

91

Line a fine sieve with cheesecloth. Add the yogurt. Place the sieve over a bowl so that the liquid may freely drain off. Drain for 1 hour; discard all liquid.

Transfer the yogurt to a medium bowl. Add the milk, lemon zest, and lemon juice. Beat until smooth.

In a small saucepan, combine ¼ cup of the water and ¼ cup of the sugar. Cook over medium heat, stirring constantly, until the sugar is dissolved. Bring to a boil. Boil, without stirring, for 6 minutes, or until a candy thermometer inserted into the syrup registers 248°F. Remove from the heat.

While the syrup is boiling, combine the egg whites and cream of tartar in a large bowl. Beat with an electric mixer on medium speed until foamy. Add the remaining 1 tablespoon sugar and beat on high speed until the whites just begin to hold a stiff peak.

Beat in the hot syrup, pouring it in a slow, steady stream. Continue to beat until the mixture is cool.

Place the remaining 1 tablespoon water in a custard cup. Sprinkle with the gelatin and let soften for 5 minutes. Bring about ½" of water to a simmer in a small skillet over medium heat. Place the custard cup in the skillet. Reduce the heat to low and stir the mixture until the gelatin is melted and the liquid is clear. Whisk into the yogurt mixture. Whisk in about one-quarter of the cooled meringue. When well-combined, fold in the remaining meringue.

Place equal portions in each of four (4-ounce) ramekins or glass bowls. Cover and refrigerate for 4 hours, or until well-chilled. When ready to serve, garnish with the mint.

YIELD: 4 SERVINGS

PER SERVING

180 CALORIES
2 G. TOTAL FAT
1 G. SATURATED FAT
8 MG. CHOLESTEROL

CONSOMMÉ WITH MINIATURE VEGETABLES

ROASTED PORK TENDERLOIN WITH VEGETABLE BRUNOISE AND POTATOES

RHUBARB COMPOTE WITH VANILLA FROZEN YOGURT

PER SERVING
752 CALORIES

16 G. TOTAL FAT (19% OF CALORIES)

5 G. SATURATED FAT

109 MG. CHOLESTEROL

CONSOMMÉ WITH MINIATURE VEGETABLES
(Consommé Arenberg)

The color and design of the tiny vegetables floating in the clear broth create a very attractive, light first course. If you don't have the required melon baller, cut the vegetables into tiny squares of equal size.

1	large carrot
1	medium turnip, peeled
	Salt
4	cups Consommé (page 35)
½	cup fresh baby peas or thawed frozen petite peas

Using a melon baller with a tiny cup, cut balls from the carrot and the turnip.

Bring a small saucepan of water to a boil over medium-high heat. Add a pinch of salt. Add the carrot balls; boil for 3 minutes. Add the turnip balls; boil for 4 minutes, or until the vegetables are just tender. Drain and rinse with cold running water. Pat dry.

Bring the consommé to a simmer in a medium saucepan over medium heat. Add the peas and simmer for 1 minute. Add the carrots and turnips. Season with the salt.

Pour equal portions into each of 4 shallow bowls.

YIELD: 4 SERVINGS

PER SERVING
78 CALORIES

1 G. TOTAL FAT

0 G. SATURATED FAT

3 MG. CHOLESTEROL

Roasted Pork Tenderloin with Vegetable Brunoise and Potatoes

(Filet de Porc Rôti avec Brunoise de Légumes et Pommes de Terre)

Lean, succulent, and very tender, pork tenderloin is a wonderful addition to the health-conscious diet. This particular recipe is filled with flavor, and the aromatic pan juices complete a marvelous dish.

3	ribs celery, cut into brunoise (page 31)
1	medium carrot, cut into brunoise (page 31)
1	medium onion, cut into brunoise (page 31)
2	cloves garlic, crushed
1	tablespoon juniper berries, crushed
1	teaspoon black peppercorns, crushed
1	teaspoon paprika
2	tablespoons gin
1	pork tenderloin (1½ pounds), trimmed of all fat
12	medium red potatoes
	Salt
3	teaspoons olive oil
½	cup dry white wine
1	teaspoon chopped fresh thyme

In a shallow baking dish large enough to hold the pork, combine the celery, carrots, onions, garlic, juniper berries, pepper, paprika, and gin. Add the pork and turn to coat all sides. Cover and marinate in the refrigerator for 8 hours.

Preheat the oven to 475°F.

Cut the potatoes into quarters and carefully shave off the edges to make slightly rounded shapes. Place the potatoes in a medium saucepan and add cold water to cover by about 1". Add a pinch of salt. Bring to a boil over high heat and cook for 4 minutes. Drain and pat dry.

Wipe any marinade from the pork, reserving the vegetables and any liquid in the dish. Lightly coat the pork with 1 teaspoon of the oil. Place the pork in a small nonstick roasting pan. Roast for 10 minutes. Reduce the heat to 375°F and roast for 10 minutes. Remove the pork from the oven and cover lightly. Do not turn the oven off.

Add the reserved vegetables and liquid to the roasting pan. Roast for 15 minutes, or until the vegetables are just tender (add water, if necessary, to keep the pan moist). Remove the pan from the oven and place over high heat on the top of the stove. Add the wine and stir constantly to deglaze the pan. Cook for 3 minutes, or until the liquid has reduced slightly.

ROASTED PORK TENDERLOIN WITH VEGETABLE BRUNOISE AND POTATOES

While the vegetables are roasting, heat the remaining 2 teaspoons oil in a large nonstick sauté pan over medium-high heat until very hot but not smoking. Add the potatoes. Sauté for 5 minutes, or until the potatoes are evenly browned and cooked through. Stir in the thyme and season with the salt.

Slice the pork crosswise into 12 slices. Place an equal portion of the potatoes at the top of each of 4 warm plates. Fan out 3 pork slices just below the potatoes. Pour the pan juices with the vegetables over the pork.

YIELD: 4 SERVINGS

PER SERVING

467 CALORIES
9 G. TOTAL FAT
2 G. SATURATED FAT
96 MG. CHOLESTEROL

RHUBARB COMPOTE WITH VANILLA FROZEN YOGURT
(*Compote à la Rhubarbe avec Glace au Yaourt*)

Tart rhubarb is a wonderful foil for ice cream or frozen yogurt. This method of broiling is a French method devised to bring out intense sweetness from an otherwise astringent plant.

10	large stalks rhubarb, peeled and cut into 1½″ chunks
3	tablespoons sugar
2	cups vanilla frozen yogurt

Place the broiler rack at least 8″ below the heating element. Preheat the broiler.

In a medium bowl, toss together the rhubarb and sugar. Spread evenly in a large nonstick baking dish or jelly-roll pan. Broil, stirring once, for 25 to 30 minutes, or until the rhubarb is very soft but not burned. Remove from the broiler and stir.

Place ½ cup of the yogurt in each of 4 dessert bowls. Spoon equal portions of the rhubarb compote over the top.

YIELD: 4 SERVINGS

PER SERVING

207 CALORIES
6 G. TOTAL FAT
3 G. SATURATED FAT
10 MG. CHOLESTEROL

ZUCCHINI SOUP

JOHN DORY WITH SPRING VEGETABLES

WARM CHOCOLATE TORTES WITH SEASONAL FRUIT

PER SERVING

549 CALORIES

12 G. TOTAL FAT (20% OF CALORIES)

4 G. SATURATED FAT

206 MG. CHOLESTEROL

ZUCCHINI SOUP
(Soupe aux Courgettes)

This unusual soup can be served either hot or chilled. When serving it cold, whisk in about 1 cup of yogurt to achieve the right consistency and add a bit more Tabasco just before serving. Do not attempt to add the yogurt when the soup is very hot or it might curdle. Additionally, the apple can be replaced with either banana or pear for an even more intriguing taste.

3	medium zucchini, halved crosswise
2	teaspoons olive oil
1	medium onion, chopped
1	clove garlic, crushed
2	small apples, peeled, cored, and diced
1	teaspoon curry powder
3	cups White Chicken Stock (page 37)
	Salt
1	cup water
¼	teaspoon Tabasco sauce
¼	cup low-fat plain yogurt

Cut 3 of the zucchini halves into 1″ cubes. Cut the remaining 3 halves into fine julienne (page 32).

(continued)

Warm the oil in a medium saucepan over medium heat. Add the onions and garlic. Sauté for 5 minutes, or until the vegetables are very soft. Stir in the apples, curry powder, and the cubed zucchini. Add the stock and bring to a boil over medium-high heat. Reduce the heat to medium-low and season with the salt. Cover and simmer for 15 minutes. Remove from the heat and allow to cool slightly.

Transfer to a blender or a food processor fitted with the metal blade. Process until very smooth. Pour into a clean saucepan.

In a small saucepan, combine the julienned zucchini and the water. Bring to a boil over high heat. Cook for 1 minute. Remove the pan from the heat and drain well. Stir into the saucepan with the soup. Add the Tabasco sauce. Taste and adjust the seasoning. Bring to a simmer over medium heat.

Pour equal portions into each of 4 shallow bowls. Place a large dollop of yogurt in the center of each.

YIELD: 4 SERVINGS

PER SERVING

81 CALORIES
2 G. TOTAL FAT
0.3 G. SATURATED FAT
5 MG. CHOLESTEROL

JOHN DORY WITH SPRING VEGETABLES
(Filets de Saint-Pierre aux Légumes de Printemps)

Only recently available in the United States, John Dory has long been a favorite fish of European chefs. If you can't find it in your fish market, any mild, delicately textured fish can replace it.

6 ounces haricots verts or small green beans, trimmed
  Salt
4 tender ribs celery, cut into julienne (page 32)
2 leeks, white parts only, well-washed and cut into julienne (page 32)
1 medium carrot, cut into julienne (page 32)
¼ cup water
1 teaspoon unsalted butter
4 John Dory fillets (6 ounces each)
  Freshly ground white pepper
¾ cup Fish Stock (page 40)
¼ cup nonfat sour cream
2 tablespoons chopped fresh flat-leaf parsley

Place the haricots verts or beans in a medium saucepan. Add cold water to cover by about 1″. Add a pinch of salt. Bring to a boil over high heat. Reduce the heat to medium and simmer for 4 minutes, or until crisp-tender. Drain and rinse with cold running water.

In a medium saucepan, combine the celery, leeks, carrots, water, and butter. Season with the salt. Bring to a boil over medium heat. Cover and cook for 5 minutes, or until the vegetables are crisp-tender and the water has evaporated. Add the haricots verts or beans. Set aside.

Season the fillets with the salt and pepper.

Bring the stock to the boiling point in a large sauté pan over high heat. Gently add the fillets. Reduce the heat to medium and cover. Simmer for 2 minutes.

Using a slotted spoon, carefully transfer a fillet to each of 4 warm dinner plates.

Raise the heat under the sauté pan and bring the liquid to a boil. Boil for 3 minutes, or until the liquid has reduced by half. Remove from the heat and whisk in the sour cream. Stir in the parsley and the reserved vegetables. Taste and adjust the seasoning. Spoon an equal portion of the sauce and vegetables over the fillets.

YIELD: 4 SERVINGS

PER SERVING

201 CALORIES
4 G. TOTAL FAT
1.2 G. SATURATED FAT
92 MG. CHOLESTEROL

WARM CHOCOLATE TORTE WITH SEASONAL FRUIT

WARM CHOCOLATE TORTES WITH SEASONAL FRUIT
(*Gâteaux au Chocolat Chaud aux Fruits de Saison*)

This scrumptious, traditional, meringue-based flourless cake can be made with any berry or with pitted cherries. If you are amenable to a few more calories, unmold the tortes and serve them in a pool of lightly whipped cream or French Custard Sauce (page 57).

2	teaspoons plus 3 tablespoons sugar
2	large egg whites
½	cup chocolate pastry cream (see note)
1	cup fresh raspberries

Spray four (4-ounce) ramekins with nonstick spray. Using 2 teaspoons of the sugar, lightly dust the interior of the ramekins.

Preheat the oven to 350°F.

Place the egg whites in a medium bowl. Beat with an electric mixer on medium speed until foamy. Gradually add the remaining 3 tablespoons sugar and beat on high speed until the whites are stiff and shiny. Fold in the pastry cream.

Transfer to a pastry bag fitted with a star tip. Pipe the mixture into the prepared ramekins, piping in a spiral motion to fill the ramekins halfway. Divide the raspberries over the meringue. Pipe 2 additional circles of meringue over the berries.

Place the ramekins on a baking sheet. Bake for 5 to 7 minutes, or until the meringue is just set. Serve warm.

Chef's Note: To make chocolate pastry cream, see the recipe for Vanilla Pastry Cream (page 56) and make the adjustments suggested.

YIELD: 4 SERVINGS

PER SERVING

207 CALORIES
6 G. TOTAL FAT
2.4 G. SATURATED FAT
109 MG. CHOLESTEROL

PEA AND MINT SOUP

FILLET OF TROUT GRENOBLOISE

BURNT CUSTARD

<u>PER SERVING</u>

565 CALORIES

17 G. TOTAL FAT (27% OF CALORIES)

6 G. SATURATED FAT

253 MG. CHOLESTEROL

PEA AND MINT SOUP
(Soupe de Pois Frais avec Feuilles de Menthe)

For the most delicate flavor, this soup is best made with fresh early spring peas. This light soup is wonderful served either warm or chilled. If you serve it cold, however, be sure to chill it in a tightly covered glass container, as exposure to oxygen will cause the bright green color to fade.

1	teaspoon unsalted butter
1	teaspoon canola oil
1	large leek, white part with a little green, well-washed and sliced crosswise into ¼″ pieces
4	cups water
	Salt and freshly ground white pepper
3½	cups fresh baby peas or thawed frozen petite peas
10	large leaves fresh mint
4	large croutons (optional)
4	small sprigs fresh mint (optional)

Combine the butter and oil in a medium saucepan. Place over medium-low heat until the butter is melted. Add the leeks and cook slowly for 10 minutes. Do not brown. Add the water. Season with the salt and pepper.

Bring to a boil over medium-high heat. Reduce the heat to medium-low and simmer for 10 minutes. Add the peas. Cover and cook for 3 minutes, or until the mixture just begins to boil. Uncover and cook for 2 minutes. Do not overcook or the peas

PEA AND MINT SOUP

will begin to lose their bright color and sweet taste. Stir in the mint leaves. Remove from the heat and allow to cool slightly.

Transfer to a blender or a food processor fitted with the metal blade. Process until very smooth.

Pour equal portions into each of 4 shallow soup bowls. If desired, garnish with a crouton topped with a sprig of mint.

YIELD: 4 SERVINGS

PER SERVING

150 CALORIES
3 G. TOTAL FAT
0.8 G. SATURATED FAT
3 MG. CHOLESTEROL

FILLET OF TROUT GRENOBLOISE
(*Filet de Truite Grenobloise*)

In this classic French preparation, butter is one of the predominant flavors. If you are on a restricted diet, don't hesitate to use only canola oil. The flavor will be changed, but the final dish will still be delicious.

1	lemon
¼	cup all-purpose flour
4	trout fillets (4 ounces each)
	Salt and freshly ground black pepper
1	teaspoon canola oil
1	teaspoon plus 1 tablespoon unsalted butter
2	tablespoons capers, well-drained
2	tablespoons chopped fresh flat-leaf parsley
2	slices white bread, crusts removed, cut into ¼″ dice, and oven-toasted
4	slices lemon
4	sprigs fresh flat-leaf parsley

Peel the lemon, removing all the white pith. Cut the flesh into small dice. Discard any seeds.

Place the flour in a shallow bowl or plate. Season the fillets with the salt and pepper and then dip into the flour, coating evenly and shaking off any excess.

Combine the oil and 1 teaspoon of the butter in a large nonstick sauté pan. Place over medium-high heat. When very hot but not smoking, place the fillets, skin side down, in the pan. Cook for 1 to 1½ minutes, or until golden. Carefully turn the fillets. Cook for 2 minutes, or until the fish flakes easily when tested with a fork.

Using a wide spatula, lift the fillets from the pan and place in the center of 4 warm dinner plates.

Remove the sauté pan from the heat and, using a paper towel, carefully wipe the interior clean. Return the pan to medium heat. Add the remaining 1 tablespoon butter. Cook for 2 minutes, or until the butter just begins to brown and emit a nutty aroma. Remove the pan from the heat and stir in the capers, parsley, and diced lemon. Return the pan to medium heat and add the bread. Toss to coat.

Immediately spoon an equal portion of the mixture over the fillets. Garnish with a lemon slice and a sprig of parsley.

YIELD: 4 SERVINGS

PER SERVING

243 CALORIES
10 G. TOTAL FAT
4 G. SATURATED FAT
105 MG. CHOLESTEROL

BURNT CUSTARD
(*Crème Brûlée*)

This classic French dessert was made famous in America at New York's Le Cirque restaurant by Chef Alain Sailhac. We have lowered its fat and calories by lessening the number of eggs and using 1% low-fat milk. We think that it is still one of the best desserts in the world!

2	large eggs
2	large egg yolks
¼	cup plus 7 tablespoons sugar
2	tablespoons all-purpose flour
1¾	cups 1% low-fat milk
½	vanilla bean, split lengthwise

In a small bowl, combine the eggs, egg yolks, and ¼ cup plus 1 tablespoon of the sugar. Whisk until well-blended.

Place the flour in a medium nonstick saucepan. Gradually whisk in ½ cup of the milk until smooth. Scrape the seeds from the vanilla bean into the saucepan, then add the bean. Whisk in the remaining 1¼ cups milk.

Cook over medium heat, stirring frequently, for 3 minutes, or until very hot.

Whisking constantly, pour about ¾ cup of the milk mixture into the egg mixture to warm it and keep it from curdling when added. Whisking constantly, add the egg mixture to the milk. Continue cooking, stirring constantly, for 2 minutes, or until the mixture comes to a boil.

Reduce the heat to medium-low and simmer, stirring constantly, for 5 minutes, or until the mixture has thickened. Strain through a very fine sieve into a medium bowl. Pour equal portions into 6 (3-ounce) brûlée molds.

Allow to cool to room temperature, then refrigerate for at least 2 hours, or until the custard is very cold.

When ready to serve, move the broiler rack as close to the heating element as possible. Preheat the broiler.

Place the custards on a baking sheet. When the broiler is very hot, evenly sprinkle 1 tablespoon of the remaining sugar on top of each custard. Place the custards under the broiler for 1 minute, or until the sugar melts and turns very brown. Serve immediately.

YIELD: 6 SERVINGS

PER SERVING

172 CALORIES
4 G. TOTAL FAT
1.5 G. SATURATED FAT
145 MG. CHOLESTEROL

SUMMER MENUS

FOR THE COOK, SUMMER IS THE MOST WELCOME SEASON. THE FIELD AND GARDEN ARE OVERFLOWING WITH NATURE'S BOUNTY JUST WAITING FOR THE PICKING. THIS IS THE TIME FOR SIMPLE PREPARATIONS TO HIGHLIGHT THOSE JUST-PICKED FLAVORS OF THE LUSH FRUITS AND SWEET VEGETABLES. IN FRANCE, THE WARMTH OF THE SOUTH SEEMS TO ENFOLD THE ENTIRE COUNTRY AS COLORFUL PROVENÇAL FABRICS ARE THROWN OUT ON THE LAWN OR OVER THE TERRACE TABLE FOR THE MUCH-LOVED *PICNIQUE*. AT NO OTHER TIME DOES NATURE PRODUCE MORE FRAGRANT HERBS, SENSUAL FRUITS, AND BOLD-TASTING VEGETABLES. WE HOPE THAT OUR RECIPES, EVEN WITH AN EYE TO HEALTH-CONSCIOUS DINING, WILL BRING YOU AN APPRECIATION OF THE EPICUREAN DELIGHTS OF FRANCE IN THE SUMMER.

SWISS CHARD GRATIN

BAKED BLUEFISH WITH PARSLEY AND TOMATOES

RASPBERRY FLOATING ISLANDS

<u>PER SERVING</u>

699 CALORIES

17 G. TOTAL FAT (22% OF CALORIES)

7 G. SATURATED FAT

165 MG. CHOLESTEROL

SWISS CHARD GRATIN
(*Blettes au Gratin*)

The rich egg and cheese content of this time-honored French recipe has been considerably lessened to create a low-fat, low-cholesterol classic.

½	cup Low-Fat Béchamel Sauce (page 44)
¼	cup shredded Gruyère cheese
¼	cup freshly made dry bread crumbs
2	tablespoons grated Parmesan cheese
½	teaspoon unsalted butter
2	bunches Swiss chard
	Salt and freshly ground black pepper

In a medium bowl, combine the béchamel sauce and Gruyère. Mix well.

In a small bowl, combine the bread crumbs and Parmesan. Mix well.

Coat four (4-ounce) ramekins with the butter.

Preheat the oven to 350°F.

Remove the stems from the chard and cut out the thick triangular core from each leaf (see note). Slice the leaves.

Bring a large pot of water to a boil and add a pinch of salt. Add the chard and cook for 2 minutes, or until wilted. Drain well. Cool slightly, then squeeze out all the excess moisture. Add to the béchamel mixture. Season with the salt and pepper. Mix well.

Divide among the prepared ramekins. Sprinkle with the bread-crumb mixture.

Place the ramekins on a baking sheet. Bake for 25 minutes, or until the gratins are set and the tops have lightly browned.

Chef's Note: The triangular core that you remove from the chard can be chopped and sautéed with onions and garlic for a tasty side dish.

YIELD: 4 SERVINGS

PER SERVING

94 CALORIES
4 G. TOTAL FAT
2 G. SATURATED FAT
2 MG. CHOLESTEROL

BAKED BLUEFISH WITH PARSLEY AND TOMATOES
(Bluefish Rôti au Persil et Tomates)

Any fine-textured, white-fleshed fish can replace the bluefish in this simple but delicious recipe.

1	bluefish (4 pounds), gills removed, cleaned, and scaled with head and tail left on
	Salt and freshly ground black pepper
1	large very ripe tomato, peeled, cored, and cut into ¼″ slices
3	tablespoons chopped fresh flat-leaf parsley
1	tablespoon unsalted butter, cut into small pieces
1½	pounds small red new potatoes, halved
½	cup dry white wine
1	lemon, trimmed and cut crosswise into ⅛″ slices

Preheat the oven to 400°F.

Rinse the fish with cold running water. Pat dry. Generously season, inside and out, with the salt and pepper. Place in a small nonstick roasting pan. Place the tomato slices around the fish and sprinkle with 1 tablespoon of the parsley. Dot with the butter.

Roast, basting every 3 minutes, for 30 minutes, or until the fish flakes easily when tested with a fork. Remove the pan from the oven and carefully lift the fish and tomatoes to a warm serving platter. Cover loosely and keep warm.

While the fish is roasting, place the potatoes in a large saucepan and add cold water to cover by about 1″. Add a pinch of salt. Bring to a boil over high heat. Reduce the heat to medium and cook for 15 minutes, or until tender when pierced with a fork. Drain well and toss with the remaining 2 tablespoons parsley.

(continued)

BAKED BLUEFISH WITH PARSLEY AND TOMATOES (PAGE 109)

Place the roasting pan on top of the stove over high heat. Add the wine and bring to a boil. Boil for 3 minutes, or until slightly reduced. Taste and adjust the seasoning. Pour over the fish. Arrange the potatoes and lemon slices around the fish.

YIELD: 4 SERVINGS   PER SERVING

414 CALORIES
11 G. TOTAL FAT
4 G. SATURATED FAT
108 MG. CHOLESTEROL

RASPBERRY FLOATING ISLANDS
(*Oeufs à la Neige aux Framboises*)

This classic "nursery" dessert is a perfect low-fat treat. Usually poached in milk, our meringues are gently baked to cut calories. Beautiful in presentation and very satisfying in taste.

4	large egg whites
¼	cup sugar
¼	cup raspberry jam
1	cup French Custard Sauce (page 57)

Preheat the oven to 350°F.

Place the egg whites in a large bowl. Beat with an electric mixer on medium speed until foamy. Gradually beat in the sugar and beat on high speed until the whites are stiff and shiny. Using a rubber spatula, fold in the jam until well-blended.

Transfer to a pastry bag fitted with a ¾″ tip and pipe the meringue into eight (3- to 4-ounce) cups or into a muffin tin; pipe so that the meringue mounds slightly in the center. Place the cups or muffin tin in a shallow roasting pan; add enough hot water to come halfway up the cups or tin. Carefully place in the oven.

Bake for 5 minutes, or just until the meringues feel quite firm when touched. Remove the pan from the oven and lift the cups or tin from the water. Place on a wire rack to cool.

When ready to serve, cover the bottom of each of 4 shallow soup bowls with the custard sauce. Place 2 meringues in the center of each bowl.

YIELD: 4 SERVINGS

PER SERVING

191 CALORIES
2 G. TOTAL FAT
1 G. SATURATED FAT
55 MG. CHOLESTEROL

FRESH TOMATO SOUP

TARRAGON ROASTED CHICKEN

APRICOT TART

PER SERVING

518 CALORIES

13 G. TOTAL FAT (16% OF CALORIES)

4 G. SATURATED FAT

117 MG. CHOLESTEROL

FRESH TOMATO SOUP
(*Velouté aux Tomates de l'Été*)

For the sweetest taste, use only very ripe summer tomatoes to make this soup. Low in calories and fat, this is a wonderful summer first course or luncheon dish.

2	teaspoons olive oil
1	medium onion, thinly sliced
5	medium very ripe tomatoes, cored and cut into 8 pieces each
1	clove garlic, crushed
1	sprig fresh thyme, chopped
	Pinch of sugar
2½	cups White Chicken Stock (page 37)
½	cup whole milk (optional)
	Salt and freshly ground black pepper
4	sprigs fresh chervil or 12 leaves fresh flat-leaf parsley

Warm the oil in a medium nonstick saucepan over medium-low heat. Add the onions and cook for 10 minutes, or until very soft but not brown. Add the tomatoes, garlic, thyme, and sugar. Raise the heat to medium and simmer for 10 minutes. Stir in the stock and bring the mixture to a boil. Boil for 2 minutes. Remove from the heat and allow to cool slightly.

112

Transfer to a blender or a food processor fitted with the metal blade. Process until smooth.

Strain the soup through a medium-fine sieve into a clean saucepan. Bring to a boil over medium-high heat. Reduce the heat to medium-low. Stir in the milk (if using). Season with the salt and pepper. Simmer for 1 minute.

Place equal portions in each of 4 shallow soup bowls. Garnish with the chervil or parsley.

YIELD: 4 SERVINGS

PER SERVING

93 CALORIES
3 G. TOTAL FAT
0.5 G. SATURATED FAT
6 MG. CHOLESTEROL

TARRAGON ROASTED CHICKEN
(*Poulet Rôti à l'Estragon*)

We think that this is the most perfect roast chicken. If desired, you may serve the chicken with rice, roasted potatoes, or Parsleyed Noodles (page 194). The delicate, tarragon-scented meat makes great-tasting leftovers for chicken salads or sandwiches.

1	roasting chicken (3–4 pounds)
	Salt and freshly ground black pepper
5	sprigs fresh tarragon
1	small onion, halved
1	teaspoon olive oil
2	tablespoons water
1	medium carrot, chopped
1	medium onion, chopped
1	clove garlic
10	sprigs fresh parsley
2	sprigs fresh thyme
1	bay leaf
½	cup dry white wine
½	cup White Chicken Stock (page 37)
1	teaspoon chopped fresh tarragon

113

TARRAGON ROASTED CHICKEN (PAGE 113)

Preheat the oven to 450°F.

Wash the chicken, inside and out, with cold running water. Pat dry. Generously season, inside and out, with the salt and pepper. Place the tarragon sprigs and halved onion in the cavity. Tuck the wing tips under. Tie the legs together with butcher's twine.

Warm the oil in a medium nonstick roasting pan over medium heat. Place the chicken, on its side, in the pan. Roast, basting every 5 minutes, for 15 minutes.

Turn the chicken on its other side and add the water. Reduce the oven heat to 400°F. Roast, basting every 5 minutes, for 15 minutes.

Turn the chicken on its back. Add the carrots, chopped onions, and garlic. Tie the parsley, thyme, and bay leaf in a small square of cheesecloth. Add to the pan. Roast, basting every 5 minutes, for 15 minutes, or until an instant-read thermometer inserted in the center of the breast registers 170°F.

Remove the chicken from the oven and carefully lift it onto a warm platter. Cover loosely with foil and keep warm.

Place a strainer over a bowl. Pour the vegetables and fat into the strainer. Discard the cheesecloth bundle and the fat. Return the vegetables to the roasting pan.

Place the roasting pan over medium heat and add the wine and stock. Bring to a boil and deglaze the pan, stirring constantly with a wooden spoon to remove all of the browned bits from the bottom. Cook for 5 minutes, or until the liquid has reduced slightly. Strain through a fine sieve into a clean saucepan and stir in the chopped tarragon. Season with the salt and pepper. Keep warm.

Cut the breast and legs from the chicken. Remove and discard the skin. Slice each breast, on the bias, into 2 pieces. Separate the drumsticks from the thighs.

Place equal portions of the breast meat on 4 warmed dinner plates. Add 1 piece of leg meat to each plate. Spoon the sauce over the meat.

Or, place the whole chicken on a large serving plate along with a mélange of vegetables, if desired. Carve at the table and serve the sauce alongside the chicken. Remove and discard the skin before eating.

YIELD: 4 SERVINGS

PER SERVING

243 CALORIES
7 G. TOTAL FAT
2 G. SATURATED FAT
106 MG. CHOLESTEROL

APRICOT TART
(*Tarte aux Abricots*)

It is impossible to make a fat-free tart in the classic French method. However, phyllo dough is a truly wonderful low-fat replacement for pâte brisée *or* pâte sucrée. *It's crunchy and satisfying with just the hint of butter for flavor.*

4   sheets phyllo dough
2   teaspoons unsalted butter, melted
4   tablespoons apricot jam
10 very ripe apricots, pitted and cut into 8 slices each
4   teaspoons packed light brown sugar

115

Preheat the oven to 350°F.

Place 1 sheet of the phyllo on a piece of parchment paper; keep the remainder covered with a damp paper towel. Using a pastry brush, lightly coat the phyllo with some of the butter. Place a second sheet on top and brush with more of the butter. Repeat the process to use the remaining 2 sheets and the remaining butter.

Coat four (4″) tart pans with removable bottoms with nonstick spray.

Using a 6″ pastry ring, carefully cut out 4 circles from the phyllo, pressing down gently but firmly to cut through all of the layers. Fit each circle into a tart pan. Place a circle of parchment paper in each pan and fill with dried beans, rice, or pie baking weights to hold down the dough.

Place the tart pans on a baking sheet. Bake for 10 minutes. Remove from the oven and carefully remove the weights and parchment. Allow to cool on wire racks for 5 minutes.

Raise the oven heat to 375°F.

Spread 1 tablespoon of the jam in the bottom of each shell. Arrange 20 of the apricot slices in each shell, fitting them in tightly. Sprinkle 1 teaspoon of the brown sugar over the top of each tart.

Bake for 20 minutes, or until the apricots are cooked and the top is nicely glazed. Serve warm or at room temperature.

YIELD: 4 SERVINGS

PER SERVING

182 CALORIES
3.4 G. TOTAL FAT
1.4 G. SATURATED FAT
5 MG. CHOLESTEROL

SALAD OF ARTICHOKE, CUCUMBER, AND TOMATO

RED SNAPPER IN PARCHMENT PAPER

PEACHES POACHED IN RIESLING WITH FRESH CURRANTS

PER SERVING

473 CALORIES

15 G. TOTAL FAT (29% OF CALORIES)

3 G. SATURATED FAT

55 MG. CHOLESTEROL

SALAD OF ARTICHOKE, CUCUMBER, AND TOMATO
(Éventail d'Artichauts en Salade avec Concombres et Tomates)

We prepared the artichokes for this recipe in the classic French technique of cooking in a blanc *(a mixture of flour, lemon juice, and water) to preserve their color and enhance their flavor. Prepared in this manner, artichokes will keep, refrigerated, for up to 5 days.*

2	tablespoons fresh lemon juice
4	large fresh artichokes
4	cups cold water
2	tablespoons all-purpose flour
	Juice of ½ lemon
1	teaspoon olive oil
	Salt
2	hothouse (or English) cucumbers
4	very ripe plum tomatoes, peeled, cored, seeded, and chopped
¾	cup Citrus Vinaigrette (page 52)
6	ounces mesclun (salad mix), washed and dried

Fill a large bowl with cold water. Add the 2 tablespoons lemon juice and set aside.

Remove 1 or 2 layers, depending on the bruising, of the outer leaves from each artichoke. Holding an artichoke in the palm of your hand and a sharp paring knife in

(continued)

SALAD OF ARTICHOKE, CUCUMBER, AND TOMATO (PAGE 117)

the other, slowly rotate each artichoke while peeling away the base leaves with the knife. Continue turning until all of the green has been peeled off. Lay the artichoke on its side and cut off the top leaves at the point where they turn green. You should now have a 1½″ to 2½″ round disk. As each artichoke is prepared, place it in the bowl of water to prevent it from turning brown.

In a medium saucepan, combine the water, flour, lemon juice, oil, and a pinch of salt. Whisk until well-combined. Drain the artichokes and add to the pan. Cook over medium heat for 20 minutes, or until tender but still firm when tested with the point of a sharp knife. Drain well.

Carefully cut out the choke (the hairy center). Place the artichokes on a plate and refrigerate for 30 minutes so that they will be easier to slice.

Using a vegetable peeler, shave off long paper-thin strips from the cucumbers. Place the strips in a bowl of ice water and refrigerate until ready to use.

Using a mandoline (see page 29), slice the artichokes into paper-thin slices. Fan equal portions of the artichokes around the edge of each of 4 well-chilled salad plates.

Drain the cucumber strips and pat dry. Place in a medium bowl. Add the tomatoes and ¼ cup of the vinaigrette. Toss to coat.

Place the mesclun in a large bowl. Add the remaining ½ cup vinaigrette and toss to coat. Taste and adjust the seasoning.

Place a large mound of the mesclun in the center of each of the plates. Top with an equal portion of the cucumber mixture.

YIELD· 4 SERVINGS

PER SERVING

133 CALORIES
8 G. TOTAL FAT
1 G. SATURATED FAT
0 MG. CHOLESTEROL

RED SNAPPER IN PARCHMENT PAPER
(*Vivaneau en Papillote*)

Baking en papillote *is a wonderful way to concentrate flavor without the use of added fats. The aroma that perfumes the air when the diner slits open the steaming packet is extremely enticing. If you don't have parchment paper on hand, you can quite successfully create a sealed package using heavy-duty foil. Since the foil is much less attractive, open the packets in the kitchen and place the contents on a dinner plate before serving.*

4	red snapper fillets (5 ounces each)
3	teaspoons olive oil
4	sprigs fresh thyme
½	small onion, finely chopped
1	clove garlic, minced
3	shallots
8	ounces very ripe plum tomatoes, peeled, cored, seeded, and chopped
½	teaspoon sugar (optional)
	Salt and freshly ground black pepper
1	teaspoon unsalted butter
8	ounces button mushrooms, brushed clean and chopped
	Juice of 1 lemon
	Pinch of herbes de Provence (see note)
1	large carrot, cut into julienne (page 32) and blanched (page 32)
1	large leek, well-washed, cut into julienne (page 32), and blanched (page 32)
1	large rib celery, cut into julienne (page 32) and blanched (page 32)
1	tablespoon dry white wine or water
1	large egg white, lightly beaten

Using a very sharp knife, score the skin side of the fillets, making 2 shallow cuts perpendicular to each other up the center of each fillet. (This will ensure that the fillets will lay flat and cook evenly.) Using 2 teaspoons of the oil, rub both sides of the fish. Rub each fillet with a thyme sprig; place the sprig on top of the fillet. Place the fillets on a plate and loosely cover with plastic wrap. Refrigerate until ready to use.

Warm the remaining 1 teaspoon oil in a medium nonstick sauté pan over medium-low heat. Add the onions and garlic. Mince 1 of the shallots and add to the pan. Allow to cook slowly for 4 minutes. Stir in the tomatoes; if they are not very ripe and sweet, add the sugar. Cook, stirring frequently, for 5 minutes, or until the tomatoes are very soft and the excess moisture has evaporated. Season with the salt and pepper. Transfer to a medium bowl.

Clean the sauté pan. Chop the remaining 2 shallots. Melt the butter in the pan over medium heat. Add the shallots and allow them to cook slowly for 5 minutes. Do not brown. Stir in the mushrooms, lemon juice, and herbes de Provence. Cook for 4 minutes, or until there is no juice left in the pan. Season with the salt and pepper. Remove from the heat.

Place a large nonstick sauté pan over high heat until very hot but not smoking. Remove and reserve the thyme sprigs from the fillets and lay the fillets, skin side down, in the hot pan. Sear for about 30 seconds, or just until the skin has browned. Do not cook the fish; allow it just to acquire a little color. Transfer to a clean plate.

Preheat the oven to 400°F.

Cut 4 pieces of parchment paper, at least 14″ × 16″. Working with 1 piece at a time, fold the paper in half crosswise. Cutting from the folded side, cut out a large half-heart shape so that when you unfold the parchment, you will have formed a large heart. Lay the heart shapes out flat.

Divide the mushroom mixture among the hearts, placing it on 1 side of the heart and keeping it toward the center fold. Top with the tomato mixture and then the fillets. Season with the salt and pepper. Cover with the carrots, leeks, and celery. Top each with a reserved thyme sprig. Sprinkle a bit of wine or water over each serving.

Using a pastry brush, coat the edges of the paper with the egg white. Fold the 2 sides of each heart together and seal the edges by making a series of straight folds, one over the other, until you have formed a tight half heart–shaped packet. Place the packets on a baking sheet and bake for 12 minutes.

Remove from the oven and place 1 packet in each of 4 shallow soup plates. Cut open the packets at the table.

Chef's Note: Herbes de Provence is a mixture of dried herbs that often includes basil, lavender, rosemary, sage, thyme, and others. Look for it in the spice section of your supermarket.

YIELD: 4 SERVINGS

PER SERVING

223 CALORIES
7 G. TOTAL FAT
2 G. SATURATED FAT
55 MG. CHOLESTEROL

PEACHES POACHED IN RIESLING WITH FRESH CURRANTS
(Pêches Pochées au Riesling et Groseilles de Juin)

Totally fat-free, this dessert is perfect for summer's sweet fruits. Nectarines, plums, or apricots can be used in place of the peaches.

½ bottle late-harvest Riesling
2 cups water
1 cup sugar
   Zest of 1 lemon
   Zest of 1 orange
4 large ripe peaches, peeled, halved, and pitted
½ cup fresh currants
4 sprigs fresh mint

In a medium saucepan, combine the Riesling, water, sugar, lemon zest, and orange zest. Place over medium heat and stir to dissolve the sugar. Add the peaches, cut side down, and cover with an inverted plate small enough to fit in the pan to keep the peaches submerged. Bring to a boil over medium-high heat. Immediately reduce the heat to low. Simmer for 7 minutes, or until the peaches are tender when pierced with a knife. Remove the pan from the heat and allow the peaches to cool in the syrup.

Strain the liquid from the pan and measure it. Place half of the liquid in a small saucepan. Return the remainder to the pan with the peaches.

Place the small saucepan over medium heat. Bring to a simmer. Cook, skimming off any foam that forms on the top, for 4 minutes, or until the liquid has thickened slightly and become syrupy. Remove from the heat and allow to cool.

When ready to serve, remove the peaches from the liquid and pat off any excess moisture. Cut each peach lengthwise into 6 slices, leaving the slices just slightly attached at the stem end. Place 2 peach halves on each of 4 dessert plates, arranging the peaches so that the stem ends face. Scatter the currants around the peaches. Drizzle the syrup over the plates. Garnish with the mint.

YIELD: 4 SERVINGS

PER SERVING

117 CALORIES
0 G. TOTAL FAT
0 G. SATURATED FAT
0 MG. CHOLESTEROL

EGGPLANT TERRINE WITH ROASTED VEGETABLES

MARINATED GRILLED LAMB CHOPS WITH PROVENÇAL ROASTED TOMATOES

FRESH FRUIT WITH SABAYON

PER SERVING
779 CALORIES

28 G. TOTAL FAT (32% OF CALORIES)

10 G. SATURATED FAT

200 MG. CHOLESTEROL

EGGPLANT TERRINE WITH ROASTED VEGETABLES
(*Terrine d'Aubergines Arc-en-Ciel*)

This summer vegetable terrine is redolent with the flavors of Provence. It can be served warm or at room temperature. The terrine can be put together early in the day and refrigerated until ready to bake.

2   tablespoons chopped fresh basil

1   tablespoon minced garlic

3   tablespoons olive oil

1   large eggplant, cut lengthwise into ¼″ slices

1   large zucchini, cut lengthwise into ¼″ slices

1   large yellow squash, cut lengthwise into ¼″ slices
   Salt and freshly ground black pepper

10 ounces fresh spinach, washed, stems removed, and dried
   Freshly grated nutmeg

2   small red bell peppers, roasted, peeled, seeded, and cut into strips

2   ounces Gruyère cheese, sliced paper-thin

2   sprigs fresh thyme
   Tomato Vinaigrette (page 50)

Preheat the oven to 400°F.

In a small bowl, combine the basil, garlic, and 2 tablespoons of the oil.

Lightly brush 3 baking sheets with the remaining 1 tablespoon oil. Place the eggplant, zucchini, and yellow squash in single layers on the sheets. Lightly brush the vegetables with some of the basil mixture. Bake for 5 minutes, or until the vegetables are tender but still firm. Remove from the oven. Season the vegetables with the salt and black pepper.

Lightly brush a large nonstick sauté pan with some of the remaining basil mixture. Add the spinach. Sauté over medium heat for 4 minutes, or until the spinach has wilted. Remove from the heat and drain through a fine strainer, pressing on the spinach to extract all excess liquid. Place in a small bowl and season with the salt, black pepper, and nutmeg.

Lightly brush a 9″ × 5″ nonstick loaf pan with the remaining basil mixture. Lay 1 or 2 eggplant slices, skin side down, in the pan to cover the bottom. Arrange the remaining eggplant slices, skin side down and slightly overlapping, around the sides of the pan, allowing them to overhang the edge of the pan by about 2″.

Place a layer of zucchini in the pan. Top with a layer of red peppers, a layer of Gruyère, a layer of yellow squash, and a layer of spinach. Repeat to use all the vegetables and cheese. Bring the eggplant slices up over the edge to enclose the terrine. Place the thyme on top. Cover the pan with foil.

Place in a small roasting pan. Add enough hot water to the outer pan to come at least 2″ up the sides of the loaf pan. Bake for 30 minutes. Remove from the oven and allow to cool for at least 10 minutes.

Slice the terrine crosswise into 1½″ slices. Place the slices on salad plates. Drizzle with the vinaigrette.

YIELD: 6 SERVINGS

PER SERVING

156 CALORIES
10 G. TOTAL FAT
3 G. SATURATED FAT
10 MG. CHOLESTEROL

MARINATED GRILLED LAMB CHOPS WITH PROVENÇAL ROASTED TOMATOES (PAGE 126)

MARINATED GRILLED LAMB CHOPS
WITH PROVENÇAL ROASTED TOMATOES

(Côtes d'Agneau Grillées aux Herbes avec Tomates Provençales)

This is a quick and simple dish for easy backyard entertaining. Add a green salad, crusty bread, and a great red wine for a perfect summer meal.

8	baby lamb chops, trimmed of all fat
3	cloves garlic
2	sprigs fresh thyme
1	sprig fresh rosemary
4	large ripe tomatoes, halved crosswise and seeded
2	teaspoons coarse salt
½	cup freshly made dry bread crumbs
2	tablespoons grated Parmesan cheese
2	tablespoons chopped fresh flat-leaf parsley
½	teaspoon fresh thyme leaves
1	teaspoon olive oil
	Salt and freshly ground black pepper
4	sprigs fresh flat-leaf parsley

Place the lamb chops in a shallow baking dish. Crush 2 cloves of the garlic and halve them. Add to the dish. Add the thyme sprigs and rosemary. Cover and refrigerate for 4 hours.

When ready to serve, preheat the broiler. Preheat the grill to high.

Sprinkle the tomatoes with the salt and place them, cut side down, on a wire rack placed over a jelly-roll pan. Allow to drain for 15 minutes.

In a small bowl, combine the bread crumbs, Parmesan, chopped parsley, thyme leaves, and oil. Mince the remaining 1 clove garlic and add to the bowl. Mix well.

Fit the tomatoes, cut side up, into a small baking dish just large enough to hold them. Divide the bread-crumb mixture among the tomatoes. Broil for 10 minutes, or until the tomatoes have softened slightly and the tops are golden brown. Remove from the broiler. Cover lightly with foil and keep warm.

While the tomatoes are broiling, season both sides of the chops with the salt and pepper. Grill for 3 minutes per side for medium-rare.

Place 2 tomato halves in the center of each of 4 warm dinner plates. Crisscross 2 chops over the tomatoes on each plate. Garnish each with a sprig of parsley.

YIELD: 4 SERVINGS

PER SERVING

301 CALORIES
14 G. TOTAL FAT
5 G. SATURATED FAT
79 MG. CHOLESTEROL

FRESH FRUIT WITH SABAYON
(Sabayon aux Fruits d'Été)

Sabayon is a classic dessert sauce also known as zabaglione in Italian cuisine. Very rich-tasting, this frothy custard can be served alone or as a sauce for cakes, pastries, or fruit. You can use just one fruit or any combination you like for this recipe.

2	small bananas, sliced crosswise
2	small peaches, peeled and sliced lengthwise
1	mango, peeled and sliced lengthwise
¾	cup fresh blueberries
¾	cup fresh raspberries
	Juice of ½ lemon
2	large egg yolks
¼	cup plus 2 tablespoons sugar
½	cup Sauternes wine
1	tablespoon heavy cream

In a medium bowl, combine the bananas, peaches, mangoes, blueberries, raspberries, and lemon juice. Mix well. Cover and set aside.

In a medium stainless-steel bowl, whisk together the egg yolks and sugar until they are quite pale. Add the wine and cream and whisk to combine.

Half fill a 2-quart saucepan with water. Bring to a boil over high heat. Place the stainless-steel bowl over the water, without allowing the bottom of the bowl to touch the water. Rapidly whisk the egg mixture, allowing it to warm and become frothy and thick. To prevent the mixture from heating too quickly and curdling, it may be necessary to remove the bowl from the heat from time to time.

When the sauce has thickened, pour equal portions into 4 shallow dessert bowls (or cover the surface of the sauce with plastic wrap to keep it from forming a skin until ready to serve). Place equal portions of the fruit in each bowl.

YIELD: 4 SERVINGS

PER SERVING

322 CALORIES
4 G. TOTAL FAT
2 G. SATURATED FAT
111 MG. CHOLESTEROL

SALAD NIÇOISE

SEA BASS WITH SAUTÉED CUCUMBERS

FROZEN BLUEBERRY SOUFFLÉS

PER SERVING

604 CALORIES

11 G. TOTAL FAT (16% OF CALORIES)

3 G. SATURATED FAT

150 MG. CHOLESTEROL

SALAD NIÇOISE
(Salade Niçoise)

To be called niçoise, a dish must have tomatoes, olives, and anchovies—ingredients typically used in the south of France. This is our low-fat version.

4	small red new potatoes
	Salt
¾	cup Vegetable Vinaigrette (page 52)
1	small green bell pepper
4	canned anchovy fillets
1	head Boston lettuce, washed, leaves pulled apart, and dried
1½	cups haricots verts or small green beans cut into 2″ pieces, blanched (page 32)
2	medium very ripe tomatoes, peeled, cored, seeded, and cut into 8 wedges each
1	small cucumber, peeled, seeded, and cut crosswise into thin slices
1	can (3½ ounces) tuna packed in water, well-drained, or 4 ounces grilled fresh tuna
2	hard-boiled eggs, peeled and quartered
12	niçoise olives, pitted and chopped
2	tablespoons chopped fresh flat-leaf parsley

Place the potatoes in a medium saucepan and add cold water to cover by about 1″. Add a pinch of salt. Bring to a boil over high heat. Reduce the heat to medium and simmer for 15 minutes, or until the potatoes are tender when pierced with a fork. Drain well and set aside until just cool enough to handle. Pull off the skins and cut the potatoes crosswise into ⅛″ slices. Place in a small bowl. Add 2 tablespoons of the vinaigrette. Toss well.

Using a vegetable peeler, carefully peel the skin from the pepper. Cut the pepper in half lengthwise and remove the core, seeds, and membrane. Cut lengthwise into 2″ × 1/16″ strips.

Place the anchovies in a small bowl. Add cold water to cover. Allow to soak for 5 minutes. Drain and pat dry. Cut into 1″ pieces.

Place the lettuce in a large bowl. Add 1 tablespoon of the remaining vinaigrette. Toss well. Transfer to a large shallow salad bowl or a platter.

Using the remaining 9 tablespoons vinaigrette, separately dress the haricots verts or beans, tomatoes, cucumbers, and peppers.

Place the tuna in the center of the lettuce. Arrange the vegetables in a decorative pattern around the tuna. Place the eggs around the edges. Scatter the olives and anchovies over the salad. Sprinkle with the parsley.

YIELD: 4 SERVINGS

PER SERVING

223 CALORIES
4 G. TOTAL FAT
1 G. SATURATED FAT
72 MG. CHOLESTEROL

SALAD NIÇOISE

Sea Bass with Sautéed Cucumbers
(Bar de l'Atlantique aux Concombres Poêlés)

In France, cucumbers are more frequently used as a cooked vegetable than they are in America. In this recipe, the fat-free cucumbers are a wonderful partner for the lean fish.

3	large cucumbers, peeled
	Salt
½	teaspoon unsalted butter
1½	teaspoons canola oil
	Freshly ground black pepper
¼	cup all-purpose flour
4	sea bass fillets (5 ounces each)
1	large tomato, peeled, cored, seeded, and diced

Cut the cucumbers crosswise into 3″ pieces. Using an apple corer, remove the seeds so that you create hollow tubes. Cut crosswise into ¼″ slices. Transfer to a colander. Sprinkle with 1 teaspoon of salt and toss to coat. Set the colander in the sink or over a bowl and allow the cucumbers to drain for 15 minutes. Rinse off the salt under cold running water. Pat the cucumbers dry.

Combine the butter and ½ teaspoon of the oil in a large nonstick sauté pan. Place over high heat. Add the cucumbers in a single layer and cook for 2 minutes. Turn the slices. Cover and reduce the heat to medium. Cook for 9 minutes, or until the cucumbers are nicely browned. Season with the salt and pepper. Keep warm.

Place the flour in a shallow bowl. Lightly dust each fillet with flour, shaking off any excess. Season with salt and pepper.

Warm the remaining 1 teaspoon oil in another large nonstick sauté pan over high heat. Add the fillets and cook for 1½ minutes, or until nicely browned on the bottom. Carefully turn the fillets and cook for 2 minutes, or until the fish flakes easily when tested with a fork.

Place 1 fillet in the center of each of 4 warm dinner plates. Surround each fillet with a circle of slightly overlapping cucumber slices. Sprinkle the tomatoes over the top.

Yield: 4 servings

Per serving

268 calories
7 g. total fat
2 g. saturated fat
78 mg. cholesterol

FROZEN BLUEBERRY SOUFFLÉS
(Soufflés Glacés aux Myrtilles)

This is a terrific make-ahead no-fat dessert. The blueberries can be replaced with any other berry. If using berries with large seeds, strain the puree.

1 cup pureed fresh blueberries
1 teaspoon fresh lemon juice
2 tablespoons water
¼ cup plus 2 tablespoons granulated sugar
2 large egg whites
2 tablespoons confectioners' sugar
16 fresh blueberries

In a large bowl, combine the pureed blueberries and lemon juice. Mix well.

In a small saucepan, combine the water and ¼ cup of the granulated sugar. Bring to a boil over high heat. Reduce the heat to medium and cook for 10 minutes, or until a candy thermometer inserted into the syrup registers 238° to 240°F.

While the syrup is cooking, place the egg whites in a medium bowl. Beat with an electric mixer on medium speed until foamy. Gradually beat in the remaining 2 tablespoons granulated sugar and beat on high speed until soft peaks form.

Slowly pour the hot syrup into the egg whites, beating constantly and taking care that the syrup does not hit the beaters or stick to the sides of the bowl. Continue beating until the meringue is cool.

Fold one-quarter of the meringue into the blueberry puree. When well-blended, fold in the remaining meringue.

Divide among four (4-ounce) molds, filling them to the top. Using a spatula, carefully smooth the surface of each mold. Place in the freezer for at least 1 hour or up to 24 hours. (If freezing for a longer period, tightly cover the molds with plastic wrap so that the soufflés do not absorb other odors.)

When ready to serve, remove the molds from the freezer and allow them to stand at room temperature for 15 minutes. Sprinkle with confectioners' sugar and garnish with the fresh blueberries.

YIELD: 4 SERVINGS

PER SERVING
113 CALORIES
0 G. TOTAL FAT
0 G. SATURATED FAT
0 MG. CHOLESTEROL

FENNEL À LA GRECQUE

GRILLED PORK TENDERLOIN WITH ROASTED RED PEPPER
AND TOMATO SAUCE

CHERRY CLAFOUTIS, LIMOUSIN-STYLE

<u>PER SERVING</u>

555 CALORIES

15 G. TOTAL FAT (24% OF CALORIES)

3 G. SATURATED FAT

207 MG. CHOLESTEROL

FENNEL À LA GRECQUE
(*Fenouil à la Grecque*)

Almost any vegetable can be prepared à la grecque, *one of the classic French methods. Vegetables prepared in this manner make perfect hors d'oeuvres and buffet table dishes as they are served at room temperature and can be made several days in advance of use.*

2	large bulbs fennel
2	teaspoons olive oil
1	small onion, thinly sliced
¾	cup dry white wine
	Juice of 1 lemon
½	teaspoon coriander seeds
1	bay leaf
1	large sprig fresh thyme
	Pinch of paprika
	Salt
2	lemons, cut crosswise into ¼" slices
½	cup fresh flat-leaf parsley leaves

Remove any hard or discolored outer layers from the fennel bulbs. Trim and discard the root ends and the feathery tops. Cut the bulbs in half lengthwise, then cut each half into 8 wedges, leaving the core intact to keep the fennel from falling apart when cooked.

Warm the oil in a large nonstick sauté pan over medium heat. Add the onions and sauté for 10 minutes, or until soft but not browned. Stir in the wine, lemon juice, coriander seeds, bay leaf, thyme, paprika, and fennel. Season with the salt. Cover and simmer for 15 minutes, or until the fennel is tender when pierced with a knife. Allow to cool to room temperature. Remove and discard the bay leaf and thyme sprig.

Place equal portions of the fennel in the center of each of 4 salad plates. Surround with a circle of alternating lemon slices and parsley leaves.

YIELD: 4 SERVINGS

PER SERVING

64 CALORIES
3 G. TOTAL FAT
0.3 G. SATURATED FAT
0 MG. CHOLESTEROL

FENNEL À LA GRECQUE

GRILLED PORK TENDERLOIN WITH ROASTED RED PEPPER
AND TOMATO SAUCE

(Filet de Porc Grillé aux Poivrons Rouges et Sauce Tomate)

Pork tenderloin is an extremely lean and flavorful meat. Marinated and grilled, it offers a wonderful addition to the low-fat diet.

¼	cup fresh orange juice
1	tablespoon sherry vinegar
1	tablespoon Dijon mustard
2	teaspoons herbes de Provence (see note)
1	pork tenderloin (1½ pounds), trimmed of all fat
	Salt and freshly ground black pepper
1	cup Roasted Red Pepper and Tomato Sauce (page 46)
2	tablespoons chopped fresh flat-leaf parsley

In a small bowl, combine the orange juice, vinegar, mustard, and herbes de Provence. Mix well.

Place the pork in a small nonstick roasting pan. Pour the orange-juice mixture over the pork, then turn to coat evenly. Cover with plastic wrap and refrigerate for 4 hours.

Preheat the grill to medium.

Wipe any excess marinade from the pork; discard the marinade. Season the pork with the salt and pepper. Grill, turning frequently, for 20 minutes, or until the pork is medium-well with an internal temperature of 150° to 160°F. Transfer to a warm platter and allow to stand for 5 minutes.

Place the tomato sauce in a small saucepan. Warm over medium heat. Taste and adjust the seasoning.

Cut the tenderloin crosswise into 1″ slices. Pool about ¼ cup of the sauce on each of 4 warm dinner plates. Place equal slices of pork on the plates. Sprinkle with the parsley.

Chef's Note: Herbes de Provence is a mixture of dried herbs that often includes basil, lavender, rosemary, sage, thyme, and others. Look for it in the spice section of your supermarket.

YIELD: 4 SERVINGS

PER SERVING

259 CALORIES
8 G. TOTAL FAT
2 G. SATURATED FAT
98 MG. CHOLESTEROL

CHERRY CLAFOUTIS, LIMOUSIN-STYLE
(*Clafoutis de Cerises Limousin*)

Clafoutis is a traditional French homestyle dessert. Usually made with summer's ripest cherries, it can also be made with any fruit or berry that you choose.

1¾	cups 1% low-fat milk
½	vanilla bean, split lengthwise
3	large eggs
⅓	cup sugar
1	tablespoon all-purpose flour
2	tablespoons kirschwasser (clear cherry brandy)
2	cups pitted Bing (or other sweet) cherries

Preheat the oven to 300°F.

Coat a 9″ quiche dish with nonstick spray.

Place the milk in a small saucepan. Scrape the seeds from the vanilla bean into the saucepan, then add the bean. Cook over medium heat for 3 minutes, or until the milk is very hot but not boiling. Remove from the heat. Remove and discard the vanilla bean.

In a medium bowl, combine the eggs and sugar. Whisk well to combine. Whisk in the flour, beating until no lumps are visible. Whisk in the kirschwasser. Whisking constantly, slowly add about ½ cup of the milk. Then whisk in the remaining milk.

Place the cherries in a single layer over the bottom of the quiche dish. Pour the batter through a fine sieve over the cherries. Bake for 30 minutes, or until puffed and set. Cool slightly before serving. When ready to serve, cut into wedges.

YIELD: 6 SERVINGS

PER SERVING

232 CALORIES
4 G. TOTAL FAT
1 G. SATURATED FAT
109 MG. CHOLESTEROL

SORREL SOUP

TROPICAL MARINATED CHICKEN BREASTS WITH WARM FRENCH
POTATO SALAD

PEACH AND NECTARINE PURSES

PER SERVING

894 CALORIES

14 G. TOTAL FAT (14% OF CALORIES)

4 G. SATURATED FAT

250 MG. CHOLESTEROL

SORREL SOUP
(Soupe à l'Oseille)

Intensely acidic, sorrels make a very light and flavorful soup that can be served either hot or chilled. If desired, a last-minute sprinkling of chopped fresh herbs such as chives or chervil will add another dimension to the very refreshing taste.

1	teaspoon unsalted butter
1	teaspoon canola oil
1	large leek, white part with a little green attached, trimmed, halved lengthwise, well-washed, and cut crosswise into ¼″ slices
1	small onion, chopped
1	small clove garlic, crushed
1	medium all-purpose potato, peeled and cubed
3½	cups White Chicken Stock (page 37)
3	ounces sorrel, stems trimmed to 1″ below the leaves, washed, and dried
	Salt and freshly ground black pepper
½	cup 2% reduced-fat milk

Warm the butter and oil in a large nonstick saucepan over medium-low heat. Add the leeks, onions, and garlic. Sauté for 15 minutes, or until the vegetables have softened but have not browned. Stir in the potatoes and stock.

SORREL SOUP

Bring to a boil over medium-high heat. Reduce the heat to medium. Simmer, stirring occasionally, for 15 minutes, or until the potatoes are soft. Add the sorrel. Season with salt and pepper. Cook for 3 minutes. Remove from the heat; cool slightly.

Transfer to a blender or a food processor fitted with the metal blade. Process until very smooth. Pour into a clean saucepan. Stir in the milk. Taste and adjust the seasoning. Bring to a simmer over medium heat. Pour equal portions of the soup into each of 4 soup bowls.

YIELD: 4 SERVINGS

PER SERVING

125 CALORIES
4 G. TOTAL FAT
1 G. SATURATED FAT
12 MG. CHOLESTEROL

TROPICAL MARINATED CHICKEN BREASTS
WITH WARM FRENCH POTATO SALAD

(Suprêmes de Volaille Sautés avec Salade de Pommes de Terre)

Easy and light—the perfect summer entrée! You could add a tossed salad and a glass of chilled white wine for the complete meal.

4	boneless, skinless chicken breasts (5 ounces each)
¾	cup Tropical Vinaigrette (page 53)
2	tablespoons nonfat plain yogurt
1½	pounds small red new potatoes
	Salt
¼	cup dry white wine
2	tablespoons sherry vinegar
1	teaspoon Dijon mustard
1	tablespoon olive oil
2	large shallots, minced
2	tablespoons chopped fresh flat-leaf parsley
	Freshly ground black pepper
4	sprigs fresh flat-leaf parsley

Place the chicken in a shallow glass baking dish.

In a small bowl, combine the vinaigrette and yogurt. Mix well and pour over the chicken to evenly cover. Cover with plastic wrap and refrigerate for at least 4 hours.

About 45 minutes before serving, place the potatoes in a large saucepan and add cold water to cover by about 1″. Add a pinch of salt. Bring to a boil over high heat. Reduce the heat to medium and simmer for 15 minutes, or until the potatoes are just tender when pierced with a fork. Drain and set aside until just cool enough to handle.

In a small bowl, combine the wine, vinegar, and mustard. Whisk well. Slowly whisk in the oil. Season with the salt.

Peel and quarter the potatoes. Place in large bowl. Add the shallots, chopped parsley, and wine mixture. Season with the salt and pepper. Toss to mix well. Keep warm.

Preheat the grill to medium.

Wipe the marinade from the chicken; discard the marinade. Season with salt and pepper. Grill for 5 to 7 minutes, or until golden brown and cooked through when tested with a knife. Let stand for 3 minutes. Cut each breast on the bias into 4 pieces.

Place a mound of the potato salad in the center of each of 4 warm plates. Fan a chicken breast in front of the salad and garnish with a parsley sprig.

YIELD: 4 SERVINGS

460 CALORIES
7 G. TOTAL FAT
2 G. SATURATED FAT
131 MG. CHOLESTEROL

PEACH AND NECTARINE PURSES
(Pêches et Brugnons en Portefeuille)

Crêpes can be made up to a day or two in advance and stored, separated by parchment paper or plastic wrap, tightly covered and refrigerated. They are great to keep on hand for an easy dessert filled with simple fresh fruit or a more elaborate preparation such as this.

2	large eggs
½	cup skim milk
¼	cup plus 2 tablespoons sugar
½	cup all-purpose flour
	Zest of 1 lemon
	Zest of 1 orange
½	vanilla bean, split lengthwise
3	medium peaches, peeled, pitted, and sliced
3	medium nectarines, peeled, pitted, and sliced
2	tablespoons honey
2	tablespoons rum
1	vanilla bean

In a medium bowl, combine the eggs, milk, and ¼ cup of the sugar. Whisk well. Whisk in the flour, lemon zest, and orange zest until smooth. Scrape the seeds from the ½ vanilla bean into the bowl. Mix well.

Lightly coat a nonstick crêpe pan with nonstick spray. Place over medium heat. When very hot, pour about 2 tablespoons of the batter into the pan and swirl it around to lightly and evenly coat the bottom. Cook for 30 seconds, or until the bottom is just set. Flip the crêpe by gently lifting 1 side with a knife or fork and then quickly and carefully turning it. Cook for 30 seconds, or until the crêpe just starts to brown. Transfer to a plate. Continue making crêpes until all of the batter has been used. You should have 8 crêpes.

(continued)

In a medium bowl, combine the peaches, nectarines, and honey. Toss to mix.

Place a medium nonstick sauté pan over medium-high heat until very hot. Add the remaining 2 tablespoons sugar. Cook, stirring frequently, for 3 minutes, or until the sugar has caramelized. Add the fruit and cook for 2 minutes. Pour in the rum. Remove the pan from the heat and carefully ignite the fruit with a long match. Allow the flame to burn out, then return the pan to the heat. Cook for 10 minutes, or until the fruit begins to break apart. Add up to ¼ cup water if the pan gets too dry. Allow to cool slightly.

Cut the whole vanilla bean lengthwise into 8 very thin strips.

Lay 8 crêpes on a work surface. Place an equal portion of the fruit in the center of each crêpe. Gather the sides of each crêpe up and around the fruit to make a pouch. Using a vanilla bean strip, tie each pouch closed. Place 2 pouches on each of 4 plates. Place any remaining fruit or fruit juices on each plate.

YIELD: 4 SERVINGS

PER SERVING

309 CALORIES
3 G. TOTAL FAT
1 G. SATURATED FAT
107 MG. CHOLESTEROL

GAZPACHO

BAKED COD WITH TOMATOES, CAPERS, AND TURMERIC
ON SAUTÉED SPINACH

PEACHES MELBA

PER SERVING

443 CALORIES

11 G. TOTAL FAT (22% OF CALORIES)

3 G. SATURATED FAT

56 MG. CHOLESTEROL

GAZPACHO
(Gazpacho)

Although this uncooked chilled soup has its origins in Spain, it has been adopted by many cuisines. It is refreshing, low in fat and calories, and absolutely delicious.

6	medium very ripe tomatoes, peeled, cored, seeded, and chopped
1	clove garlic, chopped
1	cucumber, peeled, seeded, and finely diced
½	cup water
1	tablespoon sherry vinegar
1	tablespoon olive oil
½	teaspoon Tabasco sauce
	Juice of 1 lemon
	Salt
	Pinch of cayenne pepper
1	red bell pepper, seeded and finely diced
20	large leaves fresh basil, cut into chiffonade (page 31)

In a blender or a food processor fitted with the metal blade, combine the tomatoes, garlic, and half of the cucumbers. Process until very smooth. Add the water,

(continued)

GAZPACHO (PAGE 141)

vinegar, oil, Tabasco sauce, and lemon juice. Process to blend. Season with the salt and cayenne. Transfer to a large glass bowl. Cover and refrigerate for at least 1 hour, or until well-chilled.

Pour equal portions of the soup into each of 4 chilled soup bowls. Place equal portions of the red peppers and the remaining cucumbers in each bowl. Sprinkle with the basil.

YIELD: 4 SERVINGS

PER SERVING

88 CALORIES
4 G. TOTAL FAT
1 G. SATURATED FAT
1 MG. CHOLESTEROL

BAKED COD WITH TOMATOES, CAPERS, AND TURMERIC ON SAUTÉED SPINACH
(Casserole de Morue Fraîche sur Feuilles d'Épinards Sautées)

Low in fat and cholesterol, this dish sings of the flavors of Provence. Any green can be substituted for the spinach and any lean, firm white fish for the cod.

1	teaspoon unsalted butter
2	teaspoons olive oil
2	large very ripe tomatoes, peeled, cored, seeded, and diced
1	cup Fish Stock (page 40)
3	tablespoons capers, well-drained
1	tablespoon turmeric
	Salt and freshly ground black pepper
⅓	cup freshly made dry bread crumbs
1	tablespoon chopped fresh chives
1	tablespoon chopped fresh flat-leaf parsley
4	cod fillets (5 ounces each)
1	pound fresh spinach, washed and stems removed

Preheat the oven to 450°F.

Using ½ teaspoon of the butter, lightly coat a casserole large enough to hold the fish in a single layer.

Warm 1 teaspoon of the oil in a medium sauté pan over medium-high heat. Add the tomatoes and sauté for 3 minutes. Add the stock, capers, and turmeric. Bring to a boil. Reduce the heat to medium-low and simmer for 10 minutes. Season with the salt and pepper. Cover and keep warm.

In a small bowl, combine the bread crumbs, chives, parsley, and the remaining 1 teaspoon oil. Mix well.

Season the cod on both sides with salt and pepper. Lay the fillets in the prepared casserole. Top each fillet with an equal amount of the bread-crumb mixture. Bake for 8 minutes, or until the cod is just slightly underdone.

Turn on the broiler and broil for 1 minute, or until the tops are golden and the fish flakes easily when tested with a fork. Remove from the broiler. Cover lightly and keep warm.

Melt the remaining ½ teaspoon butter in a large nonstick sauté pan over high heat. Shake excess water from the spinach and add to the pan. Season with the salt and pepper. Cover and cook over medium heat for 2 minutes, or until the spinach has wilted. Drain, if necessary.

(continued)

Place equal portions of the spinach in the center of each of 4 warm dinner plates. Place a cod fillet on top and pour the sauce around the edge of the spinach.

YIELD: 4 SERVINGS

PER SERVING

228 CALORIES
6 G. TOTAL FAT
1 G. SATURATED FAT
55 MG. CHOLESTEROL

PEACHES MELBA
(*Pêches Melba*)

This is a low-fat version of the famous dessert created by Auguste Escoffier, a great French chef, for Dame Nellie Melba, a turn-of-the-century opera diva.

6   cups water
1   cup sugar
    Zest of 1 lemon, cut into long, thin strips
4   small pieces crystallized ginger
4   large ripe peaches, peeled, halved, and pitted
1   cup fresh raspberries
2   cups nonfat vanilla frozen yogurt

In a medium saucepan, combine the water, sugar, lemon zest, and ginger. Bring to a boil over medium heat. Carefully lower the peaches into the liquid. Reduce the heat to low and gently simmer for 10 minutes, or until the peaches are tender when pierced with a knife. Using a slotted spoon, remove the peaches from the poaching liquid and place on a plate to cool.

Transfer ¼ cup of the poaching liquid to a blender or a food processor fitted with the metal blade. Add the raspberries. Process until very smooth.

Cut each peach half lengthwise into 4 wedges. Place 4 wedges in the bottom of each of 4 well-chilled parfait glasses or dessert bowls. Place ½ cup of the frozen yogurt on top of the peaches. Top each with 4 of the remaining peach wedges. Spoon the reserved raspberry puree over the top.

YIELD: 4 SERVINGS

PER SERVING

127 CALORIES
1 G. TOTAL FAT
0.5 G. SATURATED FAT
0 MG. CHOLESTEROL

TOMATO TARTS

MUSSELS IN WHITE WINE

BABY GREENS

MELON SOUP

PER SERVING

828 CALORIES

20 G. TOTAL FAT (22% OF CALORIES)

4 G. SATURATED FAT

62 MG. CHOLESTEROL

TOMATO TARTS
(*Tartes aux Tomates du Jardin*)

Summer perfection! Sweet, ripe tomatoes with just a hint of cheese. These would also make a lovely luncheon entrée, prepared as a full-size tart.

      Savory Pastry (page 55)
3   medium very ripe tomatoes, peeled, cored, and sliced
      crosswise paper thin
2   tablespoons grated Parmesan cheese
      Salt and freshly ground black pepper
2   tablespoons fresh basil cut into chiffonade (page 31)

Preheat the oven to 375°F. Lightly coat a nonstick baking sheet with nonstick spray.

On a lightly floured surface, roll out the pastry to about ⅛″ thickness. Using a 6″ round pastry cutter with decorative edges, cut out 4 circles. Place the circles on the prepared baking sheet. Randomly prick the circles with a fork. Bake for 5 minutes. Remove from the oven but do not turn off the heat.

Place the tomato slices, slightly overlapping, in concentric circles on each pastry circle, leaving ½″ of pastry around the outside edge. Place 2 or 3 tomato slices in

(continued)

TOMATO TARTS (PAGE 145)

the center to completely cover each circle. Sprinkle the tomatoes with the Parmesan, salt, and pepper. Bake for 8 minutes, or until the tomatoes are cooked and the pastry is golden. Sprinkle the basil over the top.

YIELD: 4 SERVINGS

PER SERVING

175 CALORIES
7 G. TOTAL FAT
2 G. SATURATED FAT
42 MG. CHOLESTEROL

MUSSELS IN WHITE WINE
(Moules au Vin Blanc)

We have added the bread and greens to make a complete low-fat meal in 15 minutes. However, you could serve the mussels with any vegetable or salad you like. Just don't forget the bread—it is needed to absorb the delicious, aromatic cooking liquid.

3	pounds fresh mussels
1½	teaspoons olive oil
4	small shallots, minced
2	cloves garlic, minced
1½	cups dry white wine
2	bay leaves
4	very ripe plum tomatoes, peeled, cored, and chopped
	Salt and freshly ground black pepper
2	tablespoons chopped fresh flat-leaf parsley
1	baguette, warmed and sliced crosswise into ½″ pieces

Squeeze each mussel in the palm of your hand and discard any whose shells open. Scrub the remaining mussels to remove grit; cut off the beards. Wash in 3 changes of cold water.

Warm the oil in a large nonstick sauté pan over medium-high heat. Add the shallots and sauté for 1 minute. Add the garlic and sauté for 1 minute, or until the garlic just begins to brown. Add the wine and bay leaves. Stir in the mussels. Cover and cook for 4 minutes, or until the mussels open. Remove the pan from the heat and, using a slotted spoon, transfer the mussels to a large bowl. Discard any mussels that do not open. Strain the cooking liquid through a fine sieve into a medium saucepan.

When the mussels are cool enough to handle, use a spoon to slightly loosen the meat in each mussel. Place equal portions in each of 4 large shallow soup bowls.

Add the tomatoes to the saucepan. Bring to a boil over high heat and cook for 2 minutes. Season with the salt and pepper. Pour over the mussels. Sprinkle with the parsley and serve the bread on the side.

YIELD: 4 SERVINGS

PER SERVING

350 CALORIES
12 G. TOTAL FAT
2 G. SATURATED FAT
20 MG. CHOLESTEROL

BABY GREENS
(*Mesclun*)

A small amount of extra-virgin olive oil gives great flavor without a lot of fat to this delicious vinaigrette.

5 cups mixed baby greens
2 tablespoons water
2 teaspoons sherry vinegar
1 teaspoon fresh lemon juice
½ teaspoon Dijon mustard
1 tablespoon extra-virgin olive oil
Salt and freshly ground black pepper

Place the greens in a medium bowl.

In a small bowl, combine the water, vinegar, lemon juice, and mustard. Whisk well. Whisk in the oil. Season with the salt and pepper. Pour over the greens and toss to coat.

YIELD: 4 SERVINGS

PER SERVING
29 CALORIES
2.4 G. TOTAL FAT
0 G. SATURATED FAT
0 MG. CHOLESTEROL

MELON SOUP
(*Soupe de Melon Glacé*)

This dessert soup can be made up to a day in advance. Store it tightly covered in the refrigerator. For the sweetest taste, be sure that the melons you use are very ripe.

1 cup water
¾ cup fresh orange juice
¼ cup sugar
2 large very ripe cantaloupes, halved and seeded
1 large very ripe honeydew, halved and seeded
Juice of ½ lemon
1 tablespoon fresh mint cut into chiffonade (page 31)

In a small bowl, combine the water, orange juice, and sugar. Whisk for 2 minutes, or until the sugar has dissolved.

Using a large spoon, scoop the flesh from the cantaloupes and half of the honeydew. Place in a blender or a food processor fitted with the metal blade. Add the orange-juice mixture and process until very smooth. Pour into a large glass bowl. Cover and refrigerate for at least 1 hour, or until well-chilled.

Using a melon baller, scoop small balls from the remaining honeydew half. Place in a small bowl. Add the lemon juice and toss to combine.

When ready to serve, pour equal portions of the chilled soup into 4 glass bowls. Garnish with the honeydew balls and mint.

YIELD: 4 SERVINGS

PER SERVING

303 CALORIES
1 G. TOTAL FAT
0 G. SATURATED FAT
0 MG. CHOLESTEROL

SMOKED SALMON CANAPÉS

BASQUE-STYLE OMELETS

SOUR CREAM–BLUEBERRY TARTS

<u>PER SERVING</u>

556 CALORIES

21 G. TOTAL FAT (34% OF CALORIES)

5 G. SATURATED FAT

313 MG. CHOLESTEROL

SMOKED SALMON CANAPÉS
(*Saumon Fumé sur Canapés*)

Salmon tartare can also be served on toast points or crackers for cocktail hors d'oeuvres. Be sure that you purchase very fresh salmon for this dish since it is served raw.

8	ounces skinless, boneless smoked salmon fillet, all gray flesh removed and well-chilled
2	tablespoons finely diced red onions
1	tablespoon chopped fresh dill
1	tablespoon chopped fresh flat-leaf parsley
½	teaspoon chopped fresh tarragon
½	teaspoon minced fresh ginger
¼	jalapeño pepper, seeded and minced (wear plastic gloves when handling)
1	teaspoon olive oil
1	teaspoon capers, well-drained and chopped
½	teaspoon Dijon mustard
	Salt and freshly ground black pepper
12	thin baguette slices, toasted
2	tablespoons chopped fresh chives

SMOKED SALMON CANAPÉS

Using a sharp chef's knife, chop the salmon into very small cubes.

In a medium bowl, combine the onions, dill, parsley, tarragon, ginger, and jalapeño peppers. Mix well. Stir in the oil, capers, and mustard. Add the salmon and toss to combine. Season with the salt and black pepper.

Neatly mound equal portions of the salmon tartare on each toast piece. Garnish with a sprinkle of chives.

YIELD: 4 SERVINGS

PER SERVING

193 CALORIES
7 G. TOTAL FAT
1 G. SATURATED FAT
40 MG. CHOLESTEROL

BASQUE-STYLE OMELETTES
(Omelettes Basquaises)

The flavors of the Basque country are prominent in these delightful low-fat omelettes.

3   teaspoons olive oil
1   small onion, thinly sliced
1   clove garlic, minced
1   small green bell pepper, halved, seeded, and cut lengthwise into thin strips
3   ripe plum tomatoes, peeled, cored, seeded, and chopped
   Salt and freshly ground black pepper
8   large egg whites
4   large eggs
2   tablespoons minced fresh flat-leaf parsley

Warm 1 teaspoon of the oil in a medium nonstick sauté pan over medium heat. Add the onions and garlic. Sauté for 3 minutes. Add the green peppers. Sauté for 10 minutes, or until the vegetables are very soft but not brown. Add the tomatoes and season with the salt and black pepper. Simmer for 15 minutes, or until the tomatoes are very soft and the mixture has thickened. Remove from the heat.

In a small bowl, whisk together 2 of the egg whites and 1 of the eggs. Stir in 1 heaping tablespoon of the tomato mixture and a pinch of the parsley. Season with the salt and black pepper.

Preheat the broiler.

Heat ½ teaspoon of the remaining oil in a medium ovenproof sauté pan over medium heat until very hot but not smoking. Add the egg mixture and cook for 5 seconds. With a spatula or wooden spoon, lightly scramble the eggs. Then bang the bottom of the pan on the burner to help set the eggs and smooth out the bottom of the omelette. Immediately place the pan under the broiler and broil for 1 minute, or until the eggs are soft but not runny. Slip the omelet onto a warm plate. Place 1 heaping tablespoon of the tomato mixture in the center of the omelette. Sprinkle the top with parsley. Keep warm.

Repeat with the remaining ingredients to make 3 additional omelettes.

YIELD: 4 SERVINGS

PER SERVING

166 CALORIES
9 G. TOTAL FAT
2 G. SATURATED FAT
212 MG. CHOLESTEROL

SOUR CREAM–BLUEBERRY TARTS
(*Tartes aux Myrtilles*)

This is a very satisfying low-fat version of one of France's favorite summer tastes. Fat free sour cream adds great body and smooth consistency to the tart.

5	whole graham crackers, which can be broken into 4 sections each
1	tablespoon unsalted butter, melted
½	teaspoon plus 2 tablespoons sugar
1	large egg
1	large egg white
1	cup nonfat sour cream
½	teaspoon grated lemon zest
¾	cup fresh blueberries

Preheat the oven to 300°F.

Place the graham crackers in a blender or a food processor fitted with the metal blade. Pulse until very fine crumbs form. Transfer to a bowl. Add the butter and ½ teaspoon of the sugar. Mix well. Press an equal portion into each of four (4″ to 5″) individual tart tins.

In a small bowl, combine the egg, egg white, and the remaining 2 tablespoons sugar. Whisk well. Whisk in the sour cream and lemon zest.

Place an equal portion of blueberries in each of the tart tins. Pour the custard mixture over the top. Bake for 20 minutes, or until the custard is set in the middle and a knife inserted in the center comes out clean. Cool on wire racks. Remove the tarts from the tins.

YIELD: 4 SERVINGS

PER SERVING

197 CALORIES
5 G. TOTAL FAT
2.4 G. SATURATED FAT
61 MG. CHOLESTEROL

AUTUMN MENUS

THE WANING WARMTH OF THE FALL OF THE YEAR HEIGHTENS

OUR SENSE OF THE COMING COLD WINTER MONTHS. ROOT

VEGETABLES; COLORFUL PEPPERS; TENDER CHESTNUTS; SWEET

FIGS; SQUASHES OF ALL COLORS, SHAPES, AND TEXTURES; AND

AROMATICS SUCH AS LEEKS, GARLIC, AND TEAR-MAKING JUICY

ONIONS—ALL BOUNTY FROM THE AUTUMN HARVEST—COM-

BINE WITH RICH MEATS AND SUCCULENT FISH TO CREATE THE

HEARTY MENUS WE CRAVE. IN FRANCE, FALL SIGNALS THE

TIME OF THE HUNT . . . FOR MUSHROOMS AND TRUFFLES, FOR

WILD BOAR AND GAME BIRDS, AND FOR THE PERFECT GLASS

OF WINE TO WARM BOTH THE BODY AND THE SOUL.

IN THIS CHAPTER, SEASONAL FAVORITES ARE SHOWCASED IN

EACH MENU. WE UNITE INTENSE FLAVORS AND SENSUAL

ESSENCES TO PRESENT SOUL-SATISFYING AND HEART-HEALTHY

AUTUMN MEALS.

AUTUMN VEGETABLE SOUP

SEA SCALLOPS WITH FRESH GINGER SAUCE

ROASTED PINEAPPLE WITH PASSION FRUIT SORBET

PER SERVING

763 CALORIES

19 G. TOTAL FAT (22% OF CALORIES)

6 G. SATURATED FAT

49 MG. CHOLESTEROL

AUTUMN VEGETABLE SOUP
(*Potage Cultivateur*)

In France, many people tend a small plot of land, a potager, so almost anyone has a chance to be a cultivateur—a farmer or gardener. This soup reflects the seasonal availability of vegetables from the garden. Fall root vegetables produce a soup that can easily become a highly nutritious, low-fat meal with a loaf of crusty bread, a bit of cheese, and a glass of red wine. If desired, you can prepare the soup with half water and half White Chicken Stock (page 37).

1	ounce slab bacon with rind removed, cubed
2	teaspoons olive oil
2	leeks, white parts only, well-washed and thinly sliced
1	carrot, cut into paysanne (page 32)
1	rib celery, sliced
2	ounces cabbage leaves, cut into chiffonade (page 31)
6	cups water
	Salt
1	large potato, peeled and cut into paysanne (page 32)
1	medium turnip, peeled and cut into paysanne (page 32)
	Freshly ground black pepper

1   ounce haricots verts or small green beans, trimmed
    and thinly sliced (optional)
1   ounce fresh or thawed frozen green peas (optional)
16 very thin baguette slices
2   ounces Gruyère cheese, shredded

Bring a small saucepan of water to a boil. Add the bacon and cook for 5 minutes. Drain and pat dry.

Warm the oil in a large nonstick saucepan over low heat. Add the bacon and cook slowly for 3 minutes. Do not brown. Stir in the leeks, carrots, and celery. Cook slowly for 10 minutes. Stir in the cabbage.

Add the water and season with the salt. Bring to a simmer over medium heat. Cook for 10 minutes. Add the potatoes and turnips. Simmer for 10 minutes, or until the vegetables are tender. Season with the pepper.

Add the haricots verts or beans (if using) and simmer for 3 minutes. Add the peas (if using).

Preheat the oven to 375°F. Place the baguette slices on a baking sheet and sprinkle evenly with the Gruyère. Bake for 3 minutes, or until the cheese has melted.

Place an equal portion of the soup in 4 warm shallow soup bowls. Place 1 baguette slice on the side or floating in the center; serve the remainder on the side.

YIELD: 4 SERVINGS

PER SERVING

312 CALORIES
12 G. TOTAL FAT
4.5 G. SATURATED FAT
22 MG. CHOLESTEROL

SEA SCALLOPS WITH FRESH GINGER SAUCE

SEA SCALLOPS WITH FRESH GINGER SAUCE
(Noix de Saint Jacques au Gingembre Frais)

By using nonstick cookware and replacing heavy cream with fat-free sour cream, we were able to reduce the fat content of this recipe from 80% of total calories to 22%. The sour cream is a particularly useful low-fat cooking aid as it does not "break" when used in sauces.

4	leeks
1	teaspoon unsalted butter
4	teaspoons olive oil
	Salt and freshly ground white pepper
3	shallots, minced
½	cup Mushroom Stock (page 40) or water
6	tablespoons dry vermouth
3	tablespoons fresh ginger cut into julienne (page 32)
3	sprigs fresh flat-leaf parsley
3	sprigs fresh thyme
1	cup nonfat sour cream
1	teaspoon minced fresh ginger, blanched (page 32)
8	sea scallops (1½"–2"), trimmed of muscle and cut in half crosswise

Trim the root end and green tops from the leeks; reserve the green part of 1 leek. Cut the white parts in half lengthwise and wash and dry thoroughly. Cut the white parts into fine julienne (page 32) and set aside. Thoroughly wash and dry the green leaves. Coarsely chop and set aside.

Warm the butter and 1 teaspoon of the oil in a medium nonstick sauté pan over medium heat. When bubbling, add the julienned leeks and sauté for 3 minutes, or until just soft. Season with the salt and pepper. Remove from the heat and keep warm.

Warm 2 teaspoons of the remaining oil in a medium saucepan over medium heat. Add the shallots and sauté for 2 minutes, or until just slightly browned. Add the leek greens and sauté for 2 minutes. Stir in the stock or water, vermouth, julienned ginger, parsley, and thyme. Cover and cook for 5 minutes, or until the liquid is reduced by half.

Strain through a fine sieve into a clean saucepan. Place the pan over medium heat and whisk in the sour cream until it is completely incorporated. Continue to cook, whisking constantly, for 3 minutes, or until the sauce has reduced slightly. Add the minced ginger and season with the salt and pepper. Remove from the heat and keep warm.

(continued)

Lightly brush a large nonstick sauté pan with the remaining 1 teaspoon oil. Place over high heat until hot but not smoking. Pat the scallops very dry and season 1 side with the salt and pepper. Carefully place, seasoned side down, in the hot pan. Cook for 1 to 2 minutes, or until the scallops are opaque and just brown around the edges. Season the tops of the scallops with the salt and pepper. Turn the scallops and immediately turn off the heat. Whisk any scallop juice that has formed in the pan into the sauce.

Place 4 small mounds of julienned leeks in the center of each of 4 warm shallow bowls. Spoon the sauce over the leeks and let it spill out onto the plates. Carefully place the scallops on the leeks.

YIELD: 4 SERVINGS

PER SERVING

283 CALORIES
7 G. TOTAL FAT
1.5 G. SATURATED FAT
27 MG. CHOLESTEROL

ROASTED PINEAPPLE WITH PASSION FRUIT SORBET
(Ananas Rôti avec le Sorbet Fruit de la Passion)

When you caramelize both the natural and added sugars in a fruit dish, you achieve an intense concentration of flavor. This is a healthful way to satisfy a sweet tooth.

⅓   cup granulated sugar
⅔   cup water
1   cup passion fruit juice
½   large very ripe pineapple
2   tablespoons packed light brown sugar
4   sprigs fresh mint

In a small saucepan, combine the granulated sugar and water. Bring to a boil over high heat and boil for 2 minutes. Remove from the heat and allow to cool. Stir in the passion fruit juice and pour into the container of an ice cream machine. Process according to the manufacturer's directions. Keep frozen until ready to use.

Preheat the oven to 375°F.

Trim the pineapple of all skin and brown spots. Cut crosswise into ¾" rings. Remove the core by cutting it out with a very small, round hors d'oeuvres cutter or a paring knife. Place the rings on a nonstick baking sheet. Sprinkle with the brown sugar.

Bake for 8 minutes, or until the pineapple is glazed and slightly cooked. Cool to room temperature.

When ready to serve, place a pineapple ring on each of 4 chilled dessert plates. Spoon any juices that have accumulated on the baking sheet over the pineapple. Place a scoop of passion fruit sorbet in the center of each ring. Garnish with the mint.

YIELD: 4 SERVINGS

PER SERVING

168 CALORIES
0.4 G. TOTAL FAT
0 G. SATURATED FAT
0 MG. CHOLESTEROL

ROASTED EGGPLANT ROULADE WITH OREGANO
AND MARINATED GOAT CHEESE

CHICKEN LIVER FLANS WITH TOMATO COULIS

CRISPY HATS WITH PLUMS AND RAISINS

PER SERVING
646 CALORIES
22 G. TOTAL FAT (31% OF CALORIES)
9 G. SATURATED FAT
198 MG. CHOLESTEROL

ROASTED EGGPLANT ROULADE WITH OREGANO
AND MARINATED GOAT CHEESE
(Ballotine d'Aubergines au Chèvre Mariné)

This beautiful roulade is a great addition to the home cook's entertaining menu because it is easier to cut and serve when made a day ahead. The nutritional analysis is for a 2" slice of roulade, but you can make the slices as thin or as thick as you desire.

1	log (4 ounces) fresh goat cheese
2	cloves garlic
1	tablespoon fresh oregano leaves
3	teaspoons olive oil
	Freshly ground black pepper
1	large eggplant
	Salt
10	ounces fresh spinach, washed and stems removed
2	small red bell peppers, roasted, peeled, seeded, and diced
3	very ripe plum tomatoes, peeled, cored, seeded, and diced
3	tablespoons coarsely chopped fresh basil

Juice of 1 lemon
12   radicchio leaves
12   small celery leaves

Place the goat cheese in a large bowl. Mince 1 clove of garlic and sprinkle over the cheese. Sprinkle with the oregano and 1 teaspoon of the oil. Season with the black pepper. Cover with plastic wrap and set aside to marinate at room temperature.

Trim the stem end from the eggplant. Cut lengthwise into ⅛"-thick slices. Place the slices on a nonstick baking sheet and lightly sprinkle with the salt. Let stand for 10 minutes.

Preheat the oven to 450°F.

Using a paper towel, blot away the liquid released by the eggplant. Pat the skin very dry. Brush both sides of the eggplant with 1 teaspoon of the remaining oil. Roast for 5 minutes, or just until the slices begin to color. Remove from the oven.

Warm the remaining 1 teaspoon oil in a large nonstick sauté pan over medium heat. Crush the remaining 1 clove of garlic and add to the pan. Sauté for 1 minute, or just until the garlic begins to turn golden. Shake excess water from the spinach and add to the pan. Season with the salt and black pepper. Cover and cook over medium heat for 2 minutes, or until the spinach has wilted. Remove from the heat and drain through a fine strainer, pressing on the spinach to extract all excess liquid. Discard the garlic.

Add the spinach to the bowl with the goat cheese. Add the red peppers. Toss to mix well and break up the cheese.

Line a 12" × 8" baking dish with plastic wrap. Place the eggplant in the dish in overlapping slices so that there are no uncovered spaces. Evenly spread the spinach mixture over the eggplant. Carefully lift up an edge of the plastic from a 12" side and gently roll the eggplant into a firm roll. Tightly twist 1 end of the plastic wrap and then tightly twist the opposite end to make an even, round shape. Place in the refrigerator and chill for at least 8 hours.

When ready to serve, combine the tomatoes, basil, and lemon juice in a small bowl. Season with the salt and black pepper.

With the roll still encased in the plastic, use a serrated knife to cut four (2"-thick) slices; reserve the remainder for another meal. Remove the plastic after cutting.

Place 3 radicchio leaves together to form a cup in the center of each of 4 well-chilled luncheon plates. Fill each cup with 2 tablespoons of the tomato mixture. Place a roulade slice on top of the tomatoes. Garnish with 3 celery leaves set into the tomatoes.

YIELD: 6 SERVINGS

PER SERVING

112 CALORIES
6.7 G. TOTAL FAT
3 G. SATURATED FAT
9 MG. CHOLESTEROL

CHICKEN LIVER FLANS WITH TOMATO COULIS
(*Flans de Foie de Volaille au Coulis de Tomates*)

The classic recipe for these individual flans originated in the late nineteenth century, when it was served with a rich crayfish sauce. Our adaptation, eliminating the egg yolks and 90% of the butter, is creamy and satisfying. The tomato coulis replaces the rich sauce for a refreshing highlight to the rich liver. Although chicken liver is high in cholesterol, it is relatively low in total fat and calories and is a good source of iron, folate, and vitamins A and B_2.

6	ounces chicken livers
1	teaspoon unsalted butter
2	cloves garlic
	Salt and freshly ground black pepper
3	large egg whites, lightly beaten
1	cup 2% reduced-fat milk, warmed slightly
1	teaspoon olive oil
2	tablespoons chopped onions
6	ounces very ripe plum tomatoes, halved and seeded
1	tablespoon tomato paste
1	tablespoon chopped fresh tarragon
	Sugar (optional)
	Red wine vinegar (optional)
4	sprigs fresh chervil
8	thin baguette slices, toasted

In a blender or a food processor fitted with the metal blade, combine the chicken livers, butter, and 1 clove of the garlic. Season with the salt and pepper. Process until smooth. With the motor running, slowly add the egg whites and process until well-incorporated. Keeping the motor running, slowly add ½ cup of the milk. When the mixture is smooth, add the remaining ½ cup milk and process until well-blended. Transfer the mixture to a fine sieve and strain, pushing with a rubber spatula, into a medium bowl.

Preheat the oven to 300°F.

Fill four (4-ounce) ramekins three-quarters full with the liver mixture. Place in a small roasting pan and add boiling water to come halfway up the sides of the ramekins. Bake, without allowing the water to boil, for 40 minutes, or until set. Remove from the oven and let stand for 10 minutes in the hot water.

While the flans are baking, brush a medium nonstick sauté pan with the oil. Place over medium-low heat and add the onions. Mince the remaining 1 clove of garlic and add to the pan. Cook slowly for 3 minutes, or until translucent. Add the tomato halves, cut side down. Add the tomato paste and stir with a wooden spoon. Cook, stirring occasionally, for 5 minutes, or until the tomatoes have released their liquid and begun to cook down and thicken. Add the tarragon and season with the salt and pepper. Taste the sauce. If the mixture seems too acidic, add a little sugar; if it seems too bland, add a little vinegar. Strain through a fine sieve, pushing with a rubber spatula, into a clean saucepan. Keep warm over low heat or serve at room temperature.

Remove the flans from the ramekins by running a sharp knife around the inside of each container. Holding a clean kitchen towel in your hand, carefully turn 1 ramekin at a time upside down on the towel to allow all excess liquid to drain from the flan. Invert onto a warm luncheon plate and gently tap the bottom of the ramekin to release the flan.

Carefully ladle equal portions of the coulis around each flan. Garnish with the chervil. Serve with the baguette slices on the side.

YIELD: 4 SERVINGS

PER SERVING

228 CALORIES
7 G. TOTAL FAT
3 G. SATURATED FAT
179 MG. CHOLESTEROL

CRISPY HATS WITH PLUMS AND RAISINS
(*Chapeaux à Claque aux Prunes Fraîches et Raisins*)

Phyllo dough once again serves as a crispy, satisfying replacement for other richer doughs. The addition of fresh fruit sorbet makes this a very special end to a light meal.

4	sheets phyllo dough
4	teaspoons unsalted butter, melted
2	tablespoons confectioners' sugar
½	cup water
¼	cup raisins
4	large Italian plums, pitted and cut into 8 slices each
5	teaspoons granulated sugar
1	tablespoon rum
2	cups plum or passion fruit sorbet
4	sprigs fresh mint

Preheat the oven to 350°F.

Place 1 sheet of the phyllo on a piece of parchment paper; keep the remainder covered with a damp paper towel. Using a pastry brush, coat the phyllo with some of the butter. Fold the piece in half and brush the top with more of the butter. Place the con-

(continued)

CRISPY HAT WITH PLUMS AND RAISINS (PAGE 165)

fectioners' sugar in a sifter and sift evenly over the top. Repeat to use the remaining phyllo sheets, butter, and confectioners' sugar.

Line a baking sheet with parchment paper. Place four (4-ounce) custard cups upside down on the sheet. Drape a folded sheet of phyllo, sugared side down, over each cup; push the phyllo down and over each cup to form a neat cup shape. Bake for 10 minutes, or until golden and crisp. Remove from the oven. While still warm, carefully remove the phyllo cups from the custard cups. Cool the phyllo cups on a wire rack until ready to use.

Bring the water to a boil in a small saucepan over high heat. Remove from the heat. Add the raisins. Allow to soak for 10 minutes, or until the raisins are nicely plumped. Drain and, using your hands, squeeze out all of the excess liquid. Place the raisins in a small bowl and add the plums. Toss to mix.

Place a small nonstick saucepan over medium-high heat. When it is very hot but not smoking, add the granulated sugar. Cook, stirring constantly, for 4 minutes, or until the sugar is a golden brown liquid. Add the plum mixture and cook for 2 minutes. Stir in the rum. Remove the pan from the heat and carefully ignite the fruit with a long match to burn off some of the alcohol. Allow the flame to burn out, then return the pan to the heat. Reduce the heat to medium and cook for 3 minutes, or until the fruit softens and begins to fall apart. If the liquid begins to evaporate from the fruit, add up to ¼ cup water and continue to cook until the fruit is soft. Remove from the heat and keep warm.

Invert onto 4 dessert plates. Fill the cups with an equal portion of the cooked fruit. Top each with a scoop of sorbet and garnish with the mint.

YIELD: 4 SERVINGS

PER SERVING

306 CALORIES
8 G. TOTAL FAT
3 G. SATURATED FAT
10 MG. CHOLESTEROL

BEET SALAD WITH ENDIVE AND WALNUTS

ROASTED QUAIL STUFFED WITH RICE

FIGS POACHED IN PORT AND PEPPERCORNS

<u>PER SERVING</u>

736 CALORIES

21 G. TOTAL FAT (26% OF CALORIES)

6 G. SATURATED FAT

79 MG. CHOLESTEROL

BEET SALAD WITH ENDIVE AND WALNUTS
(Salade de Betteraves aux Endives et Noix)

Although Roquefort is a high-fat cheese, it is such a perfect partner for beets and walnuts that we used it sparingly to give a hint of the traditional flavor. By using the low-fat Beet Vinaigrette, the flavor of the salad is intensified while calories remain low.

2	large beets (about 4 ounces each)
¾	cup Beet Vinaigrette (page 50)
12	ounces Belgian endive
8	walnut halves, toasted and coarsely chopped
1	ounce Roquefort cheese
1	tablespoon chopped fresh flat-leaf parsley
1	teaspoon minced fresh thyme
½	clove garlic, minced
	Salt and freshly ground black pepper
8	small celery leaves

Preheat the oven to 450°F.

Trim off all but 1″ of the beet greens; scrub the beets well. Wrap the beets in foil, making sure that the edges are sealed. Place the foil packet on a baking sheet. Roast for 1 hour, or until the beets are just tender when pierced with a knife.

Unwrap the beets and allow them to cool. Peel and trim off the stem ends. Cut crosswise into ⅛″ slices and then into julienne (page 32). Place in a medium bowl and add ½ cup of the vinaigrette.

Tear off and discard any damaged outer leaves from the endives. Cut off and discard the root ends. Cut 3″ off the tip end of each endive; cut the remainder into ¼″ pieces.

In a small bowl, combine the walnuts, Roquefort, parsley, thyme, and garlic. Mix into a paste. Stir in the remaining ¼ cup vinaigrette. Pour over the beets. Season with the salt and pepper. Mix well.

Place an equal portion of endive tips, tip facing out, around the edge of each of 4 chilled salad plates. Place an equal portion of chopped endive in the center of each plate, mounding slightly. Top each with an equal portion of the beet mixture. Garnish with 2 celery leaves placed on opposite sides. Or simply toss and serve.

YIELD: 4 SERVINGS

PER SERVING

160 CALORIES
7 G. TOTAL FAT
1.8 G. SATURATED FAT
6 MG. CHOLESTEROL

BEET SALAD WITH ENDIVE AND WALNUTS

ROASTED QUAIL STUFFED WITH RICE
(*Cailles Farcies Rôties sur Canapés*)

Quail, like most game, is relatively low in fat. Boneless birds are now available from most butchers, many supermarkets, and a score of mail-order companies. When roasting at a high temperature as we do here, do not open the oven door because the temperature will drop by almost half and the roasting method will not be as effective.

½	teaspoon olive oil
¼	cup chopped onions
¼	cup carrots cut into brunoise (page 31)
½	cup long-grain white rice
½	cup mushrooms cut into brunoise (page 31)
1	bay leaf
1¾	cups White Chicken Stock (page 37)
1	sprig fresh thyme
	Salt
½	cup zucchini cut into brunoise (page 31)
4	boneless quail
1½	teaspoons unsalted butter, melted
	Freshly ground black pepper
½	cup dry white wine
12	ounces carrots, sliced on the diagonal ⅛″ thick
10	ounces zucchini, sliced on the diagonal ⅛″ thick

Warm the oil in a medium nonstick saucepan over medium heat. Add the onions and cook slowly for 5 minutes. Do not brown. Add the brunoise carrots and cook for 5 minutes. Stir in the rice, mushrooms, bay leaf, and ¾ cup of the stock. Strip the leaves from the thyme and add to the saucepan; discard the stem. Season with the salt. Bring to a boil. Reduce the heat to medium-low, cover, and simmer for 15 minutes.

Stir in the brunoise zucchini. Cover and cook for 5 minutes, or until all of the liquid has been absorbed. Remove from the heat and set aside to cool. Remove and discard the bay leaf.

Preheat the oven to 450°F.

Cut eight (7″ × 7″) pieces of heavy-duty foil. Sandwich 2 of the pieces together, with the shiny sides facing out; form into an open box by folding over 1″ of the edges on all sides. Repeat to make 4 shallow boxes.

Wash the quail, inside and out, with cold running water. Pat dry. Gently pull up and out on the skin of the quail to cover the entire breast and neck area; fold any excess skin over the neck opening. Stuff the cavity of each quail with the rice mixture. Cross the legs and tie closed with butcher's twine. Brush off any rice mixture that might be clinging to the skin as it will burn during the roasting.

Slip each quail, breast side up, into a box. Push the box up and around the quail to cover not more than half of the quail. Using ½ teaspoon of the butter, brush the quail breasts. Season with the salt and pepper.

Transfer, breast side up, to a small roasting pan. Roast for 12 minutes. Turn on the broiler. Broil for 2 minutes, or until golden brown and an instant-read thermometer inserted in the center of each breast registers 170°F. Remove from the heat and place the quail on a warm platter. Cover lightly and keep warm.

Place the roasting pan over medium heat. Add the wine and the remaining 1 cup stock. Bring to a boil and deglaze the pan, stirring constantly with a wooden spoon to remove all of the browned bits from the bottom. Boil for 2 minutes. Remove from the heat and keep warm.

While the quail are roasting, prepare the vegetables. Brush the carrot slices and zucchini slices with the remaining 1 teaspoon butter. Place the carrots in a medium sauté pan over medium heat. Add water to come halfway up the carrots. Cover and cook over medium-high heat for 5 minutes, or until almost all of the liquid has evaporated and the carrots are just tender. Remove the carrots from the pan. Season with the salt and pepper and keep warm.

Place the zucchini in the same sauté pan over medium heat. Sauté for 4 minutes, or until lightly colored and just tender. Remove from the heat and season with the salt and pepper.

Fan alternating slices of carrots and zucchini in a small circle around each of 4 warm dinner plates. Remove the quail from their pouches and place, breast side up, in the center of each plate. Spoon the sauce over the top.

YIELD: 4 SERVINGS

PER SERVING

330 CALORIES
14 G. TOTAL FAT
4 G. SATURATED FAT
73 MG. CHOLESTEROL

FIGS POACHED IN PORT AND PEPPERCORNS
(*Figues Pochées au Porto et Baies de Poivre*)

If you can't find fresh figs, you can use dried. However, you will have to increase the liquid considerably because the dried fruit will absorb a great deal of liquid as it rehydrates.

1	large orange
1	large lemon
1	cup port
8	peppercorns
1	stick cinnamon
½	cup sugar
1	vanilla bean, split lengthwise
12	fresh figs
¼	cup water

Using a zester, carefully remove lengthwise sections of zest from half of the orange and half of the lemon. Place 1 strip of orange zest and 1 strip of lemon zest in a medium saucepan. Julienne (page 32) the remaining zest and set aside. Reserve the fruit for another use.

To the saucepan, add the port, peppercorns, cinnamon stick, and ¼ cup of the sugar. Scrape the seeds from the vanilla bean into the saucepan, then add the bean. Stir over medium heat until the sugar has dissolved. Add the figs and cook for 8 minutes, or until tender but still holding their shapes. Do not overcook.

Using a slotted spoon, carefully remove the figs from the syrup and set them aside. Pour any liquid that flows out of the figs back into the saucepan. Simmer the liquid for 5 minutes, or until it reaches a thin syrup (it will thicken as it cools). Remove from the heat. Remove and discard the vanilla bean.

Bring a small nonstick saucepan of water to a boil over high heat. Add the julienned orange zest and lemon zest. Boil for 1 minute. Drain and pat dry.

Return the zest to the saucepan. Add the ¼ cup water and the remaining ¼ cup sugar. Bring to a simmer over medium-high heat. Reduce the heat to medium-low and barely simmer for 20 minutes, or until the zest is very tender. Remove from the heat and, using a fork, lift the zest from the syrup. Place in an even layer on a piece of parchment paper to cool and dry.

Place 3 figs in the center of each of 4 dessert plates. Pour an equal portion of the syrup over the figs and let it freely flow onto the plates. Sprinkle with the zest.

YIELD: 4 SERVINGS

PER SERVING

246 CALORIES
0.3 G. TOTAL FAT
0 G. SATURATED FAT
0 MG. CHOLESTEROL

POTATO-MUSHROOM GALETTES

FILLETS OF SOLE OVER SAUTÉED BOSTON LETTUCE

LIGHT CARAMEL CREAMS WITH ORANGE ESSENCE

PER SERVING

588 CALORIES

11 G. TOTAL FAT (17% OF CALORIES)

3 G. SATURATED FAT

152 MG. CHOLESTEROL

POTATO-MUSHROOM GALETTES
(Galettes de Pommes de Terre aux Champignons)

A potato galette is not only a tasty first course but also the base for an entrée of grilled or roasted meat or game. It can even be served for a light lunch with a tossed green salad on the side. To achieve the required thin, uniform potato slices, you will need a mandoline (see page 29). You can prepare the galettes up to 1 hour in advance of serving and reheat them on a baking sheet for no more than 3 minutes in a very hot oven.

1	teaspoon canola oil
1	teaspoon unsalted butter
4	cups sliced mushrooms
2	small shallots, minced
3	sprigs fresh thyme
	Salt and freshly ground black pepper
3	large russet potatoes, peeled and sliced lengthwise into paper-thin slices
1	tablespoon olive oil

Warm the canola oil and butter in a large sauté pan over medium heat. Add the mushrooms and cook slowly, stirring frequently, for 5 minutes, or until the mushrooms release their juices. Continue cooking until all the moisture evaporates. Add the shal-

(continued)

POTATO-MUSHROOM GALETTES (PAGE 173)

lots and cook for 3 minutes. Strip the leaves from the thyme sprigs and add to the pan; discard the stems. Season with the salt and pepper. Remove from the heat.

Place the potatoes in a large bowl. Drizzle with the olive oil and toss until well-coated.

Place 2 medium nonstick sauté pans over medium-low heat. Place 1 potato slice in the center of each pan. Using one-quarter of the potatoes per pan, carefully form circles of slightly overlapping potato slices around the center slices, letting them fall slightly over the edge of the pan. Season with the salt and pepper. Cook for 4 minutes. If any gaps form between the slices, patch with slices cut to fit the gap.

Place one-quarter of the mushroom mixture in the center of each galette and evenly spread it out to cover the potatoes. As the potatoes become soft and flexible, begin folding them inward so that they slightly enclose the mushrooms and form a perfect disk-shaped galette. Cook for 25 minutes, turning occasionally so that the potatoes cook through and the galette is evenly browned, taking care not burn it. As you turn, season each side with salt and pepper.

Remove from the pans and place in a warm, dry spot. Repeat to make 2 more galettes using the remaining potatoes and mushroom mixture. Serve with the most evenly browned, symmetrical side of the galette facing up.

YIELD: 4 SERVINGS

PER SERVING

90 CALORIES
3 G. TOTAL FAT
0.6 G. SATURATED FAT
1 MG. CHOLESTEROL

FILLETS OF SOLE OVER SAUTÉED BOSTON LETTUCE
(Filets de Sole avec Coeur de Laitue Sauté)

The delicate lettuce sauté is a perfect foil for the sweet sole. The lemon heightens the flavors for a rich-tasting main course that is both calorie- and fat-conscious.

2	heads Boston lettuce
1½	teaspoons unsalted butter
	Salt and freshly ground black pepper
½	cup all-purpose flour
4	sole fillets (6 ounces each), trimmed and cut in half lengthwise
2	teaspoons canola oil
	Juice of 1 lemon

Remove the leaves from the lettuce, reserving the center core. Wash and dry the leaves and cut into chiffonade (page 31). Cut the core crosswise into ¼" coins.

Melt ¼ teaspoon of the butter in a large nonstick sauté pan over medium heat. Add the lettuce chiffonade and season with the salt and pepper. Cover and cook, stirring occasionally, for 10 minutes, or until all the liquid evaporates.

While the chiffonade is cooking, melt ¼ teaspoon of the remaining butter in a medium nonstick saucepan over medium heat. Add the lettuce coins in a single layer and sauté for 5 minutes, or until tender and golden brown.

Place the flour on a large plate and season with the salt and pepper Dredge the sole in the flour, shaking off all excess.

(continued)

Warm the oil and the remaining 1 teaspoon butter in a very large sauté pan over medium-high heat. Add the sole and cook, turning once, for 3 minutes, or until the fish is just cooked through and golden brown. Remove the fish from the pan and keep warm. Add the lemon juice to the pan and stir to deglaze the pan.

Place a mound of lettuce in the center of each of 4 warm dinner plates. Place the 2 halves of each fillet on top of the lettuce. Pour the pan juices over each serving. Garnish the fillets with the lettuce coins.

YIELD: 4 SERVINGS

PER SERVING

253 CALORIES
6 G. TOTAL FAT
1.6 G. SATURATED FAT
94 MG. CHOLESTEROL

LIGHT CARAMEL CREAMS WITH ORANGE ESSENCE
(Crèmes au Caramel Parfumé à l'Orange)

We have lightened the traditional, very rich classic French dessert by using 1% low-fat milk and cutting back on the number of whole eggs. It is still extremely satisfying and delicious. If you don't have a vanilla bean, use ½ teaspoon pure vanilla extract.

1	orange
⅓	cup plus ½ cup sugar
1	tablespoon water
1½	cups 1% low-fat milk
¼	vanilla bean, split lengthwise
1	large egg
2	large egg whites

Bring 4 to 6 cups water to a boil.

Grate the zest from the orange and set aside. Using a paring knife, remove the skin and outer membrane from the orange and carefully cut out each section, catching any dripping juice in a small bowl as you cut. Reserve the sections. Squeeze juice from the orange membranes into the bowl. Strain the juice and reserve 2 teaspoons.

In a small nonstick saucepan, combine ⅓ cup of the sugar and the water. Cook over medium-high heat, stirring frequently, for 5 minutes, or until the sugar syrup caramelizes and reaches a rich amber-brown color. Remove from the heat. Very carefully stir in the reserved orange juice (hot syrup may spatter).

Pour an equal portion of the syrup into each of four (4-ounce) ramekins, tilting and rotating so that the caramel covers the bottom and goes partially up the sides of the ramekins. Refrigerate the coated ramekins while you prepare the custard.

In a medium nonstick saucepan, combine the milk and the reserved orange zest. Scrape the seeds from the vanilla bean into the saucepan, then add the bean. Cook over medium heat for 2 minutes, or until just hot. Turn off the heat, cover, and allow the mixture to steep for 15 minutes. Remove and discard the vanilla bean.

Preheat the oven to 300°F.

Combine the egg and egg whites in a large bowl. Whisk with the remaining ½ cup sugar until well-blended. Slowly whisk the milk into the egg mixture. Strain through a fine sieve into a clean bowl. Remove any foam or bubbles from the surface by running a ladle or metal spoon over the top.

Remove the ramekins from the refrigerator. Pour an equal portion of the hot custard into each ramekin. Place the filled ramekins in a small roasting pan and add the boiling water to come halfway up the sides of the ramekins. Bake for 55 minutes, or until the custard is stable when the pan is gently shaken. Remove the roasting pan from the oven and carefully lift the ramekins onto a wire rack. Allow to cool completely.

When ready to serve, invert each ramekin onto a chilled dessert plate. Garnish each custard with 2 orange sections.

YIELD: 4 SERVINGS

PER SERVING

245 CALORIES
2.3 G. TOTAL FAT
1 G. SATURATED FAT
57 MG. CHOLESTEROL

LEEK AND ROASTED PEPPER TARTLETS

NOISETTES OF VENISON WITH CRANBERRY SAUCE

CELERY ROOT PUREE

MANGO MOUSSE

PER SERVING
999 CALORIES

21 G. TOTAL FAT (19% OF CALORIES)

7 G. SATURATED FAT

296 MG. CHOLESTEROL

LEEK AND ROASTED PEPPER TARTLETS
(Tartelettes de Poireaux et Poivrons Rôtis)

These tarts are a terrific do-ahead first course as they can be prepared in the morning and reheated in a 350°F oven just before serving. Light, fragrant, and filling, they can also be cut into quarters for a cocktail party hors d'oeuvre.

1   teaspoon unsalted butter
1   teaspoon olive oil
3   leeks, with a little green attached, well-washed and
        thinly sliced
2   red bell peppers, roasted, peeled, seeded, and diced
     Salt and freshly ground black pepper
1   large egg
3   large egg whites
     Savory Pastry (page 55)

Preheat the oven to 375°F.

Warm the butter and oil in a medium nonstick sauté pan over medium heat. Add the leeks and cook slowly, stirring frequently, for 5 minutes, or until tender. Do not brown. Add the red peppers and season with the salt and black pepper. Cook for 2 minutes. Remove from the heat.

In a small bowl, whisk together the egg and egg whites. Season with the salt and black pepper.

Divide the pastry among four (4″ to 5″) individual tart tins. Place on a baking sheet. Fit a small square of foil into each. Add some pastry weights or dried beans. Bake for 10 minutes. Remove the tins from the oven and carefully remove the weights or beans and the foil. Do not turn off the oven.

Place an equal portion of the leek mixture in each tart shell. Strain an equal portion of the egg mixture into each tart shell, allowing the mixture to come just below the top edge of the shell. Bake for 20 minutes, or until the center is set.

YIELD: 4 SERVINGS

PER SERVING

274 CALORIES
10 G. TOTAL FAT
2 G. SATURATED FAT
109 MG. CHOLESTEROL

NOISETTES OF VENISON WITH CRANBERRY SAUCE
(Noisettes de Chevreuil avec Sauce d'Airelles)

Farm-raised venison is a very lean red meat; therefore, it must be quickly seared and served medium-rare or it will be quite dry. When serving, if you nap both the plate and the venison with some of the sauce, extra moisture will be added to the final taste.

1	cup fresh cranberries
1	teaspoon sugar
2	teaspoons unsalted butter
	Freshly ground black pepper
8	venison medallions (2½ ounces each and ½″–¾″ thick)
	Salt
2	small shallots, minced
2	cups quartered domestic or wild mushrooms
1	cup dry red wine
½	cup red wine vinegar
1	cup White Chicken Stock (page 37)
1	tablespoon red currant jelly

In a small nonstick sauté pan, combine the cranberries, sugar, and 1 teaspoon of the butter. Season with the pepper. Cook over low heat for 3 minutes. Remove from the heat.

(continued)

NOISETTES OF VENISON WITH CRANBERRY SAUCE (PAGE 179) AND CELERY ROOT PUREE

Season the venison with the salt and pepper. Melt the remaining 1 teaspoon butter in a large nonstick sauté pan over medium-high heat. Add the venison and sear for about 1½ minutes, or until the bottoms have colored slightly. Turn and sear for 2 minutes, or until well-colored and medium-rare in the center. The meat will continue to cook as it stands. Transfer to a warm platter, cover lightly, and keep warm.

Return the sauté pan to medium heat. Add the shallots and sauté for 2 minutes. Stir in the mushrooms and sauté for 3 minutes. Add the wine and vinegar and stir with a wooden spoon to remove the browned bits from the bottom.

Raise the heat to medium-high and cook for 10 minutes, or until the liquid is reduced to about ½ cup. Stir in the stock and cook for 10 minutes. Stir in the jelly. Taste and adjust the seasoning.

Spoon a small amount of the cranberry sauce on each of 4 warm dinner plates and place 2 venison medallions on top of the sauce. Spoon additional sauce over the top of each serving.

YIELD: 4 SERVINGS

PER SERVING

440 CALORIES
9 G. TOTAL FAT
4.3 G. SATURATED FAT
135 MG. CHOLESTEROL

CELERY ROOT PUREE
(Purée de Céleri-Rave)

1   pound all-purpose potatoes, peeled and cubed
1   celery root, peeled and cubed
      Salt
½   cup 1% low-fat milk
1   teaspoon unsalted butter
      Freshly ground black pepper

Place the potatoes and celery root in a large saucepan and add cold water to cover by about 1". Add a pinch of salt. Bring to a boil over high heat. Reduce the heat to medium and cook for 15 minutes, or until the vegetables are tender when pierced with a fork. Drain, reserving 1 cup of the cooking liquid.

Push the potatoes and celery root through the fine disk of a food mill into a medium bowl. Beat in the milk and butter. Add salt and pepper to taste. If the mixture is dry, add the reserved cooking liquid, a few tablespoons at a time.

(continued)

181

Chef's Note: If not using the puree immediately, place it in the top half of a double boiler over simmering water. Cover the top with a piece of parchment paper to keep the puree moist. Keep warm until ready to use.

YIELD: 4 SERVINGS

PER SERVING

164 CALORIES
4 G. TOTAL FAT
2.4 G. SATURATED FAT
10 MG. CHOLESTEROL

MANGO MOUSSE
(Mousse aux Mangues)

This is a very light dessert. If desired, you can eliminate the cake base and serve the mousse by itself in small glass bowls with some fresh mango cubes and mint as garnish.

5	large egg whites
½	cup plus 2 teaspoons sugar
2	large egg yolks
½	cup all-purpose flour, sifted
2	large very ripe mangoes, peeled, pitted, and chopped
	Juice of ½ lemon
5	tablespoons cold water
1	packet unflavored gelatin

Preheat the oven to 375°F.

Coat a baking sheet with nonstick spray and cover with a piece of parchment paper.

Place 2 of the egg whites in a small bowl. Beat with an electric mixer on medium speed until soft peaks form. Gradually beat in ¼ cup of the sugar and beat on high speed until shiny. Beat in the egg yolks, one at a time. Beat for 1 minute. Gently fold in the flour until well-incorporated.

Spread the batter on the baking sheet, smoothing the top to make an even layer, 1″ larger than the circumference of four (4-ounce) molds. Bake for 7 minutes, or until the cake is golden and springs back when lightly touched. Remove from the oven and allow to cool on a wire rack.

In a blender or a food processor fitted with the metal blade, combine the mangoes and lemon juice. Process until smooth. Transfer to a fine sieve. Push through the sieve with the back of a spoon into a medium bowl.

Lightly coat four (4-ounce) molds with nonstick spray.

Place 3 tablespoons of the water in a custard cup. Sprinkle with the gelatin and let soften for 5 minutes. Bring about ½″ of water to a simmer in a small skillet over medium heat. Place the custard cup in the skillet. Reduce the heat to low and stir the mixture until the gelatin is melted and the liquid is clear. Pour into the bowl with the mango puree and mix well.

In a small saucepan, combine ¼ cup of the remaining sugar and the remaining 2 tablespoons water. Cook over medium heat, stirring constantly, for 3 minutes, or until the sugar has dissolved and the syrup is bubbling. Stop stirring and turn the heat to low.

Place the remaining 3 egg whites in a medium bowl. Beat with an electric mixer on medium speed until foamy. Gradually beat in the remaining 2 teaspoons sugar and beat on high speed until thick and shiny.

Raise the heat under the sugar syrup and boil for 4 minutes, or until a candy thermometer inserted into the syrup reads 248°F. Immediately remove from the heat and pour the syrup into a heatproof glass measuring cup to stop the cooking.

Slowly pour the hot syrup into the egg whites, beating constantly and taking care that the syrup does not hit the beaters or stick to the sides of the bowl. Fold the egg-white mixture into the mango puree.

Cut the cooled cake into 4 circles of the exact circumference of the prepared molds; reserve the extra cake for another use. Pour an equal portion of the mousse into each mold. Place a cake circle on top. Cover with plastic wrap and refrigerate for at least 8 hours, or until the mousse is very firm.

When ready to serve, remove the mousse from the refrigerator and quickly dip the bottom of each mold into very hot water. Immediately wipe the molds dry and invert the mousse onto each of 4 well-chilled dessert plates.

YIELD: 4 SERVINGS

PER SERVING

285 CALORIES
1.6 G. TOTAL FAT
0.5 G. SATURATED FAT
53 MG. CHOLESTEROL

CHESTNUT, PORCINI, AND PEARL BARLEY SOUP

SALMON COOKED IN ITS OWN JUICES WITH BROCCOLI FLORETS

CELERY ROOT CHIPS

CHOCOLATE MERINGUE COOKIES

PER SERVING

528 CALORIES

12 G. TOTAL FAT (20% OF CALORIES)

2 G. SATURATED FAT

84 MG. CHOLESTEROL

CHESTNUT, PORCINI, AND PEARL BARLEY SOUP
(Velouté d'Orge Perlé aux Champignons et Marrons)

Dried porcini mushrooms and chestnuts are a great taste combination. In many instances, they even grow in the same area. Add the sweetness of celery root, and you have the perfect marriage of fall flavors. You can re-place fresh chestnuts with canned or frozen ones, but their essence will be far less concentrated.

½   ounce dried porcini mushrooms
8   ounces fresh chestnuts
8   ounces celery root, peeled and diced
¾   cup chopped button mushrooms
1   leek, white part only, well-washed and chopped
2   cups White Chicken Stock (page 37)
3½ cups water
    Salt and freshly ground black pepper
¼   cup pearl barley
4   Celery Root Chips (page 187)

184

Place the dried mushrooms in a small bowl and add very warm water to cover. Allow to soak for 20 minutes. Carefully strain through a fine sieve into another small bowl, discarding the bottom liquid holding any mushroom sediment. Add the mushrooms to the bowl and set aside.

Preheat the oven to 400°F.

Using a paring knife, cut an X into the flat side of the chestnut shells. Place the nuts, in a single layer, on a baking sheet. Roast for 30 minutes, or until the chestnuts are tender when pierced with a knife. Remove from the oven and allow to cool slightly. When cool enough to handle, peel and place in a medium saucepan.

To the saucepan, add the celery root, chopped mushrooms, leeks, stock, and 2 cups of the water. Add the reserved mushrooms and their liquid. Season with the salt and pepper. Cover and bring to a boil over medium heat. Reduce the heat to medium-low and simmer for 30 minutes.

Bring the remaining 1½ cups water to a boil in a small saucepan over high heat. Add a pinch of salt. Add the barley. Reduce the heat to medium-low, cover, and simmer for 45 minutes, or until the barley is soft; if necessary, add additional boiling water.

Transfer the chestnut mixture to a blender or a food processor fitted with the metal blade. Process until smooth.

Pour into a clean saucepan and fold in the barley. Warm over medium heat. Pour an equal portion into each of 4 warm shallow soup bowls. Garnish each with a celery root chip.

YIELD: 4 SERVINGS

PER SERVING

226 CALORIES
2.4 G. TOTAL FAT
0.6 G. SATURATED FAT
6 MG. CHOLESTEROL

SALMON COOKED IN ITS OWN JUICES WITH BROCCOLI FLORETS
(Saumon Cuit dans Son Jus avec Fleurons de Brocoli)

This is a quick and very healthy meal for a lazy day. Even Chef Alain Sailhac calls it Lazy Bum Salmon! Served hot, you can add rice or roasted potatoes for a hearty main course. Chilled, the salmon is wonderful with a fresh vegetable vinaigrette. Feel free to replace the broccoli with any vegetable you like.

4	boneless, skinless salmon fillets (5 ounces each)
½	teaspoon ground coriander
	Coarse salt
7	sprigs fresh thyme
1	lemon, thinly sliced
1	teaspoon unsalted butter
1	teaspoon canola oil
12	ounces broccoli, broken into florets and blanched (page 32)
	Freshly ground black pepper

Cut a piece of heavy-duty foil large enough to enclose the salmon fillets. Place the salmon in the center of the foil and sprinkle with the coriander and salt. Strip the leaves from 3 of the thyme sprigs and sprinkle over the salmon; discard the stems. Reserve 4 lemon slices; place the remaining slices over the top of the salmon. Fold the foil up and over the salmon and then fold the edges together to make a tight seal.

Place about ½" of water in a large sauté pan. Lay the foil packet in the pan. Cover and bring to a simmer over medium-high heat. Simmer for 8 minutes. Uncover and carefully lift the packet from the water.

When the salmon is almost cooked, prepare the broccoli. Combine the butter and oil in a medium sauté pan. Warm over medium heat. Add the broccoli and season with the salt and pepper. Sauté for 2 minutes, or until the broccoli is heated through and nicely flavored.

Carefully open the foil packet and transfer a salmon fillet to each of 4 warm dinner plates. Spoon any juices from the packets onto each fillet. Place equal portions of the broccoli along the side. Stick a small thyme sprig into each of the reserved lemon slices. Lay the lemon slice over the salmon.

YIELD: 4 SERVINGS

PER SERVING

207 CALORIES
9 G. TOTAL FAT
1.4 G. SATURATED FAT
78 MG. CHOLESTEROL

CELERY ROOT CHIPS
(Chips de Céleri-Rave)

½   teaspoon canola oil
½   teaspoon unsalted butter, melted
16   paper-thin celery root slices
     Salt

Preheat the oven to 400°F.

In a custard cup, combine the oil and butter. Mix well. Lightly brush both sides of each celery root with the mixture. Lightly sprinkle with the salt. Place in a single layer on a nonstick baking sheet. Bake for 6 minutes, or until golden brown. Remove from the oven and drain on paper towels. Serve at room temperature.

YIELD: 16 CHIPS

PER CHIP

18 CALORIES
1.8 G. TOTAL FAT
0.2 G. SATURATED FAT
0 MG. CHOLESTEROL

CHOCOLATE MERINGUE COOKIES
(Meringues au Chocolat)

These wonderfully light but satisfying cookies are almost fat-free. You could serve a couple of them nestled into a small portion of nonfat vanilla yogurt or ice cream for a very special dessert.

3   large egg whites
⅛   teaspoon cream of tartar
¾   cup granulated sugar
3   tablespoons unsweetened cocoa powder
¼   cup confectioners' sugar (optional)

187

CHOCOLATE MERINGUE COOKIES (PAGE 187)

Preheat the oven to 300°F.

Cover 2 baking sheets with parchment paper.

Place the egg whites and cream of tartar in a medium bowl. Beat with an electric mixer on medium speed until soft peaks form. Gradually beat in the granulated sugar and beat on high speed until the whites are stiff and shiny.

Sift the cocoa over the egg whites and gently fold in until just blended.

Drop tablespoonfuls of batter, 1″ apart, on the prepared baking sheets. Bake for 30 to 35 minutes, or until the cookies are dry. Carefully peel the cookies from the paper and cool on a wire rack. When cool, sprinkle the cookies with the confectioners' sugar (if using). Store, covered, at room temperature.

YIELD: 24 COOKIES

PER 3 COOKIES

95 CALORIES
0.8 G. TOTAL FAT
0 G. SATURATED FAT
0 MG. CHOLESTEROL

CAULIFLOWER SOUP

CHICKEN BREASTS CHASSEUR

SAUTÉED CARROTS AND CELERY ROOT

PARSLEYED NOODLES

MINT FLANS IN ORANGE SAUCE

PER SERVING

792 CALORIES

19 G. TOTAL FAT (22% OF CALORIES)

5 G. SATURATED FAT

138 MG. CHOLESTEROL

CAULIFLOWER SOUP
(*Crème du Barry*)

This is a classic French soup made light with minimal use of fats and without the traditional addition of cream. Garnish the soup with a few tiny blanched cauliflower florets for an added dimension.

1	teaspoon canola oil
1	teaspoon unsalted butter
2	leeks, white parts only, well-washed and chopped
1	head cauliflower, broken into florets
1	medium all-purpose potato, cubed
6	cups White Chicken Stock (page 37)
	Salt and freshly ground white pepper
½	cup 1% low-fat milk (optional)
4	leaves fresh parsley

Combine the oil and butter in a large saucepan. Warm over medium-low heat. Add the leeks and, stirring frequently, allow them cook slowly for 10 minutes. Do not brown.

Stir in the cauliflower, potatoes, and stock. Season with the salt and pepper. Bring to a boil over high heat. Reduce the heat to medium, cover, and simmer for 20 minutes, or until the vegetables are very tender. Remove from the heat and allow to cool slightly.

Transfer to a blender or a food processor fitted with the metal blade. Process until smooth. Transfer to a clean saucepan and place over medium heat. Bring to a simmer. Taste and adjust the seasoning. If the soup is too thick, thin with the milk.

Pour an equal portion into each of 4 warm soup bowls. Lay a parsley leaf in the center.

YIELD: 4 SERVINGS

PER SERVING
144 CALORIES
4 G. TOTAL FAT
1 G. SATURATED FAT
16 MG. CHOLESTEROL

CHICKEN BREASTS CHASSEUR
(Suprêmes de Volaille Chasseur)

"In the style of chasseur" (the hunter) usually means a whole fowl sautéed with the bounty of the fall mushroom hunt. Here, we substitute chicken breasts and use button mushrooms to make a healthier, less expensive but still aromatic dish.

4	bone-in chicken breasts with skin (6 ounces each)
	Salt and freshly ground black pepper
2	teaspoons olive oil
1	medium carrot, chopped
½	cup chopped onions
2	cups Brown Veal Stock (page 34)
2	cups sliced button mushrooms
2	shallots, minced
2	tablespoons cognac
⅓	cup dry white wine
2	tablespoons chopped fresh tarragon

Preheat the oven to 350°F.

Season the chicken with the salt and pepper. Warm 1 teaspoon of the oil in a large nonstick sauté pan over medium heat. Carefully lay the chicken breasts, skin side down, in the pan. Sear for 3 minutes, or until the skin has nicely browned. Transfer the chicken, skin side up, to a nonstick jelly-roll pan. Reserve the sauté pan.

(continued)

191

CHICKEN BREASTS CHASSEUR (PAGE 191), SAUTÉED CARROTS AND CELERY ROOT, AND PARSLEYED NOODLES (PAGE 194)

Bake the chicken for 20 minutes, or until the juices run clear when the chicken is pierced with a knife.

While the chicken is cooking, remove most of the fat from the sauté pan. Add the carrots and onions to the pan. Sauté over medium heat for 3 minutes, or until the vegetables begin to caramelize. Add the stock and raise the heat to high. Bring to a boil, then reduce the heat to medium. Simmer for 10 minutes, or until the liquid has reduced by half. Strain through a fine sieve into a small bowl; skim off any fat that rises to the surface.

Warm the remaining 1 teaspoon oil in a medium sauté pan over medium heat. Add the mushrooms and shallots. Sauté for 5 minutes, or until the mushrooms are golden. Season with the salt. Remove the pan from the heat and add the cognac. Carefully ignite the cognac with a long match. Allow the flame to burn out, then add the wine. Return the pan to the heat.

Bring to a boil over medium-high heat. Reduce the heat to medium and simmer for 10 minutes, or until the liquid has reduced by half. Add the reserved stock and simmer for 5 minutes, or until the sauce is thick enough to coat the back of a spoon. Stir in the tarragon. Taste and adjust the seasoning.

Remove the skin from the chicken breasts. Carefully cut the breast meat from the breast bone and then cut each breast, on the diagonal, into 2 pieces. Place a divided chicken breast in the center of each of 4 warm dinner plates.

Or, place Parsleyed Noodles (page 194) on 4 dinner plates. Top each with a chicken breast and the mushroom sauce. Sprinkle with the Sautéed Carrots and Celery Root (below). Remove and discard the skin from the chicken before eating.

YIELD: 4 SERVINGS

PER SERVING

269 CALORIES
10 G. TOTAL FAT
2.4 G. SATURATED FAT
77 MG. CHOLESTEROL

SAUTÉED CARROTS AND CELERY ROOT
(Sauté de Carottes et Céleri-Rave)

This crisp-tender vegetable dish is a very pleasing combination of flavors. For extra savor, add some chopped fresh tarragon or parsley just before serving.

3	medium carrots, sliced
½–1	cup water
2	teaspoons unsalted butter
1	teaspoon sugar
½	large celery root, peeled and cut into 1″ cubes
	Salt and freshly ground black pepper

In a large sauté pan, combine the carrots, ½ cup of the water, and butter. Sprinkle the sugar over the top and bring to a boil over medium-high heat. Cover and reduce the heat to medium. Simmer for 10 minutes, or until the carrots are almost tender. Add the celery root (add more water if the mixture is dry). Cook for 5 minutes, or until the celery root is just tender. Season with the salt and pepper.

YIELD: 4 SERVINGS

PER SERVING

29 CALORIES
1 G. TOTAL FAT
0.6 G. SATURATED FAT
3 MG. CHOLESTEROL

PARSLEYED NOODLES

(*Nouilles Persillées*)

The sweeter flat-leaf or Italian parsley gives the best flavor to this dish. The parsley may also be replaced with any herb you particularly like.

8 ounces dried egg noodles
2 teaspoons unsalted butter
1 tablespoon minced fresh flat-leaf parsley
    Salt and freshly ground black pepper

Cook the noodles in a large saucepan of boiling water according to the package directions. Drain, reserving 2 tablespoons of the water. Place the noodles in a warm bowl. Add the butter and reserved cooking water. Toss to coat. Add the parsley and season with the salt and pepper. Toss to coat.

YIELD: 4 SERVINGS

PER SERVING

151 CALORIES
1.7 G. TOTAL FAT
0.4 G. SATURATED FAT
37 MG. CHOLESTEROL

MINT FLANS IN ORANGE SAUCE
(*Flans à la Menthe avec Sauce à l'Orange*)

This is a light, refreshing end to a rich fall meal.

1	cup 2% reduced-fat milk
2½	tablespoons sugar
6	sprigs fresh mint
3	tablespoons cold water
1	packet unflavored gelatin
½	cup frozen orange juice concentrate
5	ounces fresh orange juice
1	tablespoon apricot jam
1	cup fresh raspberries
1	cup fresh blueberries

In a small saucepan, combine the milk and sugar. Place over medium heat until warm. Remove from the heat and stir in the mint. Cover and let steep for 1 hour. Strain through a fine sieve into a small bowl.

Place the water in a custard cup. Sprinkle with the gelatin and let soften for 5 minutes. Bring about ½" of water to a simmer in a small skillet over medium heat. Place the custard cup in the skillet. Reduce the heat to low and stir the mixture until the gelatin is melted and the liquid is clear. Stir into the milk and mix well.

Pour equal portions into each of four (4-ounce) ramekins. Cover lightly with plastic wrap and refrigerate for 8 hours.

In a small saucepan, combine the orange juice concentrate and orange juice. Bring to a simmer over medium heat. Reduce the heat to medium-low and simmer for 5 minutes, or until reduced by half. Remove from the heat and stir in the jam.

When ready to serve, spoon an equal portion of the orange sauce onto each of 4 chilled dessert plates. Remove the flans from the refrigerator and quickly dip the bottom of each ramekin into hot water. Wipe dry and quickly unmold a flan onto each plate. Sprinkle the raspberries and blueberries around each flan.

YIELD: 4 SERVINGS

PER SERVING

199 CALORIES
2 G. TOTAL FAT
0.8 G. SATURATED FAT
5 MG. CHOLESTEROL

LEEKS VINAIGRETTE WITH ROASTED RED PEPPERS

LAMB STEW WITH GLAZED TURNIPS AND PEARL ONIONS

ROASTED APPLES WRAPPED IN PHYLLO, BOURDELOT-STYLE

PER SERVING

740 CALORIES

23 G. TOTAL FAT (28% OF CALORIES)

6 G. SATURATED FAT

142 MG. CHOLESTEROL

LEEKS VINAIGRETTE WITH ROASTED RED PEPPERS
(Poireaux Vinaigrette avec Julienne de Poivrons Rouges)

In French, leeks are called L'Asperge du Pauvre, or poor man's asparagus, which gives you some idea of their culinary value. They can be used both as a vegetable and as an aromatic flavoring but are particularly fine served in a vinaigrette as an appetizer.

1	tablespoon sherry vinegar
1½	tablespoons plus 1 teaspoon olive oil
	Salt and freshly ground black pepper
1	large red bell pepper, roasted, peeled, seeded, and cut into julienne (page 32)
1	shallot, minced
1	clove garlic, minced
1	tablespoon minced fresh flat-leaf parsley
1	sprig fresh rosemary, chopped
1	sprig fresh thyme, chopped
8	large leeks, white parts only, well-washed and trimmed

In a cup, whisk together the vinegar and 1½ tablespoons of the oil. Season with the salt and black pepper.

In a small bowl, combine the red peppers, shallots, garlic, parsley, rosemary, thyme, and the remaining 1 teaspoon oil. Season with the salt and black pepper. Toss to combine.

LEEKS VINAIGRETTE WITH ROASTED RED PEPPERS

Place the leeks in a medium saucepan. Add cold water to cover by about 1″. Add a pinch of salt. Bring to a boil over medium-high heat. Reduce the heat to medium-low and simmer for 15 minutes, or until the leeks are tender when pierced with a knife. Drain and place the leeks, in a single layer, on a wire rack to drain and cool.

When the leeks are well-drained and at room temperature, cut them in half lengthwise and place in a shallow bowl. Add the vinegar mixture and carefully toss to coat.

Place 4 leek halves in a crisscross pattern on each of 4 chilled salad plates. Sprinkle an equal portion of the red-pepper mixture over each plate.

YIELD: 4 SERVINGS

PER SERVING

138 CALORIES
7 G. TOTAL FAT
0.9 G. SATURATED FAT
0 MG. CHOLESTEROL

197

Lamb Stew with Glazed Turnips and Pearl Onions
(*Navarin d'Agneau aux Navets Glacés et Petits Oignons*)

This rich lamb stew is a perfect marriage of fall flavors. When browning the lamb, be sure that it is evenly glazed with no scorching. Good browning is essential to maximize the final flavor.

1	teaspoon olive oil
1½	pounds very lean lamb shoulder, cut into 2″ cubes
	Salt and freshly ground black pepper
1	small onion, chopped
1½	tablespoons all-purpose flour
½	cup dry red wine
1	tablespoon tomato paste
	Cold water
2	sprigs fresh thyme
1	bay leaf
2	medium carrots, cut into ¼″ × 2″ pieces
2	small all-purpose potatoes, peeled and quartered
12	pearl onions, peeled and blanched (page 32)
1	teaspoon sugar
1	teaspoon butter
2	turnips, peeled and cut into ¼″ × 2″ pieces
1	tablespoon chopped fresh flat-leaf parsley

Preheat the oven to 350°F.

Warm the oil in a large sauté pan over medium-high heat. When hot, add no more than half of the lamb and sear for 3 minutes, or until the lamb has evenly browned on all sides. Do not crowd the pan or scorch the meat. Using a slotted spoon, transfer the lamb to a Dutch oven. Continue searing the lamb until all of the meat has been browned. Season with the salt and pepper.

In the same sauté pan over medium heat, sauté the chopped onions for 3 minutes, or until softened. Sprinkle with the flour and stir to mix well. Add the wine, stirring with a wooden spoon to lift the browned bits from the bottom of the pan. Pour into the Dutch oven.

Add the tomato paste and stir to blend. Add enough cold water to just cover the lamb. Stir in the thyme and bay leaf. Bring to a simmer over medium heat. Cover and place in the oven. Adjust the heat, if necessary, to keep the liquid from boiling. Bake, stirring occasionally, for 1 hour.

Add the carrots; cover and bake for 15 minutes. Add the potatoes; cover and bake for 45 minutes. Remove and discard the bay leaf and thyme sprigs.

While the stew is baking, prepare the vegetables. In a small nonstick sauté pan, combine the pearl onions, ½ teaspoon of the sugar, and ½ teaspoon of the butter. Add enough cold water to cover the onions by half. Bring to a simmer over medium-high heat, swirling the pan from time to time to evenly glaze the onions. Reduce the heat to medium-low and simmer for 10 minutes, or until the onions are tender and the water has evaporated. Season with the salt and pepper. Using a slotted spoon, remove the onions to a warm plate. Lightly cover and keep warm.

Place the turnips, the remaining ½ teaspoon sugar, and the remaining ½ teaspoon butter in the same sauté pan. Add enough cold water to cover the turnips by half. Bring to a simmer over medium-high heat, swirling the pan from time to time to evenly glaze the turnips. Reduce the heat to medium-low and simmer for 10 minutes, or until the turnips are tender and the water has evaporated. Season with the salt and pepper. Using a slotted spoon, remove the turnips and add to the pearl onions.

Remove the stew from the oven. Taste and adjust the seasoning.

Place an equal portion in each of 4 warm shallow soup bowls. Add an equal portion of the onions and turnips to each bowl. Sprinkle with the parsley.

YIELD: 4 SERVINGS

PER SERVING

386 CALORIES
14 G. TOTAL FAT
5 G. SATURATED FAT
115 MG. CHOLESTEROL

ROASTED APPLES WRAPPED IN PHYLLO, BOURDELOT-STYLE
(*Pommes Genre Bourdelot*)

In this traditional French dessert, phyllo dough replaces the rich pâte brisée to make a much lighter dish.

4	large cooking apples (such as Cortlands)
2	tablespoons granulated sugar
2	tablespoons Calvados (dry apple brandy)
8	squares (6″) phyllo dough
	Water
2	tablespoons packed light brown sugar
1	large egg, lightly beaten

Preheat the oven to 375°F.

Carefully core the apples, making sure that you do not cut through the bottom.

Place 1½ teaspoons of the granulated sugar in each apple. Pour 1½ teaspoons of the Calvados into each apple.

Place 4 of the phyllo squares in a row on a work surface; keep the remainder covered with a damp paper towel. Using a pastry brush, lightly coat each square with water. Dust each square with brown sugar. Top each square with another piece of phyllo. Brush with water and dust with brown sugar.

Place an apple in the center of each layered phyllo square. Bring the sides up, folding and tucking as necessary, to completely cover the apple. Tuck any excess dough down into the core area of the apple. Using a pastry brush, lightly coat each apple with the egg.

Place on a nonstick baking sheet. Bake for 20 minutes, or until the apples are tender when pierced with a knife and the phyllo is crisp and golden brown.

YIELD: 4 SERVINGS

PER SERVING

216 CALORIES
2 G. TOTAL FAT
0.4 G. SATURATED FAT
27 MG. CHOLESTEROL

TWO-CELERY SOUP

VEAL STEW WITH CARROTS, LA BOUTARDE

FRENCH CHEESECAKES

<u>PER SERVING</u>

897 CALORIES

27 G. TOTAL FAT (27% OF CALORIES)

13 G. SATURATED FAT

247 MG. CHOLESTEROL

TWO-CELERY SOUP

(Soupe aux Deux Céleris)

Celery and celery root are at their best in the autumn. Almost sweet, crunchy, and low in fat and calories, they're a perfect way to start a meal. You can also serve this soup "chunky style"—just be sure to cut the vegetables into uniform pieces and reduce the cooking time by 5 minutes to keep a bit of crispness. This soup is equally good hot or chilled.

2	teaspoons canola oil
1	teaspoon unsalted butter
2	leeks, with a little green attached, well-washed and chopped
2	large ribs celery, chopped
1	medium celery root, peeled and cubed
1	small all-purpose potato, peeled and cubed
3	cups water
2	cups White Chicken Stock (page 37)
	Salt and freshly ground black pepper
1	cup whole milk
1	tablespoon chopped fresh flat-leaf parsley

Warm the oil and butter in a medium nonstick saucepan over medium heat. Add the leeks and celery. Sauté for 10 minutes. Add the celery root, potatoes, water, and stock. Season with the salt and pepper. Bring to a boil.

Cover, reduce the heat to medium-low, and simmer for 30 minutes, or until the vegetables are very tender. Remove from the heat and let cool for 5 minutes.

Transfer to a blender or a food processor fitted with the metal blade. Process until very smooth. Pour into a clean saucepan. Stir in the milk. Taste and adjust the seasoning. Bring to a simmer over medium heat.

Ladle into each of 4 soup bowls. Sprinkle with the parsley.

YIELD: 4 SERVINGS

PER SERVING

158 CALORIES
5 G. TOTAL FAT
1.7 G. SATURATED FAT
12 MG. CHOLESTEROL

VEAL STEW WITH CARROTS, LA BOUTARDE
(Ragoût de Veau aux Carottes à la Boutarde)

This aromatic veal stew is a perfect fall meal. It's nourishing, filling, and wonderfully tasty—with your health requirements always in mind.

1 tablespoon olive oil
2 pounds veal rump, well-trimmed and cut into 2″ cubes
Salt and freshly ground white pepper
2 medium carrots, cut into ½″ slices
1 medium onion, chopped
1½ cups dry white wine
1 cup water
2 medium very ripe tomatoes, peeled, cored, seeded, and chopped
2 teaspoons herbes de Provence (see note)
1 bay leaf
3 small all-purpose potatoes, peeled and quartered

Warm the oil in a large sauté pan over medium-high heat. When hot, add no more than half of the veal and sear for 3 minutes, or until the veal has evenly browned on all sides. Do not crowd the pan or scorch the meat. Using a slotted spoon, transfer the veal to a Dutch oven. Continue searing the veal until all of the meat has been browned. Season with the salt and pepper.

In the same sauté pan over medium heat, sauté the carrots and onions for 3 minutes, or until the onions are translucent. Reduce the heat and stir in the wine. Using a wooden spoon, stir vigorously to lift the browned bits from the bottom of the pan. Pour into the Dutch oven. Add the water, tomatoes, herbes de Provence, and bay leaf.

Place the Dutch oven over medium heat and bring the stew to a boil. Reduce the heat to medium-low, cover, and simmer for 1 hour. Add the potatoes and simmer for 35 minutes, or until the potatoes are tender. Taste and adjust the seasoning. Remove and discard the bay leaf.

Place an equal portion of the stew in each of 4 warm shallow soup bowls.

Chef's Note: Herbes de Provence is a mixture of dried herbs that often includes basil, lavender, rosemary, sage, thyme, and others. Look for it in the spice section of your supermarket.

YIELD: 4 SERVINGS

PER SERVING

437 CALORIES
12 G. TOTAL FAT
4 G. SATURATED FAT
149 MG. CHOLESTEROL

FRENCH CHEESECAKES
(*Gâteaux au Fromage Blanc*)

Fromage blanc is a very soft, fresh, and light French cream cheese most often used as a dessert cheese with fresh fruit. It is available in cheese shops, specialty food stores, and some supermarkets.

1	large egg
1	large egg white
½	cup sugar
1	teaspoon pure vanilla extract
1	cup fromage blanc
4	ounces reduced-fat cream cheese, at room temperature
	Zest of 1 lemon
	Zest of 1 orange
3	tablespoons strawberry jam
2	teaspoons fresh lemon juice
1	cup sliced hulled fresh strawberries
2	tablespoons water (optional)

Preheat the oven to 300°F. Bring 6 cups water to a boil.

In a small bowl, combine the egg, egg white, sugar, and vanilla. Beat with an electric mixer until pale yellow.

In a medium bowl, combine the fromage blanc, cream cheese, lemon zest, and orange zest. Beat with an electric mixer until very smooth and creamy. Add the egg mixture and beat until well-blended.

Coat four (4-ounce) ramekins with nonstick spray. Place an equal portion of the cheese batter in each ramekin. Place the ramekins in a small baking dish. Add enough boiling water to come halfway up the sides of the ramekins. Bake for 45 minutes, or until the center is set.

Remove the ramekins from the oven and baking dish. Place on a wire rack to cool. Refrigerate for 3 hours.

Place the jam, lemon juice, and ½ cup of the strawberries in a blender or a food processor fitted with the metal blade. Process until smooth. If the sauce is too thick, thin with the water. Transfer to a small bowl. Cover and refrigerate until ready to use.

When ready to serve, remove the ramekins from the refrigerator. Dip the bottom of the ramekins into very hot water for no more than 10 seconds. Wipe dry and

FRENCH CHEESECAKE

invert each ramekin into a chilled dessert bowl. Drizzle an equal portion of sauce over
each plate and top with the remaining strawberries.

YIELD: 4 SERVINGS

PER SERVING

302 CALORIES
10 G. TOTAL FAT
7 G. SATURATED FAT
86 MG. CHOLESTEROL

PUMPKIN AND TURNIP SOUP

MONKFISH OSSO BUCO

CHOCOLATE SOUFFLÉS

<u>PER SERVING</u>

650 CALORIES

17 G. TOTAL FAT (24% OF CALORIES)

5 G. SATURATED FAT

118 MG. CHOLESTEROL

PUMPKIN AND TURNIP SOUP
(*Velouté de Potiron et Navets*)

The rather bland pumpkin is brought to life by the piquant turnip to make this delicious low-fat soup. To mellow the flavor, prepare the soup a few days in advance of serving.

1	teaspoon canola oil
½	teaspoon unsalted butter
2	medium leeks, with a little green attached, well-washed and thinly sliced
3	white turnips, peeled and cubed
1	small pumpkin, peeled, seeded, and cubed
1	small all-purpose potato, peeled and cubed
5	cups White Chicken Stock (page 37)
	Salt and freshly ground black pepper
⅓	cup whole milk

Warm the oil and butter in a medium saucepan over medium heat. Add the leeks and sauté for 15 minutes, or until the leeks are very soft. Add the turnips, pumpkin, potatoes, and stock. Season with the salt and pepper. Cover and simmer for

40 minutes, or until the vegetables are very soft. Remove from the heat and allow to cool slightly.

Transfer to a blender or a food processor fitted with the metal blade. Process until very smooth. Pour through a fine sieve into a clean saucepan. Bring to a simmer over low heat. Stir in the milk. Taste and adjust the seasoning.

YIELD: 4 SERVINGS

PER SERVING

160 CALORIES
4.5 G. TOTAL FAT
1 G. SATURATED FAT
18 MG. CHOLESTEROL

MONKFISH OSSO BUCO
(Osso Buco de Lotte aux Tomates de Septembre)

The flavor and texture of this dish is nicely balanced when served over a grain. Couscous or polenta will absorb the sauce particularly well, but almost any grain or starch will make a tasty pairing.

¼	cup all-purpose flour
	Salt and freshly ground black pepper
8	monkfish medallions (3 ounces each)
1	tablespoon olive oil
1	small onion, chopped
1	small carrot, chopped
1	rib celery, chopped
2	very ripe plum tomatoes, cored and quartered
2	cloves garlic, chopped
1½	cups dry white wine
10	sprigs fresh flat-leaf parsley
2	sprigs fresh thyme
1	bay leaf
1	tablespoon chopped fresh flat-leaf parsley

Place the flour on a plate. Season with the salt and pepper. Dredge the monkfish in the flour, shaking off any excess.

Warm the oil in a large nonstick sauté pan over medium heat until hot but not smoking. Add the monkfish. Sear, turning once, for 4 minutes, or until each side is nicely browned. Transfer the monkfish to a plate.

Add the onions, carrots, and celery to the sauté pan. Cook for 5 minutes, or until the vegetables are lightly browned. Stir in the tomatoes, garlic, wine, parsley sprigs, thyme, and bay leaf. Season with the salt and pepper.

Carefully lay the fish in the sauce. Cover and bring to a simmer. Cook for 20 minutes, or until the vegetables are very tender. Remove the fish from the sauce and place it on a warm plate. Cover lightly and keep warm.

Remove and discard the parsley, thyme, and bay leaf from the sauce. Pour the sauce into a blender or a food processor fitted with the metal blade. Process until smooth. Pour the sauce through a medium sieve into a medium saucepan. Bring to a simmer over medium heat. Taste and adjust the seasoning.

Spoon an equal portion of the sauce into the center of each of 4 warm dinner plates. Place 2 monkfish medallions in the center of each plate and sprinkle with the chopped parsley.

YIELD: 4 SERVINGS

PER SERVING

326 CALORIES
6.5 G. TOTAL FAT
1 G. SATURATED FAT
43 MG. CHOLESTEROL

CHOCOLATE SOUFFLÉS
(Soufflés au Chocolat)

So low-calorie and oh, so delicious! These chocolate soufflés would be an elegant finish to any meal.

1   teaspoon unsalted butter
2   teaspoons plus 2 tablespoons sugar
1   ounce semisweet chocolate
⅛   cup chocolate pastry cream (see note)
4   large egg whites

Preheat the oven to 400°F.

Lightly coat four (4-ounce) ramekins with the butter. Using 2 teaspoons of the sugar, lightly dust the insides of the ramekins.

Place the chocolate in the top half of a double boiler. Place over boiling water until melted. Transfer to a small bowl and stir in the pastry cream. Mix well.

Place the egg whites in a medium bowl. Beat with an electric mixer on medium speed until foamy. Gradually beat in the remaining 2 tablespoons sugar and beat on high speed until soft peaks form. Fold into the pastry-cream mixture, blending well without deflating the egg whites.

Spoon an equal portion of the soufflé mixture into each of the ramekins. Place the ramekins on a baking sheet. Bake for 10 minutes, or until the soufflés have risen and set. Serve immediately.

Chef's Note: To make chocolate pastry cream, see the recipe for Vanilla Pastry Cream (page 56) and make the adjustments suggested.

YIELD: 4 SERVINGS

PER SERVING

164 CALORIES
6 G. TOTAL FAT
3.1 G. SATURATED FAT
57 MG. CHOLESTEROL

WINTER MENUS

IN FRANCE, THE WINTER MONTHS SIGNAL A RETURN TO RICH
SOUPS AND STEWS, HEARTY FOODS THAT NOURISH US FOR
THE LONG, COLD NIGHTS AHEAD. IN THIS CHAPTER, WE HAVE
TAKEN MANY OF THE CLASSIC FRENCH STEWS, SUCH AS *POT-
AU-FEU, BLANQUETTE DE VEAU,* AND *DAUBE DE BOEUF,* AND
LOWERED THE FAT AND CHOLESTEROL WHILE MAINTAINING
THEIR SAVORY, FILLING GOODNESS. YOU WILL ALSO FIND A
FEW EXOTIC FLAVORS FROM THE SOUTH OF FRANCE AND
NORTH AFRICA THAT WILL ADD A TOUCH OF SPICE TO YOUR
WINTER MEALS. REVISED WORLD-RENOWNED TRADITIONAL
FRENCH DISHES LIKE ONION SOUP, SPLIT PEA SOUP WITH
BACON, AND BOUILLABAISSE WILL BRIGHTEN ANY CHILLY DAY
WITH THEIR HEARTWARMING WHOLESOMENESS. EACH MENU
HAS BEEN CAREFULLY BALANCED, WITH THE ROBUST ENTRÉE
OFFSET BY A LIGHT APPETIZER OR A SIMPLE DESSERT. WE
HOPE THAT YOU WILL FIND THESE COLD-WEATHER MEALS
NUTRITIONALLY SATISFYING AND FULL OF GREAT TASTE.

North African Cracked Wheat Salad

Trout à la Nage

Citrus Terrines with Blueberries

PER SERVING

549 CALORIES

15 G. TOTAL FAT (25% OF CALORIES)

3 G. SATURATED FAT

82 MG. CHOLESTEROL

North African Cracked Wheat Salad
(*Salade de Taboulé Magrebienne*)

This salad is a cook's dream because it must be made the day before serving. If you would rather eat it on the same day it is made, cook the cracked wheat in boiling salted water for 2 minutes, then drain through a fine sieve. Proceed with the recipe, but serve immediately without refrigerating.

4	ounces cracked wheat
	Juice of 4 lemons
1½	tablespoons olive oil
2	tomatoes, peeled, cored, seeded, and diced
1	red bell pepper, roasted, peeled, seeded, and diced
1	green bell pepper, roasted, peeled, seeded, and diced
1	small cucumber, peeled, seeded, and diced
1	rib celery, diced
1	bunch scallions, diced
1	bunch fresh flat-leaf parsley, chopped
1	bunch fresh mint, chopped
	Salt and freshly ground black pepper

NORTH AFRICAN CRACKED WHEAT SALAD

In a large bowl, combine the cracked wheat, lemon juice, and oil. Mix well. Add the tomatoes, red peppers, green peppers, cucumbers, celery, scallions, parsley, and mint. Season with the salt and black pepper. Toss well to combine.

Cover and refrigerate for at least 8 hours, or until the wheat has softened.

YIELD: 4 SERVINGS

PER SERVING

129 CALORIES
6 G. TOTAL FAT
0.8 G. SATURATED FAT
0 MG. CHOLESTEROL

TROUT À LA NAGE
(*Truite à la Nage*)

In this recipe, the vegetables should cook very quickly. We suggest that you use a mandoline (see page 29) to achieve the necessary even, thin slices—especially for the carrots, which take longer to cook than the other vegetables. Do use caution when cutting because the blades of the slicer are very sharp. For this quick and easy meal-in-a-pot, you can change the seasonings to incorporate saffron, lemon grass, or curry. You can also substitute cod, halibut, or sole for the trout.

8	trout fillets (2½ ounces each)
2	carrots
5	very thin lemon slices
2	ribs celery, very thinly sliced
1	leek, white part only, well-washed and very thinly sliced
1	large shallot, very thinly sliced
4	sprigs fresh thyme
2	sprigs fresh tarragon
	Pinch of ground coriander (optional)
	Pinch of ground anise seed (optional)
	Salt and freshly ground black pepper
6	cups water
8	very small celery leaves

Score the skin side of the trout fillets and place them on a plate. Cover and refrigerate until ready to cook.

Use the tines of a fork to make even indentations into and down the length of each carrot. Slice very thinly into flowerlike disks. Place the carrots in a large braising pan.

Add the lemon slices, celery slices, leeks, shallots, thyme, tarragon, coriander (if using), and anise seed (if using). Season with the salt and pepper. Toss to evenly combine. Add the water and bring to a simmer over high heat. Reduce the heat to medium and simmer for 10 minutes.

Place the trout fillets, skin side down, in a single layer in the pan. Cover and cook for 3 minutes. Turn off the heat and let stand, covered, for 3 minutes.

214

Cut the fillets in half. Place 2 on each of 4 warm shallow soup plates. Cover with the vegetables and 2 more fillets. Ladle the broth over the fish and vegetables. Garnish with the celery leaves.

YIELD: 4 SERVINGS

PER SERVING

286 CALORIES
9 G. TOTAL FAT
2 G. SATURATED FAT
82 MG. CHOLESTEROL

CITRUS TERRINES WITH BLUEBERRIES
(Terrines d'Agrumes aux Myrtilles)

This light, virtually fat-free dessert makes a beautiful, almost stained glass–like presentation. It can be made a day or two in advance of serving.

3	medium oranges, peeled and sectioned
¼–½	cup fresh orange juice
2	medium grapefruit, peeled and sectioned
¼	cup cold water
1	packet unflavored gelatin
1	tablespoon orange blossom honey
28	fresh blueberries
4	sprigs fresh mint

Using a paring knife, remove the skin and outer membrane from the oranges. Carefully cut out each section from the membranes, catching any juice in a small bowl as you cut. Reserve the sections. Squeeze the juice from the membranes into the bowl. Strain the juice and add enough fresh orange juice to equal 1 cup. Repeat with the grapefruit; reserve the grapefruit juice for another use.

Place the water in a custard cup. Sprinkle with the gelatin and let soften for 5 minutes. Add 1 tablespoon of the orange juice. Bring about ½" of water to a simmer in a small skillet over medium heat. Place the custard cup in the skillet. Reduce the heat to low and stir the mixture until the gelatin is melted and the liquid is clear. Pour into a small bowl.

Add the honey and the remaining orange juice. Stir until well-blended.

Place 4 small round molds (such as coffee cups) on a work surface. Take 1 mold and place alternating sections of the orange and grapefruit very close together against the sides, leaving no space between the sections so that the terrine will hold its

(continued)

215

shape. Place 7 blueberries in the center of the mold and fill with the juice mixture. Repeat to fill the remaining 3 molds. Cover the molds with plastic wrap and refrigerate for at least 45 minutes, or until the gelatin has set.

To unmold the terrines, carefully wrap each mold in a very hot towel, loosening around the edge of the terrine with a sharp knife as it warms. Take care not to let the mold get too warm or the gelatin will melt. Unmold each terrine onto a small chilled dessert plate. Garnish with a sprig of mint.

YIELD: 4 SERVINGS

PER SERVING

134 CALORIES
0.4 G. TOTAL FAT
0 G. SATURATED FAT
0 MG. CHOLESTEROL

CELERY ROOT SALAD IN RADICCHIO CUPS

BEEF STEW IN THE STYLE OF CAMARGUE

ROASTED PEARS IN CARAMEL SYRUP

PER SERVING
762 CALORIES
17 G. TOTAL FAT (20% OF CALORIES)
5 G. SATURATED FAT
72 MG. CHOLESTEROL

CELERY ROOT SALAD IN RADICCHIO CUPS
(*Céleri-Rave dans les Nids de Salade Rouge*)

*Celery root makes a wonderful winter salad. Its sweet taste belies the fact
that it is low in fat. You can, if you wish a zestier salad, grate some fresh
horseradish into a bit of vinegar, rinse well, and then add to the dressing.
You can also use this same combination of ingredients to dress carrots
or jicama.*

1	celery root, peeled and cut into julienne (page 32)
¾	cup nonfat sour cream
1	teaspoon Dijon mustard
	Juice of 1 lemon
	Pinch of cayenne pepper
	Salt and freshly ground black pepper
12	radicchio leaves, trimmed
1	tablespoon chopped fresh flat-leaf parsley

Place the celery root in a medium bowl.

In a small bowl, combine the sour cream, mustard, lemon juice, and cayenne.
Season with the salt and black pepper. Whisk well to combine. Pour over the celery root
and toss to combine.

(continued)

217

Place 3 radicchio leaves in the center of each of 4 well-chilled salad plates. Top with equal portions of celery root salad. Sprinkle with the parsley.

YIELD: 4 SERVINGS

PER SERVING

89 CALORIES
0.3 G. TOTAL FAT
0 G. SATURATED FAT
0 MG. CHOLESTEROL

BEEF STEW IN THE STYLE OF CAMARGUE
(Daube de Boeuf Camarguaise)

This rich beef stew, part of the classic French repertoire, has been lightened considerably for a satisfying but good-for-you winter's meal.

8	small red potatoes, peeled
	Salt
16	baby carrots, peeled with a little stem attached
8	pearl onions, peeled
1½	teaspoons extra-virgin olive oil
1	pound very lean beef round, cut into 1″ cubes
	Freshly ground black pepper
1	onion, chopped
1	cup dry white wine
1	teaspoon herbes de Provence (see note)
1	large tomato, peeled, cored, seeded, and diced
¼	cup niçoise olives, pitted
2	tablespoons capers, well-drained
8	ounces haricots verts or small green beans, trimmed, cut into 1½″ lengths, and blanched (page 32)
1	tablespoon chopped fresh flat-leaf parsley
8	baguette slices (optional)

Place the potatoes in a medium saucepan and add cold water to cover by about 1″. Add a pinch of salt. Bring to a boil over high heat. Cover and reduce the heat to medium-low. Cook for 8 minutes. Add the carrots and pearl onions. Cover and cook for 8 minutes, or until the vegetables are tender but still firm when pierced with a fork. Use a slotted spoon to transfer the vegetables to a plate; reserve the cooking liquid.

Warm the oil in a large sauté pan over medium-high heat. When hot, add no more than half of the beef and sear for 3 minutes, or until the beef has evenly browned on all sides. Do not crowd the pan or scorch the meat. Using a slotted spoon, transfer the beef to a Dutch oven. Continue searing the beef until all of the meat has been browned. Season the beef with the salt and pepper.

In the same sauté pan over medium heat, sauté the chopped onions for 3 minutes, or until softened. Add the wine, stirring with a wooden spoon to lift the browned bits from the bottom of the pan. Pour into the Dutch oven.

Add the reserved cooking liquid and the herbes de Provence. Bring to a boil over medium heat. Cover and reduce the heat to medium-low. Simmer for 1½ hours, or until the beef is very tender. Taste and adjust the seasoning. (If the sauce is too thick, thin with some water. May be prepared up to a day in advance of use at this point.)

Add the reserved vegetables and bring the stew to a boil. Cook for 2 to 3 minutes, or just until the vegetables are heated through. Stir in the tomatoes, olives, and capers.

Place an equal portion in each of 4 large warm shallow bowls. Garnish with the haricots verts or beans and top with parsley. Serve with the baguette slices (if using).

Chef's Note: Herbes de Provence is a mixture of dried herbs that often includes basil, lavender, rosemary, sage, thyme, and others. Look for it in the spice section of your supermarket.

YIELD: 4 SERVINGS

PER SERVING

446 CALORIES
13 G. TOTAL FAT
3 G. SATURATED FAT
64 MG. CHOLESTEROL

ROASTED PEARS IN CARAMEL SYRUP
(Poires Rôties au Caramel)

This dessert works well at a simple weeknight supper or a formal meal.

1	tablespoon unsalted butter, melted
4	ripe pears, halved and cored
	Juice of ½ lemon
½	cup sugar
¼	cup water
1	teaspoon pear brandy (optional)

Preheat the oven to 375°F.

Using ½ teaspoon of the butter, brush the bottom of a medium ovenproof nonstick sauté pan or small roasting pan. Tightly pack the pears, cut side down, in the pan. Sprinkle with the lemon juice and then the sugar. Pour the remaining 2½ teaspoons butter over the top.

Roast for 30 minutes, or until the pears are tender and golden. Transfer the pears to a plate. Cover and keep warm.

(continued)

Place the pan over medium heat and cook for 3 minutes, or until the sugar and juices have caramelized. Add the water and bring to a boil. Boil for 2 minutes, or until a thin syrup forms. Remove from the heat and strain through a fine sieve into a small bowl. Allow to cool slightly. Add the brandy (if using).

Slice each pear half into a fan shape. Place 2 halves, opposite each other, on each of 4 warm dessert plates. Pour the syrup over the pears.

YIELD: 4 SERVINGS

PER SERVING

227 CALORIES
4 G. TOTAL FAT
2 G. SATURATED FAT
8 MG. CHOLESTEROL

ROASTED PEARS IN CARAMEL SYRUP (PAGE 219)

PROVENÇAL GARLIC SOUP

ROASTED CHICKEN WITH GRAPEFRUIT AND PINK PEPPERCORN SAUCE

SAUTÉED SPINACH

CARAMELIZED BANANA TARTS

PER SERVING

953 CALORIES

18 G. TOTAL FAT (17% CALORIES)

7 G. SATURATED FAT

132 MG. CHOLESTEROL

PROVENÇAL GARLIC SOUP
(*Tourin d'Ail Doux*)

Blanching the garlic twice allows much of the bitterness to leach out. This produces a very sweet, mellow flavor that heightens the richness of this low-fat soup.

2	large bulbs garlic
2½	cups White Chicken Stock (page 37)
1	cup whole milk
6	baguette slices
	Salt and freshly ground black pepper

Break the garlic bulbs into cloves and peel them. Place in a medium saucepan and add cold water to cover by about 1″. Bring to a boil over high heat. Reduce the heat to medium and simmer for 4 minutes. Drain well. Repeat the process. Drain and return the garlic to the saucepan.

Add the stock. Bring to a boil over high heat. Reduce the heat to medium and simmer for 10 minutes, or until the garlic is soft. Add the milk and baguette slices. Simmer for 3 minutes. Remove from the heat and allow to cool slightly.

Transfer to a blender or a food processor fitted with the metal blade. Process until smooth.

(continued)

Strain through a coarse sieve into a clean saucepan. Season with the salt and pepper. Bring to a simmer.

YIELD: 4 SERVINGS

PER SERVING

216 CALORIES
4 G. TOTAL FAT
2 G. SATURATED FAT
14 MG. CHOLESTEROL

PROVENÇAL GARLIC SOUP (PAGE 221)

Roasted Chicken with Grapefruit and Pink Peppercorn Sauce
(*Poulet Rôti à la Sauce de Pamplemousse et Poivre Rose*)

The citrus juices and mellow peppercorns make the sauce a refreshing garnish for roast chicken with the addition of no fat and only minimal calories.

1	roasting chicken (3–4 pounds)
	Salt and freshly ground black pepper
1	teaspoon olive oil
2	ribs celery, chopped
1	medium carrot, chopped
1	medium onion, chopped
1	sprig fresh thyme
1	bay leaf
3	large yellow grapefruit
3	large pink grapefruit
1½	cups Brown Chicken Stock (page 36)
1	tablespoon pink peppercorns, crushed

Preheat the oven to 425°F.

Wash the chicken, inside and out, with cold running water. Pat dry. Generously season, inside and out, with the salt and pepper. Tuck the wing tips under. Tie the legs together. Rub the chicken skin with the oil. Place the chicken on a rack in a small roasting pan. Roast for 25 minutes.

Add the celery, carrots, onions, thyme, and bay leaf to the pan. Roast for 25 minutes, or until the juices run clear when the chicken breast is pierced with a knife and an instant-read thermometer inserted in the center of a breast registers 170°F.

While the chicken is roasting, peel and section 1 yellow grapefruit and 1 pink grapefruit. Set the sections aside. Juice the remaining 2 yellow grapefruit and the remaining 2 pink grapefruit. Place the juice in a medium bowl.

Remove the chicken from the oven. Tilt the chicken so the juices run out of the cavity into the pan. Transfer the chicken to a warm platter; cover to keep warm.

Remove the rack from the roasting pan. Place the pan over medium heat and add the grapefruit juice. Bring to a boil and deglaze the pan, stirring constantly with a wooden spoon to remove all of the browned bits from the bottom. Add the stock and stir to combine. Strain through a fine sieve into a medium saucepan.

Allow the sauce to stand for 5 minutes. Using a metal spoon, lift off and discard any fat that has risen to the top. Add the peppercorns and place the pan over medium heat. Bring to a simmer and simmer for 7 minutes, or until the sauce has thickened slightly. Taste and adjust the seasoning.

(continued)

Carefully remove the skin from the chicken. Using a very sharp knife, cut each breast half from the bone, keeping each half whole. Slice each breast half on the bias into 8 pieces. Cover and keep warm. Carefully separate the drumsticks from the thighs. Cut the thighs in half lengthwise and carefully remove the bone. Reserve the drumsticks and any remaining chicken for another use.

Fan 4 slices of chicken breast in the center of each of 4 warm dinner plates. Place a thigh half on top of each portion. Fan an equal portion of grapefruit sections around the edge of each plate. Spoon the sauce over the top.

YIELD: 4 SERVINGS

PER SERVING

367 CALORIES
10 G. TOTAL FAT
3 G. SATURATED FAT
113 MG. CHOLESTEROL

SAUTÉED SPINACH
(*Épinards Sautés*)

1 teaspoon olive oil
1 clove garlic, minced
1 pound fresh spinach, washed and stems removed
   Freshly grated nutmeg
   Salt and freshly ground black pepper

Warm the oil in a large nonstick sauté pan over medium heat. Add the garlic and sauté for 2 minutes, or until the garlic is golden. Shake excess water from the spinach and add to the pan. Season with the nutmeg, salt, and pepper. Cover and cook for 2 minutes, or until the spinach is just wilted. Drain, if necessary.

YIELD: 4 SERVINGS

PER SERVING

24 CALORIES
1 G. TOTAL FAT
0.1 G. SATURATED FAT
0 MG. CHOLESTEROL

CARAMELIZED BANANA TARTS
(*Tartes aux Bananes Caramélisées*)

Absolutely scrumptious, these rich tarts are very low in fat and cholesterol but extremely satisfying to the sweet tooth—perfect for dinner-party fare or as a tea-time treat for a winter afternoon.

2 tablespoons granulated sugar
6 small ripe bananas

6   tablespoons plus 2 teaspoons packed light brown
    sugar
4   sheets phyllo dough
2   teaspoons unsalted butter, melted
¼   cup confectioners' sugar

Line a baking sheet with parchment paper. Sprinkle the paper with the granulated sugar.

Peel 2 of the bananas and place in a small bowl. Mash with a fork. Add 2 tablespoons of the brown sugar and mix well.

Preheat the oven to 400°F.

To prevent the phyllo from drying out, make 1 tart shell at a time. Carefully lay 1 phyllo sheet on a piece of parchment paper; keep the remainder covered with a damp paper towel. Using a pastry brush, lightly coat the phyllo with water. Sprinkle half of the dampened phyllo with approximately 1 teaspoon of the remaining brown sugar. Fold the phyllo in half and brush the top with water. Sprinkle half of the folded phyllo with 1 teaspoon of the remaining brown sugar. Fold the phyllo in half. Repeat to use the 3 remaining phyllo sheets and 6 teaspoons of the remaining brown sugar.

Using a pastry cutter, carefully cut a 5″ circle from each folded phyllo. Set aside; cover with a damp paper towel to keep the dough from drying out.

Using a rubber spatula, spread equal portions of the mashed bananas over the tops of the phyllo circles.

Peel the remaining 4 bananas and cut into ¼″ slices. Beginning at the outside edge of each tart, arrange slightly overlapping circles of the slices on top of the mashed bananas to completely cover the top. Lightly brush the slices with the butter. Using the remaining 2 tablespoons brown sugar, generously coat the entire top of each tart.

Place the tarts on the prepared baking sheet. Bake for 15 minutes. Turn on the broiler. Carefully remove the parchment paper from the baking sheet, leaving the tarts on the sheet. Sprinkle each tart with confectioners' sugar and place the sheet under the broiler. Broil for 2 minutes, or until the edges of the banana slices are nicely browned. Remove from the broiler and place on a wire rack to cool slightly. Serve at room temperature.

YIELD: 4 SERVINGS

PER SERVING

370 CALORIES
4 G. TOTAL FAT
2 G. SATURATED FAT
5 MG. CHOLESTEROL

ONION SOUP GRATINÉE

FISH STEW, MARSEILLE-STYLE

CARAMEL CREAM

PER SERVING

1,169 CALORIES

26 G. TOTAL FAT (20% OF CALORIES)

8 G. SATURATED FAT

186 MG. CHOLESTEROL

ONION SOUP GRATINÉE
(Soupe à l'Oignon Gratinée)

The traditional French bistro favorite is lightened up a bit for a healthier, but quite filling, start to a meal. It would work very well on its own as a winter's lunch.

1	teaspoon unsalted butter
1	teaspoon canola oil
10	ounces sweet white onions, very thinly sliced
1	clove garlic, minced
1	cup port
6	cups Brown Chicken Stock (page 36)
	Salt and freshly ground black pepper
12–16	very thin baguette slices, toasted
2	ounces Gruyère cheese, very thinly sliced

Warm the butter and oil in a large nonstick saucepan over medium-low heat. Add the onions and cook, stirring occasionally, for 25 minutes, or until very soft and sweet. Increase the heat to medium and cook, stirring frequently, for 5 minutes, or until the onions are nicely caramelized but not burned. Stir in the garlic and cook for 2 minutes.

Add the port and cook for 10 minutes, or until the liquid is reduced by half. Add the stock and bring to a simmer. Season with the salt and pepper. Cover, reduce the heat to low, and simmer for 30 minutes.

Preheat the broiler.

Place 3 or 4 baguette slices in the bottom of each of 4 heatproof soup bowls. Pour the soup over the bread, filling the bowls nearly to the rim. Place an equal number of cheese slices on top of the bowls, covering the bread and allowing the cheese to touch the edge of the bowl so that it will adhere to the sides when it is melted.

Place the bowls on a baking sheet. Broil for 2 minutes, or until the cheese melts and begins to brown.

YIELD: 4 SERVINGS

PER SERVING

335 CALORIES
10 G. TOTAL FAT
4 G. SATURATED FAT
32 MG. CHOLESTEROL

FISH STEW, MARSEILLE-STYLE
(Bouillabaisse du Cousin Marseillais)

Not the typical rich bouillabaisse of Marseille but a healthier, still-delicious alternative. Saffron remains the constant, while you can use any fish you like as long as it is fresh. The flavors and aromas of this French stew should transport you to the blue waters, blue skies, and bright sun of the south of France. It is The French Culinary Institute chefs' favorite.

12	ounces sea bass fillets
12	ounces medium shrimp, peeled and deveined
½	cup anise liqueur
8	ounces fresh mussels
1	bulb fennel
2	tablespoons olive oil
1	medium onion, very thinly sliced
1	leek, with a little green attached, well-washed and very thinly sliced
5	cloves garlic, minced
6	cups Fish Stock (page 40)
4	very ripe plum tomatoes, peeled, cored, seeded, and chopped
2	small red potatoes, peeled and halved
2	sprigs fresh thyme
3	pinches of saffron threads
	Salt and freshly ground black pepper
¼	teaspoon cayenne pepper
1	tablespoon chopped fresh flat-leaf parsley
16	thin baguette slices, toasted

227

Cut the bass into chunks and place in a large bowl. Add the shrimp and liqueur. Cover and allow to marinate at room temperature for 30 minutes.

Squeeze each mussel in the palm of your hand and discard any whose shells open. Scrub the remaining mussels to remove grit; cut off the beards. Wash in 3 changes of cold water. Place the mussels in a medium saucepan and add cold water to cover by about 1″. Bring to a boil over medium-high heat. Cover and steam for 5 minutes, or until the mussels open. Discard any mussels that do not open. Remove from the heat and carefully lift the meat from the shells; discard the shells. Return the meat to the cooking liquid.

Remove any hard or discolored outer layers from the fennel bulb. Trim the root end and feathery tops. Cut in half lengthwise; cut crosswise into very thin slices.

Warm 1 tablespoon of the oil in a large nonstick saucepan over medium heat. Add the onions, leeks, and fennel. Cook slowly for 8 minutes. If necessary, lower the heat to keep the vegetables from browning. Stir in about half of the garlic. Cook for 3 minutes.

Add the stock, tomatoes, potatoes, thyme, and 2 pinches of the saffron. Season with the salt and black pepper. Cover and simmer for 10 minutes, or until the vegetables are cooked but still firm.

To make the *rouille*, use a slotted spoon to remove the cooked potatoes from the stew. Place in a blender or a food processor fitted with the metal blade. Add the cayenne, the remaining garlic, and 1 pinch of saffron. Process until smooth. With the motor running, add ½ cup of the vegetable cooking liquid and the remaining 1 table-spoon oil. Season with the salt and black pepper. Transfer to a small bowl and set aside.

Add the marinated fish and shrimp to the stew. Strain the liquid from the mussels and add to the stew. Cover and simmer over medium heat for 8 minutes, or until the fish and shrimp are opaque. Taste and adjust the seasoning.

Ladle the stew into 4 large shallow soup bowls, making certain that each bowl contains an equal assortment of fish, shellfish, and vegetables. Sprinkle each with an equal amount of mussels and parsley. Spread the *rouille* mixture on the toast. Arrange 4 baguette slices around the edge of each plate.

YIELD: 4 SERVINGS

PER SERVING

541 CALORIES
12 G. TOTAL FAT
2 G. SATURATED FAT
43 MG. CHOLESTEROL

FISH STEW, MARSEILLE-STYLE (PAGE 227)

CARAMEL CREAM
(*Crème Caramel Minceur*)

We have lightened this traditional dessert considerably by replacing some of the whole eggs with egg whites and the cream with 1% low-fat milk. It is still a memorable French dessert.

¾ cup sugar
2 tablespoons water
2 cups 1% low-fat milk
½ vanilla bean, split lengthwise
4 large egg whites
2 large eggs
Pinch of salt

Place ¼ cup of the sugar in a small nonstick saucepan. Cook over medium heat for 3 minutes, or until the crystals begin to melt and turn brown. Cook for 2 minutes, or until the sugar turns a rich brown, taking care not to allow it to burn. Immediately remove from the heat and carefully add the water, swirling to incorporate. Return the saucepan to low heat and simmer for 1 minute. Immediately pour equal portions into each of four (6-ounce) ramekins. Refrigerate for at least 30 minutes, or until the caramel hardens.

Preheat the oven to 325°F.

Place the milk in a medium saucepan. Scrape the seeds from the vanilla bean into the saucepan, then add the bean. Warm over medium heat until an instant-read thermometer inserted in the milk reads 100°F; do not let it get too hot or it will scramble the eggs when combined with them. Remove and discard the vanilla bean.

In a large bowl, combine the egg whites, eggs, salt, and the remaining ½ cup sugar. Beat with an electric mixer on medium speed until well-combined. With the mixer running, slowly add the warm milk. When well-combined, pour through a fine sieve into a clean bowl. Skim off any foam from the top and let the custard stand for 1 minute to allow any air bubbles to break. Pour into the prepared ramekins.

Place the ramekins in a small baking dish. Add enough hot water to the baking dish to come halfway up the sides of the ramekins. Bake for 45 minutes, never allowing the water to boil.

Carefully remove the ramekins from the baking dish and run a sharp knife against the inside edge to loosen the caramel cream. One at a time, place a dessert plate on top of a ramekin. Carefully invert. Pour any caramel remaining in the ramekin over the top. Serve warm.

YIELD: 4 SERVINGS

PER SERVING

293 CALORIES
3.8 G. TOTAL FAT
1.5 G. SATURATED FAT
111 MG. CHOLESTEROL

SPLIT PEA SOUP WITH CROUTONS

LIGHT VEAL STEW BLANQUETTE

THIN APPLE TARTS

PER SERVING
997 CALORIES

18 G. TOTAL FAT (16% OF CALORIES)

5 G. SATURATED FAT

201 MG. CHOLESTEROL

SPLIT PEA SOUP WITH CROUTONS
(Velouté Saint-Germain aux Croûtons)

Modern kitchen equipment makes the preparation of pureed soups a breeze. If you prefer some texture, puree only part of the soup, perhaps up to half, and combine that with the chunkier soup base. Although much of the traditional rich flavor will be missing, you could eliminate the bacon if you choose to decrease the fat content.

2   slices white bread, crusts removed and cut into
      1″ cubes
1   teaspoon unsalted butter, melted
     Salt
     Pinch of cayenne pepper
1   ounce slab bacon, trimmed of all fat and diced
2   teaspoons olive oil
2   small carrots, diced
2   leeks, with a little green attached, well-washed and
      thinly sliced
1   small onion, chopped
1   clove garlic, minced
1½ cups dry split peas, well-washed and drained
5   cups White Chicken Stock (page 37) or water
     Freshly ground black pepper

231

Preheat the oven to 375°F.

Place the bread in a small bowl. Drizzle with the butter. Season with the salt and cayenne. Toss to coat. Spread in a single layer in a large nonstick ovenproof sauté pan. Bake for 3 minutes. Remove from the oven and place over medium heat. Sauté for 30 seconds, or until the cubes are crisp. Transfer to a plate.

Place the bacon in a medium saucepan and add cold water to cover by about ½″. Bring to a boil over medium heat. Drain well and pat the pieces dry. Dry the saucepan. Return the bacon to the saucepan. Add the oil.

Sauté over medium heat for 4 minutes, or until the bacon is lightly browned and crisp. Add the carrots, leeks, onions, and garlic. Sauté for 10 minutes, or until the vegetables are very soft but not colored. Stir in the split peas. Add the stock or water. Season with the salt and black pepper. Bring to a boil, then reduce the heat to medium-low. Cover and simmer for 45 minutes, or until the split peas are very soft.

Remove from the heat and allow to cool slightly.

Transfer to a blender or a food processor fitted with the metal blade. Process until very smooth.

Pour into a clean saucepan. Taste and adjust the seasoning. Bring to a simmer over medium heat.

Ladle equal portions into 4 warm shallow soup bowls. Garnish with the croutons.

YIELD: 4 SERVINGS

PER SERVING

346 CALORIES
5 G. TOTAL FAT
1 G. SATURATED FAT
7 MG. CHOLESTEROL

LIGHT VEAL STEW BLANQUETTE
(*Blanquette de Veau à l'Ancienne*)

This classic French veal stew has been lightened considerably by eliminating the usual cream and egg yolk liaison that serves as the thickening enrichment. However, it remains a delicious, filling winter meal. Serve over Parsleyed Noodles (page 194), rice, or boiled potatoes.

1½	pounds veal stew meat, trimmed of all fat and cut into 1″ cubes
	Coarse salt
1	small carrot, cut in half lengthwise
1	small onion, quartered with root intact
1	rib celery, cut in half lengthwise

½	leek, white part only, well-washed and cut in half lengthwise
1	clove garlic, crushed
2	sprigs fresh thyme
2	sprigs fresh flat-leaf parsley
1	bay leaf
¼	teaspoon paprika
	Freshly ground black pepper
4½	ounces pearl onions, peeled
½	teaspoon sugar
½	teaspoon unsalted butter
1½	tablespoons cornstarch
1½	cups 1% low-fat milk
¼	cup nonfat sour cream
2	tablespoons chopped fresh flat-leaf parsley

Rinse the veal cubes under cold running water. Place in a large saucepan and add cold water to cover by about 1″. Bring to a boil over high heat. Immediately remove from the heat and drain well. Rinse the veal under cold running water. Rinse out the saucepan.

Return the veal to the saucepan and add cold water to cover by about 1″. Season with the salt. Bring just to a simmer over medium-high heat. Do not allow the mixture to boil as it will cause released impurities and fat to be churned back into the liquid. Reduce the heat to medium-low and simmer for 5 minutes. Carefully skim off and discard any fat or foam that has risen to the surface.

Add the carrots, quartered onion, celery, leeks, garlic, thyme, parsley sprigs, bay leaf, paprika, and pepper. Bring to a simmer over medium-high heat. Reduce the heat to medium-low and allow the stew to simmer for 45 minutes, or until the veal is very tender. Taste and adjust the seasoning.

While stew is cooking, place the pearl onions in a medium nonstick sauté pan. Add the sugar and butter. Add cold water to come halfway up the sides of the onions. Season with the salt and pepper. Bring to a simmer over medium heat. Cover and simmer for 7 minutes, or until the onions are tender and the water has evaporated. (You may need to add more water to allow the onions to cook through.) Swirl the onions around the pan to allow the sugar and butter to glaze them. Set aside and keep warm.

Strain the veal mixture through a colander, reserving the cooking liquid. Transfer the veal to a plate, discarding any vegetables or herbs that stick to it.

Strain the cooking liquid through a fine sieve into a clean large saucepan. Bring to a simmer over medium heat.

(continued)

Place the cornstarch in a small bowl. Gradually whisk in the milk until smooth. Whisk into the cooking liquid and bring to a boil. When the mixture has thickened, add the reserved veal. Cook for 1 minute, or until the veal is heated through. Gently stir in the sour cream. Taste and adjust the seasoning.

Ladle equal portions into 4 warm shallow soup bowls. Garnish with the glazed onions and chopped parsley.

YIELD: 4 SERVINGS

PER SERVING

369 CALORIES
10 G. TOTAL FAT
3 G. SATURATED FAT
189 MG. CHOLESTEROL

THIN APPLE TARTS
(*Tartes Fines aux Pommes*)

Although phyllo dough will not be found in the classical French repertoire, it is a very useful baking alternative to the traditional pâte brisée, pâte sucrée, or puff pastry. It produces a crisp, tasty, low-fat dough when layered and sprinkled with sugar. This particular tart contains 80% less fat than one prepared with the traditional puff pastry.

- 2 tablespoons granulated sugar
- 4 sheets phyllo dough
- 4 tablespoons plus 2 teaspoons packed light brown sugar
- 4 medium apples, peeled, cored, quartered, and very thinly sliced
- 2 teaspoons unsalted butter, melted
- 2 tablespoons confectioners' sugar

Line a baking sheet with parchment paper. Sprinkle the paper with the granulated sugar.

Preheat the oven to 400°F.

To prevent the phyllo from drying out, make 1 tart shell at a time. Carefully place 1 phyllo sheet on a piece of parchment paper; keep the remainder covered with a damp paper towel. Using a pastry brush, lightly coat the phyllo with water. Sprinkle half of the dampened phyllo with approximately 1 teaspoon of the brown sugar. Fold the phyllo in half and brush the top with water. Sprinkle half of the folded phyllo with 1 teaspoon of the remaining brown sugar. Fold the phyllo in half. Repeat to use the 3 remaining phyllo sheets and 6 teaspoons of the remaining brown sugar.

(continued)

Thin Apple Tarts

Using a pastry cutter, carefully cut a 5″ circle from each folded phyllo. Set aside; cover with a damp paper towel to keep the dough from drying out.

Beginning at the outside edge of each tart, arrange slightly overlapping circles of the apples to completely cover the top; the center will be slightly higher than the outside edge. Lightly brush the slices with the butter. Using the remaining 2 tablespoons brown sugar, generously coat the entire top of each tart.

Place the tarts on the prepared baking sheet. Bake for 18 minutes, or until the apples are tender. Turn on the broiler. Carefully remove the parchment paper from the baking sheet, leaving the tarts on the sheet. Sprinkle each tart with confectioners' sugar and place the sheet under the broiler. Broil for 5 minutes, or until the edges of the apple slices are nicely browned. Remove from the broiler and place on a wire rack to cool slightly. Serve at room temperature.

YIELD: 4 SERVINGS

PER SERVING

282 CALORIES
3 G. TOTAL FAT
1 G. SATURATED FAT
5 MG. CHOLESTEROL

Spinach and Wild Mushroom Pockets

Seared Tuna with White Beans, Arugula, and Lemon Confit

Tangerine and Blood Orange Soup

PER SERVING

879 CALORIES

23 G. TOTAL FAT (24% OF CALORIES)

4 G. SATURATED FAT

145 MG. CHOLESTEROL

Spinach and Wild Mushroom Pockets
(Les Pochettes aux Épinards et Champignons Sauvages)

These savory treats would also make wonderful cocktail hors d'oeuvres if made in much smaller sizes. We like the flavor imparted by the small amount of butter, but you could replace it with canola oil, if you prefer.

1	ounce dried porcini mushrooms
¾	teaspoon unsalted butter, softened
10	ounces fresh spinach, washed and stems removed
	Salt and freshly ground black pepper
1	teaspoon canola oil
2	cups sliced button mushrooms
4	large oyster mushrooms, sliced
1	teaspoon minced fresh thyme
2	fresh sage leaves, minced
	Savory Pastry (page 55)
1	large red bell pepper, roasted, peeled, seeded, and finely diced
1	small egg, lightly beaten

Place the dried mushrooms in a small bowl and add very warm water to cover. Allow to soak for 20 minutes. Using a slotted spoon, lift the mushrooms from the soaking
(continued)

237

water and pat them dry; discard the water. Using a very sharp knife, cut the mushrooms into ½″ dice.

Lightly brush a large nonstick sauté pan with ¼ teaspoon of the butter. Shake excess water from the spinach and add to the pan. Season with the salt and black pepper. Cover and cook over medium heat for 2 minutes, or until the spinach has wilted. Remove from the heat and drain through a fine strainer, pressing on the spinach to extract all excess liquid.

Warm the oil and the remaining ½ teaspoon butter in a medium nonstick sauté pan over medium heat. Add the button mushrooms, oyster mushrooms, thyme, and sage. Season with the salt and black pepper. Sauté for 5 minutes, or until the mushrooms are tender and the liquid has evaporated. Stir in the porcini mushrooms and sauté for 3 minutes. Taste and adjust the seasoning. Remove from the heat.

Preheat the oven to 375°F.

Roll the pastry to ⅛″ thick. Using a 6″ round cutter, cut out 4 circles from the pastry. Spoon an equal portion of the mushroom mixture into the center of each circle, leaving about 1″ around the edge. Top each mushroom mound with an equal portion of the spinach and red peppers.

Carefully lift 1 side of the filled circle and fold it over the filling to create a half-moon shape. Gently press the edges together. Using a fork, crimp the edges together to seal in the filling. Using a pastry brush, generously coat the pastries with the egg. Place the pastries on a nonstick baking sheet.

Bake for 18 minutes, or until the pastry is crisp and golden brown. Remove from the oven and cool slightly on a wire rack. Serve warm or at room temperature.

YIELD: 4 SERVINGS

PER SERVING

274 CALORIES
12 G. TOTAL FAT
2 G. SATURATED FAT
81 MG. CHOLESTEROL

SEARED TUNA WITH WHITE BEANS, ARUGULA, AND LEMON CONFIT
(*Tournedos de Thon aux Haricots Blancs, Roquette et Confit de Citron*)

This wonderful combination of textures and flavors makes a very tasty and beautiful main course that is moderately low in fat.

1   cup dry small white beans
1   medium carrot, halved
1   medium onion, quartered with root intact
1   leek, white part only, well-washed and halved
1   rib celery, halved
3   sprigs fresh thyme

238

1   bay leaf
4   cups White Chicken Stock (page 37) or water
     Lemon Confit (page 240)
¼   cup crushed black peppercorns
4   tuna steaks (5 ounces each, ¾" thick)
1   teaspoon olive oil
2   ounces arugula, well-washed and dried

Place the beans in a large bowl and add cold water to cover by about 3". Allow to soak for at least 4 hours, changing the water several times. Rinse the beans with cold water; remove and discard any broken or discolored beans. Transfer the beans to a large saucepan.

Add the carrots, onions, leeks, celery, thyme, bay leaf, and stock or water. Bring to a boil over medium-high heat. Reduce the heat to medium and simmer for 45 minutes, or until the beans are just soft. Drain well; discard the liquid or reserve for another use. Remove and discard the herbs and vegetable pieces. Place the beans in a medium bowl and keep warm.

Drain the lemon confit, separately reserving the fruit and the liquid. Carefully blot excess oil from the lemon slices.

Spread the peppercorns out on a flat plate. Carefully coat 1 side of each tuna steak with the peppercorns, pressing down slightly so that they adhere.

Lightly brush a medium nonstick sauté pan with the oil. Place over medium-high heat until very hot but not smoking. Add 2 tuna steaks, peppered side down. Cook for 4 minutes. Turn and cook for 4 minutes, or until the fish flakes easily when tested with a fork. Remove from the pan and keep warm. Repeat with the 2 remaining steaks.

Arrange equal portions of the beans in the center of 4 warm dinner plates. Place 3 slices of lemon on each bean portion. Nestle a handful of arugula into the side of the beans. Using a sharp knife, carefully slice each tuna steak on the bias into ½" slices. Arrange the tuna on top of the beans, lemon, and arugula. Spoon a small amount of the reserved Lemon Confit liquid over the tuna.

YIELD: 4 SERVINGS

PER SERVING

439 CALORIES
10 G. TOTAL FAT
1.6 G. SATURATED FAT
64 MG. CHOLESTEROL

LEMON CONFIT
(*Confit de Citron*)

3 lemons, washed and dried
¼ cup sugar
2 tablespoons coarse salt
10 cloves garlic, sliced
2 shallots, sliced
¼ cup extra-virgin olive oil
¼ cup water

Bring a medium saucepan of water to a boil over high heat. Add the lemons and cook for 10 seconds. Drain well. Cut the lemons crosswise into ¹⁄₁₆″ slices. (This is most easily accomplished with a mandoline; see page 29.) Place in a large bowl.

Add the sugar, salt, garlic, and shallots. Toss to coat well. Add the oil and water. Toss well. Transfer to a small nonreactive container with a lid. Cover and refrigerate for at least 8 hours or up to 1 week.

YIELD: 30 SLICES

PER 2 SLICES
52 CALORIES
3.7 G. TOTAL FAT
0.5 G. SATURATED FAT
0 MG. CHOLESTEROL

TANGERINE AND BLOOD ORANGE SOUP
(*Soupe de Mandarines avec des Sanguines*)

Refreshing, with a glorious glow, this fruit soup is a sensational ending for any meal with its no-fat, no-cholesterol profile. Make sure when sectioning the tangerines and oranges to remove all membranes from the sections.

4 tangerines
4 blood oranges
2 tablespoons sugar
½ vanilla bean, split lengthwise
1½ cups fresh orange juice
4 sprigs fresh mint

Using a paring knife, remove the skin and outer membrane from the tangerines and oranges. Carefully cut out each section from the membranes, catching any juice in a small bowl as you cut. Place the citrus sections in a medium sauté pan. Sprinkle with the sugar.

Use your hands to vigorously squeeze the juice from the tangerine and orange membranes into the bowl.

Scrape the seeds from the vanilla bean into the sauté pan, then add the bean. Cook over medium-low heat for 3 minutes, or until the fruit just begins to simmer and the sugar has melted. Do not overcook. Add the juice from the bowl and the orange juice. Heat through. Remove and discard the vanilla bean.

Pour equal portions into 4 glass dessert bowls or wine glasses. Garnish each with a mint sprig. Serve warm.

YIELD: 4 SERVINGS

PER SERVING

166 CALORIES
0.5 G. TOTAL FAT
0 G. SATURATED FAT
0 MG. CHOLESTEROL

HARD-BOILED EGGS STUFFED WITH MUSHROOMS AND CHEESE

BOILED BEEF WITH WINTER VEGETABLES

APPLE FANTASY

PER SERVING
883 CALORIES
24 G. TOTAL FAT (24% OF CALORIES)
10 G. SATURATED FAT
217 MG. CHOLESTEROL

HARD-BOILED EGGS STUFFED WITH MUSHROOMS AND CHEESE
(*Oeufs Durs Farcis Chimay*)

This classic stuffed egg appetizer has been lightened by using mushrooms in place of the egg yolks in the stuffing and using 1% low-fat milk and cornstarch to make the béchamel—with only a small amount of cheese added to create the Mornay sauce.

1	teaspoon canola oil
½	teaspoon unsalted butter
2	shallots, minced
2	cups finely chopped button mushrooms
	Juice of ½ lemon
	Salt and freshly ground black pepper
1½	tablespoons cornstarch
1½	cups 1% low-fat milk
2	whole cloves
½	small onion
1	bay leaf
5	large eggs, hard-boiled and peeled
1	tablespoon minced fresh flat-leaf parsley
¼	cup shredded Gruyère cheese
	Cayenne pepper

Pinch of freshly grated nutmeg
4   leaves fresh flat-leaf parsley

Warm the oil and butter in a medium nonstick sauté pan over medium heat. Add the shallots and cook slowly for 3 minutes, or until soft but not brown. Stir in the mushrooms and lemon juice. Season with the salt and black pepper. Cover and cook, stirring frequently, for 10 minutes, or until the mushrooms are very soft and all the liquid has evaporated. Remove from the heat.

Place the cornstarch in a small saucepan. Slowly whisk in the milk until smooth. Stick the cloves in the onion and add to the saucepan. Add the bay leaf. Cook over low heat, stirring frequently, for 12 minutes, or until the mixture is very hot. Raise the heat to medium and simmer, stirring constantly, for 5 minutes, or until the sauce has thickened. Remove from the heat and push through a fine sieve into a clean saucepan.

Slice 4 of the eggs lengthwise. Carefully slice a small piece from the bottom of each egg white half so that it will stand flat and steady on a platter. Remove the yolks and reserve for another use.

Chop the remaining egg. Using a spatula, press it through a fine sieve into the pan with the mushrooms. Stir 3 tablespoons of the sauce into the mushroom mixture. Add the minced parsley. Season with the salt and black pepper. Cover and keep warm.

Place the remaining sauce over medium heat. Bring to a simmer, whisking constantly. Add about half of the Gruyère and continue to cook, whisking constantly, for 3 minutes, or until the cheese has melted. Season with the cayenne, nutmeg, and salt. Cover and keep warm.

Preheat the oven to 300°F.

Place an equal portion of the mushroom mixture in each egg-white half, mounding it slightly. Place the filled egg halves in a baking dish and cover lightly with the cheese sauce. Sprinkle the tops with the remaining Gruyère. Bake for 5 minutes. Turn on the broiler and broil for 2 minutes, or until golden brown and bubbly.

Place 2 egg halves on each of 4 warm salad plates. Spoon any excess sauce over the top. Garnish with the parsley leaves.

YIELD: 4 SERVINGS

PER SERVING

125 CALORIES
6 G. TOTAL FAT
2.5 G. SATURATED FAT
65 MG. CHOLESTEROL

BOILED BEEF WITH WINTER VEGETABLES

BOILED BEEF WITH WINTER VEGETABLES
(*Pot-au-Feu*)

Pot-au-feu is traditionally made with a richer piece of beef, often with marrow-filled bones. The high-calorie marrow is then served, as a separate course, on crisp toast. With this version, you can also serve the cooking liquid as a first course, followed by the meat and vegetables as an entrée.

1	small onion, halved
¼	teaspoon canola oil
1½	pounds beef shoulder steak, trimmed of all fat
10	cups water
1	medium carrot, chopped
1	rib celery, chopped
1	small leek, with a little green attached, well-washed and chopped
3	cloves garlic, chopped
3	sprigs fresh thyme
1	bay leaf
	Salt
2	medium carrots, sliced diagonally into ½″ slices
2	medium leeks, with a little green attached, well-washed and sliced crosswise into 2″ pieces
2	ribs celery, sliced crosswise into 2″ pieces
4	small potatoes, peeled, quartered, and trimmed into cocotte (page 31)
2	small turnips, peeled, quartered, and trimmed into cocotte (page 31)
½	cup nonfat sour cream
1	tablespoon Dijon mustard
1	tablespoon freshly grated horseradish or well-drained bottled horseradish
	Freshly ground black pepper

Place a small cast-iron or nonstick sauté pan over medium-high heat until hot. Rub the cut side of each onion half with the oil and place the onions, flat side down, in the pan. Cook for 3 minutes, or until the cut side of each onion has blackened. Remove from the heat.

(continued)

Combine the beef and water in a stockpot. Bring to a boil over medium-high heat. Reduce the heat to medium. Carefully skim off and discard any fat or foam that has risen to the surface. Add the onions, chopped carrots, chopped celery, chopped leeks, garlic, thyme, and bay leaf. Lightly season with the salt. Simmer for 2 hours.

Tie the sliced carrots, leeks, and celery in a piece of cheesecloth. Add to the stockpot. Cook for 40 to 60 minutes, or until the meat is very tender and the cooking liquid has become a clear, light amber color.

Place the potatoes and turnips in a small saucepan. Add some cooking liquid from the meat to just cover the vegetables. Bring to a boil over medium heat. Reduce the heat to medium-low and simmer for 10 minutes, or until the vegetables are tender when pierced with a knife. Remove from the heat.

In a small bowl, combine the sour cream, mustard, and horseradish. Mix well.

Remove the meat and cheesecloth packet from the cooking liquid. Strain the cooking liquid through a fine sieve into a clean saucepan; discard the solids. Taste the liquid and adjust the seasoning. Keep warm over low heat.

Cut the meat into 8 slices and fan them down the center of a serving platter. Open the cheesecloth and place the vegetables around the meat. Using a slotted spoon, transfer the potatoes and turnips to the platter. Pour some of the cooking liquid over the meat and vegetables. Serve with the sour-cream mixture on the side.

YIELD: 4 SERVINGS   PER SERVING

513 CALORIES
14 G. TOTAL FAT
5 G. SATURATED FAT
144 MG. CHOLESTEROL

APPLE FANTASY
(Fantaisie aux Pommes)

*Once you learn how to create these easy-to-make molded cookies, called tuiles,
you will want to end almost any meal with a healthy fantasy.*

¼	cup plus 1 tablespoon cake flour
¼	cup plus 2 tablespoons sugar
1	large egg white
1	tablespoon unsalted butter, melted
1	tablespoon 1% low-fat milk or water (optional)
4	large apples, peeled, cored, and cut into 1″ cubes
1	tablespoon Calvados (dry apple brandy)
¼	cup seedless raisins

Preheat the oven to 375°F.

In a medium bowl, combine ¼ cup of the cake flour and ¼ cup of the sugar. Add the egg white and butter. Mix until a thick paste has formed. If necessary, add the milk or water to facilitate blending.

Coat a nonstick baking sheet with a nonstick spray. Using a pastry brush, paint four (8″ × 2″) strips of the batter on the sheet. Bake for 7 minutes, or until the strips are lightly browned. Remove from the oven and allow to cool for 1 minute. While the strips are still warm and pliable, carefully peel them off the baking sheet and loosely wrap each around the outside of a 4-ounce ramekin or custard cup to form an open circle. Allow to cool to room temperature. Carefully remove from the ramekins and set aside.

Place the remaining 2 tablespoons sugar in a medium nonstick sauté pan over medium-high heat. Cook, stirring constantly, for 3 minutes, or until the sugar has caramelized. When a rich, amber color has developed, add the apples and toss to combine. Sauté for 5 minutes, or until the apples are well-caramelized. Remove from the heat and add the Calvados. Stir in the raisins. Cook over medium heat, stirring frequently, for 3 minutes; add a bit of water, if necessary, to prevent sticking. The apples should be tender but still hold their shapes. Remove from the heat and allow to cool slightly.

Place equal portions of the apple mixture in four (4-ounce) ramekins. Let stand for 5 minutes, then carefully unmold each onto a dessert plate. Carefully place a formed tuile around each apple compote. Serve warm.

YIELD: 4 SERVINGS

PER SERVING

245 CALORIES
3.6 G. TOTAL FAT
2 G. SATURATED FAT
8 MG. CHOLESTEROL

PROVENÇAL FISH SOUP

VEAL CUTLETS WITH CAULIFLOWER, POTATOES, AND SPLIT PEAS

CRÊPES IN ORANGE SAUCE

PROVENÇAL FISH SOUP
(*Soupe de Poisson à la Provençale*)

The flavors of the south of France literally sing in this soup.

1	bulb fennel
2½	teaspoons olive oil
1	medium onion, chopped
1	medium leek, with a little green attached, well-washed and chopped
1	rib celery, chopped
3	cloves garlic, chopped
1	pound red snapper fillets, cut into 6 pieces
8	cups Fish Stock (page 40)
4	very ripe plum tomatoes, peeled, cored, seeded, and chopped
1	tablespoon tomato paste
2	sprigs fresh thyme
1	bay leaf
	Pinch of saffron threads
	Salt and freshly ground black pepper
8	baguette slices, toasted

Remove any hard or discolored outer layers from the fennel bulb. Trim the root end and feathery tops. Cut the bulb in half lengthwise, then cut crosswise into thin slices.

Warm 2 teaspoons of the oil in a large saucepan over medium heat. Add the fennel, onions, leeks, celery, and garlic. Cook slowly for 10 minutes, or until the vegetables are tender but not colored. Stir in the snapper and sauté for 3 minutes. Add the stock, tomatoes, tomato paste, thyme, bay leaf, and saffron. Season with the salt and pepper. Bring the mixture to a boil over medium-high heat. Reduce the heat to medium-low and simmer for 40 minutes. Remove from the heat and allow to cool slightly. Remove and discard the bay leaf.

Transfer to a blender or a food processor fitted with the metal blade. Process until smooth.

Push the puree through a medium-fine sieve into a clean saucepan. Cook over low heat for 3 minutes, or until the soup is heated through. Taste and adjust the seasoning.

Brush the baguette slices with the remaining ½ teaspoon oil.

Pour equal portions of the soup into each of 4 warm shallow soup bowls. Serve with the bread on the side.

YIELD: 4 SERVINGS

PER SERVING

190 CALORIES
7 G. TOTAL FAT
1 G. SATURATED FAT
5 MG. CHOLESTEROL

VEAL CUTLETS WITH CAULIFLOWER, POTATOES, AND SPLIT PEAS
(Escalopes de Veau avec Chou-Fleur, Pommes de Terre, et Pois Cassés)

To reduce the fat content of the meat, have the butcher cut the veal cutlets from the leg and remove all visible fat. To speed preparation, you can make the split peas up to 2 days ahead and blanch the potatoes and cauliflower early in the day.

½	cup dry split peas, well-washed and drained
2	cups White Chicken Stock (page 37)
	Salt
1	teaspoon canola oil
2	teaspoons unsalted butter
4	veal cutlets (6 ounces each), trimmed of all fat
12	small red potatoes, boiled and halved
1	small head cauliflower, cored, broken into florets, and blanched (page 32)
2	tablespoons water
1	teaspoon minced garlic
1	teaspoon chopped fresh flat-leaf parsley
	Freshly ground black pepper
4	sprigs fresh flat-leaf parsley

249

Combine the split peas and stock in a medium nonstick saucepan. Bring to a boil over medium heat. Reduce the heat to medium-low and cook for 50 minutes, or until the split peas are very tender. Remove from the heat and cool slightly.

Transfer to a blender or a food processor fitted with the metal blade. Process until smooth. Season with the salt. Place in a small saucepan. Cover and keep warm.

Warm the oil and 1 teaspoon of the butter in a large nonstick sauté pan over medium-high heat. Add the veal and cook for 4 minutes per side, or until cooked through. Transfer to a plate, cover, and keep warm.

Melt the remaining 1 teaspoon butter in the same sauté pan over medium heat. Add the potatoes, cauliflower, water, garlic, and chopped parsley. Sauté for 3 minutes. Season with the salt and pepper.

Place an equal portion of the split-pea puree in the center of each of 4 warm dinner plates. Place a cutlet on top of the puree and arrange the cauliflower mixture around the puree. Garnish with a parsley sprig.

YIELD: 4 SERVINGS

PER SERVING

476 CALORIES
12 G. TOTAL FAT
4 G. SATURATED FAT
158 MG. CHOLESTEROL

CRÊPES IN ORANGE SAUCE
(Crêpes Façon Suzette)

This classic French dessert has been lightened with a fresh orange sauce that replaces the usual orange butter. If you have a copper chafing dish, the flambé can be done dramatically at the table for a very exciting end to a low-fat meal.

1	large orange
2	tablespoons grenadine
5	ounces fresh orange juice
5	ounces frozen orange juice concentrate
1	tablespoon orange jam or apricot jam
½	cup 1% low-fat milk
¼	cup sugar
1	large egg white
	Pinch of salt
1	tablespoon plus 1 teaspoon unsalted butter, melted
½	cup cake flour
1	tablespoon cognac

Remove the zest from the orange in long, thin strips and place in a small saucepan. Add cold water to cover by about ½". Reserve the orange for another use.

Bring the water to a boil over medium heat. Reduce the heat to medium-low and simmer for 2 minutes, or until the zest has barely softened. Remove from the heat and drain well.

Return the zest to the saucepan. Add the grenadine. Simmer over medium-low heat for 5 minutes. Using a slotted spoon, remove the zest from the saucepan and place the pieces, without touching, on a sheet of parchment paper.

Rinse out the saucepan. Add the orange juice and orange juice concentrate. Bring to a boil over medium-high heat, stirring frequently. Cook for 5 minutes, or until the liquid is reduced by half. Remove from the heat and whisk in the jam.

In a medium bowl, combine the milk, sugar, egg white, salt, and 1 tablespoon of the butter. Whisk well. Whisk in the flour until smooth.

Lightly coat a nonstick crêpe pan with nonstick spray. Place over medium heat. When very hot, pour about 2 tablespoons of the batter into the pan and swirl it around to lightly and evenly coat the bottom. Cook for 30 seconds, or until the bottom is just set. Flip the crêpe by gently lifting 1 side with a knife or fork and then quickly and carefully turning it. Cook for 30 seconds, or until the crêpe just starts to brown. Transfer to a plate. Continue making crêpes until all of the batter has been used. You should have 8 crêpes.

(continued)

Pour the orange sauce into a large sauté pan. Warm over medium heat. Do not allow the sauce to boil. One at a time, dip the crêpes into the hot sauce to just coat; fold each crêpe in half and then into quarters. Place to the side of the pan as you complete the folds. When all of the crêpes are in the pan, add the cognac. Remove the pan from the heat and carefully ignite the cognac with a long match.

When the flame has died out, lift 2 crêpes onto each of 4 warm dessert plates. Pour an equal portion of the sauce on the top and garnish with an equal portion of the reserved zest.

YIELD: 4 SERVINGS

PER SERVING

241 CALORIES
2 G. TOTAL FAT
1 G. SATURATED FAT
5 MG. CHOLESTEROL

LENTIL SOUP WITH DICED CARROTS

SMALL BEEF TENDERLOIN WITH SAUTÉED ENDIVES

BLUEBERRY-LEMON SORBET

<u>PER SERVING</u>

640 CALORIES

18 G. TOTAL FAT (25% OF CALORIES)

6 G. SATURATED FAT

86 MG. CHOLESTEROL

LENTIL SOUP WITH DICED CARROTS
(Soupe de Lentilles aux Carottes)

Lentil soup is one of the world's great comfort foods—and it is so good for you. The bright orange carrots and the lively chive garnish add great style to this low-calorie starter.

1   tablespoon olive oil
1   small onion, finely chopped
1   rib celery, finely chopped
1   pound dry green lentils, well-rinsed and drained
8   cups White Chicken Stock (page 37)
    Salt and freshly ground black pepper
3   medium carrots, cut into small dice
1   clove garlic, minced
1   small bunch fresh chives, chopped

Warm the oil in a large saucepan over medium heat. Add the onions and celery. Cook for 10 minutes, or until the vegetables are tender but have not browned. Add the lentils and stock. Season with the salt and pepper. Bring to a boil.

Reduce the heat to medium-low. Simmer for 1¼ hours, or until the lentils are very soft. Add the carrots and garlic. Cook for 30 minutes. Taste and adjust the seasoning.

(continued)

Ladle 1-cup portions into each of 4 warm shallow soup bowls (reserve the remainder for another use). Sprinkle the chives over the top.

YIELD: 8 SERVINGS

SMALL BEEF TENDERLOIN WITH SAUTÉED ENDIVES
(*Mignonette de Boeuf aux Endives Meunière*)

This tenderloin of beef dish is a fantastic dinner-party entrée with the meltingly sweet endives and rustic mushroom garnish.

1½	teaspoons unsalted butter
1½	teaspoons canola oil
8	Belgian endives, well-washed, cored, and cut in half lengthwise
	Salt and freshly ground black pepper
2	shallots, minced
½	cup dry white wine
1	cup Brown Veal Stock (page 34)
4	beef tenderloins (4 ounces each), trimmed of all fat
2	cups sliced button mushrooms
1	clove garlic, minced
2	tablespoons chopped fresh flat-leaf parsley

Warm 1 teaspoon of the butter and 1 teaspoon of the oil in a large nonstick sauté pan over medium-low heat. Add the endives in a single layer. Season with the salt and pepper. Cover and cook for 15 minutes. Turn and cook, covered, for 10 minutes. Using a slotted spoon, remove the endives from the pan. Place on a plate, cover, and keep warm.

Return the sauté pan to medium heat. Add the shallots and the remaining ½ teaspoon butter. Sauté for 4 minutes, or until the shallots are soft and transparent. Add the wine and bring to a boil. Boil for 5 minutes, or until the wine is reduced by half. Add the stock and boil for 5 minutes, or until the liquid is reduced by one-third. Remove from the heat and keep warm.

Season the tenderloins with the salt and pepper. Lightly brush a medium nonstick sauté pan with the remaining ½ teaspoon oil. Place over medium-high heat until very hot but not smoking. Add the tenderloins. Cook for 3 minutes. Turn and cook for 3 minutes for medium-rare. Place the meat on a plate, cover, and keep warm.

Return the pan to medium heat. Add the mushrooms and season with the salt and pepper. Sauté for 5 minutes, or until the mushrooms have released all of their moisture. Add the garlic and sauté for 30 seconds. Toss in the parsley.

Place a tenderloin in the center of each of 4 warm dinner plates. Arrange equal portions of endive around each tenderloin. Spoon the sauce over the tenderloins and then top with an equal portion of the mushrooms.

YIELD: 4 SERVINGS

PER SERVING
279 CALORIES
14 G. TOTAL FAT
5 G. SATURATED FAT
76 MG. CHOLESTEROL

BLUEBERRY-LEMON SORBET (PAGE 256)

BLUEBERRY-LEMON SORBET
(Sorbet Citronné aux Myrtilles)

Blueberries retain much of their flavor when frozen. They are, therefore, terrific to keep on hand for a fat-free taste of summer in the middle of winter. Serve the sorbet in sparkling glass dishes with a garnish of mint or a touch of cassis (black-currant liqueur), if desired.

2	cups frozen blueberries
¾	cup sugar
2	teaspoons fresh lemon juice
1	teaspoon grated lemon zest
4	cups lemon-flavored seltzer or lemon-lime soda

In a blender or a food processor fitted with the metal blade, combine the blueberries, sugar, lemon juice, and lemon zest. Process until well-blended. Add 2 cups of the seltzer or soda and process until smooth. Add the remaining seltzer or soda and stir to combine.

Pour into the container of an ice cream machine. Process according to the manufacturer's directions.

YIELD: 6 SERVINGS

PER SERVING

100 CALORIES
0.2 G. TOTAL FAT
0 G. SATURATED FAT
0 MG. CHOLESTEROL

SPINACH SOUFFLÉS

MOROCCAN-STYLE BRAISED LAMB OVER COUSCOUS

POACHED TANGERINES AND ORANGES

<u>PER SERVING</u>

958 CALORIES

16 G. TOTAL FAT (15% OF CALORIES)

5 G. SATURATED FAT

123 MG. CHOLESTEROL

SPINACH SOUFFLÉS
(Soufflés aux Épinards)

These light soufflés are almost fat-free. They're a perfect first course to precede a heavier entrée. When prepared in an 8-ounce ramekin, they're a delightful lunch entrée served with a salad, crisp bread, and a glass of white wine.

½	cup freshly made dry bread crumbs
½	teaspoon butter, melted
5	ounces fresh spinach, washed and stems removed
	Salt and freshly ground black pepper
1½	tablespoons cornstarch
1⅓	cups 1% low-fat milk
¼	cup shredded Gruyère cheese
	Pinch of freshly grated nutmeg
3	large egg whites
	Pinch of cayenne pepper

Coat eight (4-ounce) ramekins with nonstick spray. Sprinkle the bread crumbs into each and coat, shaking out any excess. Place the ramekins on a baking sheet.

Brush a medium nonstick sauté pan with the butter. Shake excess water from the spinach and add to the pan. Season with the salt and black pepper. Cover and cook over medium heat for 2 minutes, or until the spinach has wilted. Remove from the heat and drain through a fine strainer, pressing on the spinach to extract excess liquid.

(continued)

Transfer the spinach to a blender or a food processor fitted with the metal blade. Process until well-pureed. Transfer to a large bowl.

Preheat the oven to 400°F.

Place the cornstarch in a small saucepan. Gradually whisk in the milk until smooth. Bring to a boil over medium heat, whisking frequently. Reduce the heat to medium-low and, whisking frequently, cook for 3 minutes, or until very thick. Whisk in the Gruyère. Add to the bowl with the spinach and mix well. Season with the salt and nutmeg.

Place the egg whites in a medium bowl. Beat with an electric mixer on medium speed until firm peaks form. Beat in one-quarter of the spinach mixture. When well-blended, use a rubber spatula to carefully fold in the remaining spinach mixture.

Pour equal portions of the mixture into the prepared ramekins to fill approximately three-quarters full.

Reduce the oven heat to 375°F. Bake for 20 minutes, or until the center is firm when a ramekin is lightly tapped and the top is well-browned.

YIELD: 8 SERVINGS

PER SERVING

74 CALORIES
2 G. TOTAL FAT
1 G. SATURATED FAT
6 MG. CHOLESTEROL

MOROCCAN-STYLE BRAISED LAMB OVER COUSCOUS
(*Agneau Braisé aux Épices Marocaines avec Couscous*)

Aromatic flavors sing of the warmth and fantasy of Africa. Plus, the combination of lean lamb and couscous offers a complete meal with zesty taste.

2½	teaspoons olive oil
1	pound very lean leg of lamb, cut into 1″ cubes
	Salt and freshly ground black pepper
2	medium carrots, chopped
2	ribs celery, chopped
1	medium onion, chopped
2	teaspoons grated fresh ginger
1	tablespoon ground coriander
2	teaspoons ground cumin
1	teaspoon ground cardamom
¼	teaspoon ground cloves
2	bay leaves
1	stick cinnamon
½	cup dry white wine

1   cup chopped dates
1   cup chopped dried apricots
1   medium carrot, cut into ¼″ dice
1   small onion, cut into ¼″ dice
1   red bell pepper, seeded and cut into ¼″ dice
2   teaspoons ground turmeric
    Pinch of saffron threads
1   cup White Chicken Stock (page 37)
2   teaspoons dried currants
1½ cups medium-grain couscous
2   tablespoons all-purpose flour
¼   cup water
2   tablespoons chopped fresh flat-leaf parsley

Warm 2 teaspoons of the oil in a large nonstick sauté pan over medium-high heat. When hot, add no more than half of the lamb and sear for 3 minutes, or until the lamb has evenly browned on all sides. Do not crowd the pan or scorch the meat. Using a slotted spoon, transfer the lamb to a plate. Continue searing until all of the meat has been browned. Season with the salt and black pepper.

In the same sauté pan over medium heat, cook the chopped carrots, celery, and chopped onions for 5 minutes, or until the vegetables are very soft. Stir in the ginger, coriander, cumin, cardamom, cloves, bay leaves, and cinnamon. Add the wine and deglaze the pan, stirring constantly with a wooden spoon to remove all of the browned bits from the bottom.

Stir in the dates and apricots. Bring to a boil over medium-high heat. Reduce the heat to medium and simmer for 5 minutes. Add the lamb, along with any juices that have accumulated on the plate. Add enough cold water to just cover the lamb. Cover and simmer for 1¼ hours, or until the lamb is very tender.

Warm the remaining ½ teaspoon oil in a large saucepan over medium heat. Add the diced carrots, diced onions, and red peppers. Allow them to cook very slowly for 5 minutes. Do not brown. Stir in the turmeric and saffron. Add the stock and currants. Bring to a boil.

Remove the saucepan from the heat. Stir in the couscous. Cover and let stand for 10 minutes. Fluff with a fork. Taste and adjust the seasoning.

Using a slotted spoon, remove the lamb from the cooking liquid. Strain the liquid through a fine sieve into a clean saucepan. Bring to a boil over medium-high heat. Reduce the heat to medium and simmer for 10 minutes, or until the liquid has reduced by half.

Place the flour in a small bowl. Whisk in the ¼ cup water until smooth. Whisk into the saucepan. Cook, whisking constantly, for 3 minutes, or until the sauce is smooth and thick. Add the lamb to the saucepan. Taste and adjust the seasoning.

(continued)

259

Mound the couscous in the center of a large serving plate. Top with the lamb and sprinkle the chopped parsley over all. Drizzle the sauce around the edge and over the couscous.

YIELD: 4 SERVINGS

PER SERVING

699 CALORIES
14 G. TOTAL FAT
4 G. SATURATED FAT
117 MG. CHOLESTEROL

POACHED TANGERINES AND ORANGES
(*Mandarines et Oranges Pochées au Grand Marnier*)

Poached tangerines and oranges are a refreshing, fat-free end to a rich meal. The recipe can be made in advance and refrigerated for up to three days. Serve at room temperature for the best flavor.

3	large navel oranges
3	large tangerines
⅓	cup packed light brown sugar
⅓	cup water
4	whole cloves
2	tablespoons Grand Marnier
1	tablespoon sliced crystallized ginger
4	sprigs fresh mint

Using a paring knife, remove all the peel and outer membrane from the oranges and tangerines. Cut the fruit crosswise into ¼" slices. Carefully remove any seeds.

Place the slices in a large nonstick sauté pan. Add the brown sugar, water, and cloves. Cover and bring to a boil over medium heat. Reduce the heat and simmer for 2 minutes. Using a slotted spoon, remove the citrus slices from the liquid and place them in a large bowl.

Add the Grand Marnier to the sauté pan. Bring to a boil over high heat. Reduce the heat to medium and simmer for 5 minutes, or until the liquid is reduced and syrupy. Pour the syrup over the citrus slices. Cover and cool to room temperature. Refrigerate until needed. Before serving, remove and discard the cloves.

Place equal portions in each of 4 dessert bowls. Sprinkle with the ginger and tuck a mint sprig in the center of each bowl. Serve at room temperature.

YIELD: 4 SERVINGS

PER SERVING

185 CALORIES
0.2 G. TOTAL FAT
0 G. SATURATED FAT
0 MG. CHOLESTEROL

POACHED TANGERINES AND ORANGES

MENUS FOR EASY ENTERTAINING

THROUGHOUT THE YEAR, THERE WILL BE TIMES WHEN WE

NEED TO TOAST OUR DISCIPLINE AND SELF-CONTROL AT THE

TABLE. HOLIDAYS AND SPECIAL OCCASIONS ALWAYS CALL FOR

A BIT OF EXCITEMENT, IN THE FOOD AND DRINK WE SHARE

AND IN THE ATMOSPHERE THAT SURROUNDS US. WITH THIS

IN MIND, WE HAVE CREATED FIVE SPECIAL-OCCASION MENUS

THAT ALLOW FOR A BIT OF CELEBRATION—A FEW MORE CALO-

RIES, A LITTLE EXTRA FAT, AND A TRACE MORE CHOLESTEROL.

THESE ARE NOT EVERYDAY MEALS, ALTHOUGH SOME OF THE

RECIPES ARE EASY TO MAKE AND LIGHT TO EAT. INSTEAD,

THEY'RE GALA MEALS SHAPED TO MAKE YOU FEEL THAT EACH

SPECIAL OCCASION IS TRULY A TIME TO COMMEMORATE YOUR

GOOD HEALTH!

Backyard Barbecue

Seafood Marmite

Grilled Butterflied Leg of Lamb

Grilled Tomatoes

Grilled Radicchio

Warm French Potato Salad

Gingered Fresh Fruit Salad

PER SERVING

804 CALORIES

23 G. TOTAL FAT (26% OF CALORIES)

5 G. SATURATED FAT

141 MG. CHOLESTEROL

Seafood Marmite
(Marmite au Pêcheur)

This light but filling seafood stew could easily serve as the main course for a summer luncheon or supper. Quick to prepare, it can be doubled to allow for large entrée portions.

24	fresh mussels
2	tablespoons olive oil
3	leeks, with a little green attached, well-washed and thinly sliced crosswise
3	ribs celery, thinly sliced
3	shallots, and thinly sliced
3	cloves garlic, minced
4	plum tomatoes, peeled, cored, seeded, and chopped
4	cups Fish Stock (page 40)
2	cups dry white wine

12 fresh cherrystone clams, well-scrubbed

24 fresh littleneck clams, well-scrubbed

12 large shrimp, peeled and deveined

12 large scallops

Salt and freshly ground white pepper

½ cup fresh basil cut into chiffonade (page 31)

SEAFOOD MARMITE

Squeeze each mussel in the palm of your hand and discard any whose shells open. Scrub the remaining mussels to remove grit; cut off the beards. Wash in 3 changes of cold water. Set aside.

Warm the oil in a large saucepan over medium-high heat. Add the leeks and celery. Sauté for 7 minutes, or until the vegetables are very soft but not browned. Add the shallots and garlic. Cook for 1 minute. Add the tomatoes and cook for 2 minutes.

Add the stock and wine. Bring to a boil. Reduce the heat to medium-low and simmer for 5 minutes. Add the cherrystone clams. Cover and simmer for 3 minutes. Add the littleneck clams and mussels. Cover and simmer for 3 minutes. Stir in the shrimp and scallops. Cover and simmer for 3 minutes, or until the shrimp and scallops are opaque and the clams and mussels are opened. Discard any clams or mussels that do not open. Taste and adjust the seasoning with the salt and pepper.

Spoon equal portions into each of 12 shallow soup bowls. Garnish with the basil.

YIELD: 12 SERVINGS

PER SERVING

161 CALORIES
4 G. TOTAL FAT
0.4 G. SATURATED FAT
23 MG. CHOLESTEROL

GRILLED BUTTERFLIED LEG OF LAMB
(*Gigot d'Agneau Grillé en Papillon*)

The south of France comes alive in the flavors of this grilled lamb.

2   tablespoons minced fresh thyme
2   tablespoons minced fresh rosemary
2   cloves garlic, minced
2   tablespoons Dijon mustard
2   tablespoons red wine vinegar
1   tablespoon olive oil
    Freshly ground black pepper
1   leg of lamb (4 pounds), butterflied and trimmed
        of all fat
    Coarse salt

In a small bowl, combine the thyme, rosemary, garlic, mustard, vinegar, and oil. Generously season with the pepper. Rub the herb marinade over the lamb. Place the lamb in a large shallow container just large enough to hold it. Pour any remaining marinade over the top. Cover and refrigerate for at least 8 hours.

Adjust the rack of the grill so that it is at least 10″ above the heat source. Preheat the grill to medium.

Remove the lamb from the refrigerator. Uncover and generously season with the salt. Place the lamb on the grill. Cover and grill for 15 minutes. Turn the lamb. Cover and grill for 15 minutes more.

Reduce the heat and continue grilling to the desired doneness (about 10 additional minutes for rare; 15 to 20 minutes for medium). Throughout the grilling period, periodically check the lamb to make sure that it is cooking slowly and not charring. If it does begin to burn, move the lamb away from the greatest heat.

Place the lamb on a carving board or serving platter. Let stand for 10 minutes. Cut across the grain into thin slices. Serve warm or at room temperature.

YIELD: 12 SERVINGS

PER SERVING

271 CALORIES
12 G. TOTAL FAT
4 G. SATURATED FAT
118 MG. CHOLESTEROL

GRILLED TOMATOES (PAGE 268)

GRILLED TOMATOES
(*Tomates Grillées*)

This is a super and low-fat way to prepare summer's ripest, sweetest tomatoes. You may want to grill extras for use in sandwiches and salads.

6   large ripe tomatoes
2   teaspoons olive oil
    Salt and freshly ground black pepper

Preheat the grill to high.

Halve the tomatoes crosswise. Gently squeeze each half to remove the seeds. Lightly brush the tomatoes with the oil. Place, cut side down, on the hottest part of the grill. Grill for 1 minute. Turn the tomatoes and move to the edge of the grill or to wherever the heat is the least hot. Grill for 3 minutes, or until charred. Remove from the grill and season with the salt and pepper. Serve warm or at room temperature.

YIELD: 12 SERVINGS

PER SERVING
20 CALORIES
1 G. TOTAL FAT
0.1 G. SATURATED FAT
0 MG. CHOLESTEROL

GRILLED RADICCHIO
(*Salade de Trévise Grillée*)

If radicchio is a bit bitter for your taste, blanch it in lightly salted water for 1 minute. Drain well and then grill for a richer, sweeter taste.

3   heads radicchio
1   tablespoon olive oil
    Salt and freshly ground black pepper

Preheat the grill to low.

Remove any damaged outer leaves from the radicchio. Trim the stem and quarter the radicchio lengthwise, leaving the core intact. Lightly brush with the oil and season with the salt and pepper. Place on the grill. Grill for 8 minutes, or until tender and lightly browned. Serve warm or at room temperature.

YIELD: 12 SERVINGS

PER SERVING
16 CALORIES
1 G. TOTAL FAT
0.2 G. SATURATED FAT
0 MG. CHOLESTEROL

WARM FRENCH POTATO SALAD
(*Salade de Pommes de Terre Tièdes*)

In this recipe, it is important that the potatoes be hot when the dressing is added because this will allow the potatoes to absorb more of the dressing's flavor. The potatoes can be cooked in a combination of white wine and stock for a more aromatic taste.

20	ounces red new potatoes
	Salt
¼	cup dry white wine
2	tablespoons sherry vinegar
1	tablespoon olive oil
1	teaspoon Dijon mustard
2	shallots, minced
2	tablespoons minced fresh flat-leaf parsley
	Freshly ground black pepper

Place the potatoes in a large saucepan and add cold water to cover by about 1". Add a pinch of salt. Bring to a boil over high heat. Reduce the heat to medium and cook for 15 minutes, or until the potatoes are just tender when pierced with a fork. Drain.

In a small bowl, whisk together the wine, vinegar, oil, and mustard. Stir in the shallots and parsley. Season with the salt and pepper.

Cut the hot potatoes into eighths. Place them in a large bowl and pour the dressing over the top. Toss to combine. Let stand for 3 minutes, then toss again. Taste and adjust the seasoning. Serve warm.

YIELD: 12 SERVINGS

PER SERVING

171 CALORIES
4 G. TOTAL FAT
0.5 G. SATURATED FAT
0 MG. CHOLESTEROL

GINGERED FRESH FRUIT SALAD
(*Salade de Fruits Frais au Gingembre*)

Refreshing and nearly fat-free, this dish is the perfect ending to a summer cookout. Make the salad early in the day so that the ginger can subtly permeate the ripe fruit.

6	plums, peeled, pitted, and sliced
3	peaches, peeled, pitted, and sliced
3	oranges, peeled and sectioned
2	kiwifruit, peeled and sliced
1	cantaloupe, peeled, seeded, and cut into cubes
1	honeydew, peeled, seeded, and cut into cubes
½	small watermelon, peeled, seeded, and cut into cubes
1	pint fresh blueberries
1	pint fresh strawberries, hulled and sliced
	Juice of 1 lemon
¾	cup water
½	cup sugar
2	teaspoons grated fresh ginger

In a large bowl, combine the plums, peaches, oranges, kiwifruit, cantaloupe, honeydew, watermelon, blueberries, and strawberries. Add the lemon juice and toss to combine.

Combine the water and sugar in a small saucepan. Bring to a boil over high heat. Reduce the heat to medium-low and simmer for 3 minutes. Remove from the heat and add the ginger. Let stand for 3 minutes. Pour over the fruit and stir gently to combine. Serve immediately or cover and refrigerate until ready to serve.

YIELD: 12 SERVINGS

PER SERVING

165 CALORIES
1 G. TOTAL FAT
0 G. SATURATED FAT
0 MG. CHOLESTEROL

Autumn Evening with Friends

Fava Bean and Goat Cheese Salad

Wild Mushroom and Rice Cake

Roasted Turkey with Sweet Potatoes and Kale

Apple, Pear, and Cranberry Gratin

PER SERVING

1,004 CALORIES

24 G. TOTAL FAT (22% OF CALORIES)

10 G. SATURATED FAT

152 MG. CHOLESTEROL

Fava Bean and Goat Cheese Salad
(*Salade de Fèves au Fromage de Chèvre*)

Very popular in Mediterranean cooking, fava beans can be purchased fresh, dried, or canned. The fresh beans have a very tough outer skin that must be removed by blanching. When purchasing fresh beans, choose pods that are crisp and not bursting with large beans because large beans indicate old pods.

2	pounds fresh fava beans
	Salt
5	ounces fresh goat cheese, crumbled
5	cups frisée lettuce
¾	cup Citrus Vinaigrette (page 52)
	Freshly ground black pepper
2	heads radicchio or red leaf lettuce, cut into julienne (page 32)
2	tablespoons chopped fresh chives

FAVA BEAN AND GOAT CHEESE SALAD (PAGE 271)

Remove the fava beans from their pods. Bring a medium saucepan of water to a boil over high heat. Add a pinch of salt. Add the beans and cook for 2 minutes. Drain. Using your fingertips, push the tough outer skin from each bean.

Place the beans in a large bowl. Add the goat cheese and frisée. Gently toss to combine. Drizzle ½ cup of the vinaigrette over the salad and season with the salt and pepper. Toss to combine.

Place the radicchio or red lettuce in a medium bowl. Drizzle with the remaining ¼ cup vinaigrette and season with the salt and pepper. Toss to combine.

Place equal portions of the radicchio or red lettuce on each of 10 chilled salad plates. Top with the bean salad. Sprinkle with the chives.

YIELD: 10 SERVINGS

PER SERVING

110 CALORIES
6 G. TOTAL FAT
3 G. SATURATED FAT
11 MG. CHOLESTEROL

272

WILD MUSHROOM AND RICE CAKE
(*Gâteau de Riz aux Champignons des Bois*)

This deliciously rich rice cake could serve as a luncheon or light supper entrée when served with a crisp salad, warm bread, and a glass of great Pinot Noir. Use a mixture of mushrooms, such as button, porcini, portobello, and shiitake.

2	teaspoons unsalted butter
1	small onion, finely chopped
1½	cups long-grain white rice
4	cups White Chicken Stock (page 37)
2	sprigs fresh thyme
1	bay leaf
	Salt
1	tablespoon plus ½ teaspoon olive oil
1½	pounds mixed mushrooms, brushed clean and sliced
1	large shallot, minced
1	clove garlic, minced
½	teaspoon minced fresh oregano
½	teaspoon minced fresh thyme
½	teaspoon minced fresh rosemary
	Freshly ground black pepper
¾	cup shredded Gruyère cheese
1	tablespoon chopped fresh flat-leaf parsley
2	cups Mushroom Sauce (page 44)

Bring 6 cups water to a boil.

Melt the butter in a medium nonstick saucepan over medium heat. Add the onions and cook slowly for 5 minutes. Do not brown. Stir in the rice. Add the stock, thyme sprig, and bay leaf. Season with the salt. Bring to a boil. Reduce the heat to medium-low, cover, and simmer for 20 minutes, or until all of the liquid has been absorbed. Remove and discard the bay leaf and thyme sprig. Transfer the rice to a large bowl.

While the rice is cooking, warm 1 tablespoon of the oil in a large nonstick sauté pan over medium-high heat. Add the mushrooms and cook, tossing frequently, for 9 minutes, or until all of the moisture has evaporated. Add the shallots and garlic. Sauté for 2 minutes. Stir in the oregano, minced thyme, and rosemary. Season with the salt and pepper. Add to the bowl with the rice and toss to combine.

Preheat the oven to 375°F.

(continued)

Lightly brush a 12″ gratin dish with the remaining ½ teaspoon oil. Cut 1 piece of parchment paper to fit neatly in the bottom of the dish and another to fit the top. Place the bottom piece in the dish.

Add the Gruyère to the mushroom mixture. Season with the salt and pepper. Toss to combine. Transfer to the gratin dish and spread evenly. Cover with the remaining piece of parchment. Cover tightly with foil.

Place the dish in a larger baking dish or roasting pan. Add boiling water to come halfway up the sides of the gratin dish. Bake for 20 minutes.

Remove the pan from the oven. Carefully lift out the gratin dish. Remove and discard the foil and top parchment paper. Set the dish on a wire rack to cool for 10 minutes.

Carefully run a knife around the inside of the dish to loosen the rice cake from the sides. Place a warm large plate over the top and invert the dish onto it, unmolding the cake. Sprinkle with the parsley and spoon the mushroom sauce around the cake, serving any extra sauce on the side.

YIELD: 10 SERVINGS

PER SERVING

203 CALORIES
6 G. TOTAL FAT
3 G. SATURATED FAT
16 MG. CHOLESTEROL

ROASTED TURKEY WITH SWEET POTATOES AND KALE
(*Dinde Rôtie aux Pommes Douces et Choux Frisés*)

Here's a zesty, flavorful entrée for special occasions or holidays. You'll need to start the turkey a day ahead, allowing it to marinate in the refrigerator.

1	turkey (10 pounds), trimmed of all fat and extra skin
2	tablespoons olive oil
4	sprigs fresh thyme, chopped
2	bay leaves, chopped
	Salt and freshly ground black pepper
4	whole cloves
1	medium onion, quartered
1	lemon
2	cups Brown Chicken Stock (page 36)
1½	tablespoons cornstarch (optional)
¼	cup sherry (optional)

10   medium sweet potatoes
1   tablespoon unsalted butter
2   large bunches kale, washed

Wash the turkey, inside and out, with cold running water. Pat dry. Place in a large baking dish.

In a cup, combine 1½ teaspoons of the oil, half of the thyme, and half of the bay leaves. Mix well. Brush over the turkey skin and in the cavity. Cover and refrigerate for at least 12 hours.

Preheat the oven to 400°F.

Remove the turkey from the refrigerator. Generously season, inside and out, with the salt and pepper. Stick a clove into each onion quarter and place in the turkey cavity; add the lemon. Place in a medium nonstick roasting pan. Tuck the wing tips under. Tie the legs together with butcher's twine. Chop the neck; add to the pan.

In a cup, combine 1½ teaspoons of the remaining oil, the remaining thyme, and the remaining bay leaves. Lightly brush over the turkey. Roast for 1 hour, basting with the oil mixture every 20 minutes.

Reduce the heat to 325°F and roast, basting frequently, for 1¾ hours, or until an instant-read thermometer inserted in the center of a breast registers 170°F.

Turn off the oven and allow the turkey to remain in the hot oven for 15 minutes. Remove the turkey from the oven and transfer it to a warm platter. Cover lightly and let stand for 10 minutes.

Drain the liquid from the roasting pan through a fine sieve into a medium bowl; return the solids from the sieve to the roasting pan. Remove and discard the fat from the liquid in the bowl. Pour the defatted liquid into the roasting pan. Add the stock and bring to a boil over high heat. Boil for 3 minutes.

If you desire a thicker gravy, place the cornstarch in a cup. Add the sherry and stir until smooth. Add to the roasting pan and whisk for 1 minute. Season with the salt and pepper. Strain through a fine sieve into a small bowl.

During the last 1½ hours of turkey roasting, prepare the vegetables.

Using a dinner fork, randomly prick the sweet potatoes. Place in the oven and roast for 1¼ hours, or until very soft when gently squeezed. Remove the sweet potatoes from the oven and let cool slightly. Cut in half and scoop the pulp into a medium bowl. Add the butter and season with the salt and pepper. Gently mash until well-blended.

Bring a large saucepan of water to a boil and add a pinch of salt. Add the kale and cook for 3 minutes. Drain well and place in a bowl. Drizzle with the remaining 1 tablespoon oil. Season with the salt and pepper. Toss to coat.

Carve the turkey, discarding the skin.

(continued)

Place equal portions of sweet potatoes in the center of each dinner plate, spreading them out to make an even circle. Place an equal portion of kale over the top. Place 3 slices of white meat and 2 slices of dark meat on each plate. Drizzle gravy over the turkey.

YIELD: 10 SERVINGS

PER SERVING
440 CALORIES
9 G. TOTAL FAT
3 G. SATURATED FAT
124 MG. CHOLESTEROL

APPLE, PEAR, AND CRANBERRY GRATIN
(*Gratin aux Pommes, Poires, et Airelles*)

Autumn's best fruits combine to make a very hearty dessert with little fat. It's extra delicious with a dollop of nonfat vanilla yogurt.

1	large orange
4	cups water
1½	cups granulated sugar
1	teaspoon unsalted butter
1	large lemon
6	Granny Smith apples, peeled, cored, and cut into large chunks
6	pears, peeled, cored, and cut into large chunks
2	cups fresh cranberries
6	medium biscotti
½	cup packed light brown sugar

Remove the zest from the orange in long, thin strips and place in a large non-stick saucepan. Remove and discard the outer white pith from the orange. Section the orange, removing the membranes between sections. Set the sections aside.

Add the water, granulated sugar, and butter to the saucepan. Remove the zest from the lemon in long, thin strips. Add to the pan. Reserve the lemon for another use. Bring to a boil over high heat. Reduce the heat to medium and simmer for 3 minutes.

Add the apples and simmer for 8 minutes, or until the apples are tender but still firm. Using a slotted spoon, lift the apples from the syrup and transfer to large bowl.

Add the pears to the simmering syrup and cook for 4 minutes, or until the pears are tender but still firm. Using a slotted spoon, lift the pears from the syrup and add to the apples.

Remove the syrup from the heat. Using a slotted spoon, remove half of the orange zest from the syrup. Using a sharp knife, finely chop it. Transfer to a medium non-stick sauté pan.

Measure ⅓ cup of the syrup and add to a sauté pan. Add the cranberries. Bring to a boil over medium-high heat. Reduce the heat to medium and simmer for 2 minutes, or until the berries pop. Remove from the heat.

Lightly coat an 11″ × 7″ baking dish with butter or nonstick spray. Evenly spread the apple mixture in the dish. Spoon the cranberry mixture over the top.

Preheat the broiler.

Place the biscotti and brown sugar in a blender or a food processor fitted with the metal blade. Process until finely ground. Evenly sprinkle over the fruit. Broil for 3 minutes, or until golden. Serve warm, garnished with the reserved orange sections.

YIELD: 10 SERVINGS

PER SERVING

251 CALORIES
3 G. TOTAL FAT
1 G. SATURATED FAT
1 MG. CHOLESTEROL

Cocktail Party

Eggplant Caviar

Tuna Tapenade

Herb-Marinated Goat Cheese

Red Snapper Canapés

Cucumber, Shrimp, and Radish Canapés

Salmon Canapés

Chicken Pâté with Tarragon

White Bean Dip

PER SERVING

502 CALORIES

19 G. TOTAL FAT (34% OF CALORIES)

4 G. SATURATED FAT

76 MG. CHOLESTEROL

Eggplant Caviar
(Caviar d'Aubergines)

This delicious no-cholesterol dish has its origins in the Middle Eastern baba ghannouj. Here, we replace the usual rich tahini (sesame-seed paste) with yogurt for a lighter puree. Serve the dip at room temperature with crackers, toast points, or raw vegetable pieces.

1   large eggplant
1   tablespoon coarse salt
3   tablespoons olive oil
3   tablespoons nonfat plain yogurt
2   cloves garlic, minced
1   small red onion, minced

½   cup minced fresh flat-leaf parsley
4   teaspoons fresh lemon juice
    Salt and freshly ground black pepper

Remove the stem and cap from the eggplant; halve it lengthwise. Using a fork, randomly prick the skin sides. Sprinkle the cut sides with the salt. Place, cut side down, on a wire rack positioned over a jelly-roll pan and allow to drain for 1 hour. Rinse off the salt with cold running water and pat dry.

Preheat the oven to 400°F.

Lightly brush the cut sides of the eggplant with some of the oil. Place the eggplant, cut side down, in a clean jelly-roll pan. Add the remaining oil to the pan. Roast for 25 minutes, or until quite soft. Remove from the oven and carefully turn the eggplant over. Scoop the pulp into a medium bowl; discard the skin. Pour the oil from the pan into the bowl.

Stir in the yogurt. Add the garlic, onions, parsley, and lemon juice. Season with the salt and pepper. Mix well.

YIELD: 10 SERVINGS

PER SERVING

62 CALORIES
4 G. TOTAL FAT
0.6 G. SATURATED FAT
0 MG. CHOLESTEROL

TUNA TAPENADE
(*Thon avec Tapénade*)

Tapenade is, traditionally, a Provençal condiment made from capers, olives, anchovies, olive oil, and lemon. Occasionally, fresh tuna is added. Here, tuna is the main ingredient for a nonfat version of this French specialty. Serve with crackers, celery sticks, toasted pita triangles, or any cocktail tidbit you like.

1   can (3½ ounces) tuna packed in water, well-drained
¼   cup nonfat cream cheese, at room temperature
2   tablespoons nonfat mayonnaise
1   tablespoon fresh lemon juice
     Freshly ground white pepper
1   cup watercress leaves
½   cup chopped scallions, including the green parts
1½   tablespoons capers, well-drained
1   tablespoon chopped fresh mint

In a food processor fitted with the metal blade, combine the tuna, cream cheese, mayonnaise, lemon juice, and pepper. Process until well-blended. Add the watercress, scallions, capers, and mint. Pulse until well-blended.

YIELD: 10 SERVINGS

PER SERVING

20 CALORIES
0 G. TOTAL FAT
0 G. SATURATED FAT
3 MG. CHOLESTEROL

HERB-MARINATED GOAT CHEESE
(Fromage de Chèvre Mariné aux Herbes)

Use this simple method to add zest to any fresh cheese. If you really want to cut calories and fat, use freshly made yogurt cheese formed into disks. Serve with or without crackers.

10   fresh goat cheese disks (½ ounce each)
5   cloves garlic, halved
2   tablespoons olive oil
4   sprigs fresh thyme
    Coarsely ground black pepper

Place the goat cheese in a shallow glass dish in a single layer. Sprinkle with the garlic. Pour the oil over the top. Strip the leaves from the thyme and sprinkle over the cheese; discard the stems. Generously season with the pepper. Cover and refrigerate for at least 2 hours or up to 2 days.

YIELD: 10 SERVINGS

PER SERVING

67 CALORIES
6 G. TOTAL FAT
2 G. SATURATED FAT
6 MG. CHOLESTEROL

Herb-Marinated Goat Cheese (page 280) and Red Snapper Canapés (page 282)

RED SNAPPER CANAPÉS
(*Canapés aux Filets de Vivaneau*)

This combination of flavors creates a rich-tasting canapé that surprises with its low calorie and fat content.

2	red snapper fillets (6 ounces each), skin on
	Salt and freshly ground black pepper
1	dried red chili pepper, chopped (wear plastic gloves when handling)
1	tablespoon plus ½ teaspoon olive oil
½	bunch arugula, cut into chiffonade (page 31)
½	bunch watercress, cut into chiffonade (page 31)
10	squares peasant bread (2″ × 2″), toasted
2	red radishes, cut into julienne (page 32)

Using a very sharp knife, score the skin side of the fillets, making 2 shallow cuts perpendicular to each other up the center of each fillet. (This will ensure that the fillets will lay flat and cook evenly.) Cut each fillet into 5 equal sections. Season with the salt and black pepper.

Place in a shallow bowl. Add the chili peppers and 1 tablespoon of the oil. Mix well. Cover and refrigerate for 1 hour.

Lightly brush a large nonstick sauté pan with the remaining ½ teaspoon oil. Place over medium-high heat until hot but not smoking. Add the snapper, skin side down. Cook for 3 minutes. Turn off the heat and turn the snapper pieces over, leaving the pan on the hot burner.

In a small bowl, combine the arugula and watercress. Mix well. Neatly mound equal portions on the toast squares. Carefully place a piece of snapper on top of each. Garnish with the radishes and serve immediately.

YIELD: 10 SERVINGS

PER SERVING

74 CALORIES
2 G. TOTAL FAT
0.4 G. SATURATED FAT
10 MG. CHOLESTEROL

CUCUMBER, SHRIMP, AND RADISH CANAPÉS
(*Canapés aux Crevettes, Concombres, et Radis Rouges*)

Interesting flavors and a contrast of textures make this a very appealing hors d'oeuvre.

	White vinegar
10	small shrimp, peeled and deveined

1 medium cucumber, peeled
1 teaspoon coarse salt
¼ cup low-fat mayonnaise
2 teaspoons ketchup
2 teaspoons Dijon mustard
2 red radishes, thinly sliced crosswise

Bring a medium saucepan of water to a boil over high heat. Add a few drops of the vinegar. Add the shrimp and cook for 2 minutes, or until the shrimp are opaque. Immediately drain and rinse under cold running water. Pat dry and set aside until cool enough to handle. Slice the shrimp in half lengthwise. Cover and refrigerate until ready to use.

Cut the ends off the cucumber. Cut a 2½" section from the cucumber; reserve the remainder for another use. Using an apple corer, remove the seeds so you create a hollow tube. Cut crosswise into ¼" slices. Transfer to a colander. Sprinkle with the salt and toss to coat. Set the colander in the sink or over a bowl and allow the cucumbers to drain for 15 minutes. Rinse off the salt with cold running water and pat dry.

In a small bowl, combine the mayonnaise, ketchup, and mustard. Mix well. Lightly coat each cucumber slice with the mayonnaise mixture. Top with a radish slice. Place a dot of the mayonnaise mixture on the radish. Crisscross 2 shrimp halves over the top.

YIELD: 10 SERVINGS

PER SERVING
21 CALORIES
0.5 G. TOTAL FAT
0 G. SATURATED FAT
5 MG. CHOLESTEROL

SALMON CANAPÉS
(*Canapés de Saumon*)

You could replace the salmon in this canapé with any other smoked fish. To further lower calories and fat, you can also replace the low-fat mayonnaise with your favorite nonfat salad dressing.

1 medium cucumber, peeled
1 teaspoon coarse salt
¼ cup low-fat mayonnaise
1 tablespoon Dijon mustard
10 round pieces (1½" thick) pumpernickel bread
10 ounces thinly sliced smoked salmon
2 tablespoons chopped fresh chives

283

Cut the ends off the cucumber. Cut a 1¼″ section from the cucumber; reserve the remainder for another use. Using an apple corer, remove the seeds so you create a hollow tube. Cut crosswise into ⅛″ slices. Transfer to a colander. Sprinkle with the salt and toss to coat. Set the colander in the sink or over a bowl and allow the cucumbers to drain for 15 minutes. Rinse off the salt with cold running water and pat dry.

In a small bowl, combine the mayonnaise and mustard. Mix well. Lightly coat each pumpernickel slice with the mayonnaise mixture. Top with a cucumber slice. Place a dollop of the mayonnaise mixture on the cucumber.

Holding a salmon slice in 1 hand, turn one of the shorter ends in and gently rotate until the salmon resembles a rose. Place a salmon rose on top of each cucumber. Sprinkle with the chives.

YIELD: 10 SERVINGS

PER SERVING

85 CALORIES
2 G. TOTAL FAT
0.4 G. SATURATED FAT
16 MG. CHOLESTEROL

CHICKEN PÂTÉ WITH TARRAGON
(*Pâté de Poulet à l'Estragon*)

This has all the flavor—but little of the calories, fat, and cholesterol—of a traditional French country pâté. Serve with toast points and cornichons (French sour gherkins) or other zesty pickles.

1	pound boneless, skinless chicken breasts
2	large egg whites
⅓	cup nonfat sour cream
2	tablespoons brandy
	Salt and freshly ground white pepper
4	sprigs fresh tarragon
⅓	cup crushed pistachio nuts
10	cups Court-Bouillon (page 42)

Cut the chicken into small pieces. Place three-quarters of the chicken in a food processor fitted with the metal blade. Add the egg whites, sour cream, and brandy. Season with the salt and pepper. Process until the mixture is very smooth. Transfer to a medium bowl. Strip the leaves from the tarragon and add to the bowl; discard the stems. Fold in the pistachios and reserved chicken pieces.

Strain the court-bouillon into a large saucepan; reserve the vegetables for another use. Bring to a boil over high heat. Reduce the heat to medium-low.

Place a large sheet of parchment paper on a flat surface. Mound the chicken mixture on the paper in a neat log shape approximately 2″ × 10″, positioning it about 3″

from a long edge of the paper. Fold the 3″ of paper over the chicken mixture. Roll the paper around the chicken to form a neat cylinder. Twist the ends closed and tie firmly with butcher's twine.

Place the cylinder on a large piece of plastic wrap. Use the same technique to enclose the cylinder. Tie the ends with butcher's twine.

Place in the saucepan. Place a clean kitchen towel over the cylinder to keep it submerged. (Be sure that the towel is folded to lie inside the saucepan and not draped over the top, which could cause a fire.) Simmer for 20 minutes. Carefully remove the cylinder and allow to cool on a wire rack.

Unwrap the log. Cut crosswise into ¼″ slices. Arrange the slices in a decorative pattern on a chilled serving plate.

YIELD: 10 SERVINGS

PER SERVING

124 CALORIES
4 G. TOTAL FAT
0.7 G. SATURATED FAT
36 MG. CHOLESTEROL

WHITE BEAN DIP
(Sauce d'Haricots Blancs)

Serve this dip with crudités—raw vegetable pieces that can be created using any fresh crisp vegetable. Break broccoli or cauliflower into bite-size florets and cut other vegetables (such as green or red bell peppers, carrots, celery, large radishes, jícama, cucumber, or fennel) into decorative, uniform pieces. Leave cherry tomatoes and small radishes whole. Leftover crudités can be made into soup or added to a salad. You may want to line a nice basket with greens and then place the vegetable pieces down into them in a decorative pattern.

1½   cups cooked chick-peas or other white beans
¼   cup nonfat sour cream
¼   cup White Chicken Stock (page 37)
    Juice of ½ lemon
¼   teaspoon cayenne pepper
    Salt

In a food processor fitted with the metal blade, combine the chick-peas or beans, sour cream, stock, lemon juice, and cayenne. Season with salt. Process until well-blended.

YIELD: 10 SERVINGS

PER SERVING

49 CALORIES
0.7 G. TOTAL FAT
0 G. SATURATED FAT
0 MG. CHOLESTEROL

CHRISTMAS DINNER

CRÊPE CONSOMMÉ

LOBSTER SALAD

GREEN AND WHITE BEAN SALAD

ROASTED PHEASANT WITH CABBAGE AND CHESTNUTS

YULE LOG

PER SERVING

1,285 CALORIES

27 G. TOTAL FAT (19% OF CALORIES)

9 G. SATURATED FAT

321 MG. CHOLESTEROL

CRÊPE CONSOMMÉ
(*Consommé Célestine*)

This is an elegant and quite traditional French dish, which is a wonderful prelude to a special occasion or a holiday.

¼	cup skim milk
1	large egg white
	Salt
3	tablespoons cake flour
1	tablespoon chopped fresh tarragon
2	tablespoons chopped fresh flat-leaf parsley
1	teaspoon unsalted butter, melted
12	cups Consommé (page 35)
2	tablespoons chopped fresh chives
	Freshly ground black pepper

In a medium bowl, combine the milk, egg white, and a pinch of salt. Whisk well. Whisk in the flour until smooth. Stir in the tarragon and 1 tablespoon of the parsley.

Lightly brush a nonstick crêpe pan with some of the butter. Place over medium heat. When very hot, pour about one-quarter of the batter into the pan and swirl it around to lightly and evenly coat the bottom. Cook for 2 minutes, or until the bottom is just set. Flip the crêpe by gently lifting 1 side with a knife or fork and then quickly and carefully turning it. Cook for 1 minute, or until the crêpe just starts to brown. Transfer to a plate. Brush the pan with more of the butter and continue making crêpes until all of the batter has been used. You should have 4 crêpes. Using a sharp knife, cut the crêpes into long, thin strips (like noodles).

In a large saucepan, combine the consommé, chives, and the remaining 1 tablespoon parsley. Bring to a simmer over medium-high heat. Season with the salt and pepper.

Pour equal portions of consommé into each of 8 warm shallow soup bowls. Garnish with equal portions of the crêpes.

YIELD: 8 SERVINGS

PER SERVING

144 CALORIES
4 G. TOTAL FAT
2 G. SATURATED FAT
16 MG. CHOLESTEROL

LOBSTER SALAD
(*Salade d'Homard*)

Lobster is one luxurious foodstuff that is actually good for you. Plus, when you serve it, your guests always feel special.

¼	cup fresh orange juice
2	tablespoons balsamic vinegar
4	teaspoons Dijon mustard
	Salt and freshly ground black pepper
2	tablespoons olive oil
12	ounces fresh cranberry beans
5	cups Court-Bouillon (page 42)
2	cups water
1	cup dry white wine
3	lobsters (1½ pounds each)
2	large heads Boston lettuce
3	tablespoons chopped fresh flat-leaf parsley
5	ripe plum tomatoes, peeled, cored, seeded, and diced
4	sprigs fresh tarragon

In a small bowl, combine the orange juice, vinegar, and mustard. Whisk well. Season with the salt and pepper. Whisk in the oil.

Remove the cranberry beans from their pods. Place in a small saucepan and add cold water to cover by about 1″. Add a pinch of salt. Bring to a boil over high heat. Reduce the heat to medium and simmer for 20 minutes, or until the beans are tender. Drain well.

In a stockpot, combine the court-bouillon, water, and wine. Bring to a boil over high heat and boil for 5 minutes. Add the lobsters and return to a boil. Reduce the heat to medium and simmer for 12 minutes.

Using tongs, lift the lobsters from the pot and place them on a plate until cool enough to handle. Remove the claw and tail meat and cut it into bite-size pieces.

Remove and reserve 24 of the large outer leaves from the lettuce. Cut the remaining leaves into chiffonade (page 31). Place the chiffonade in a large bowl.

Add the lobster meat to the bowl. Add the parsley, half of the tomatoes, and half of the beans. Strip the leaves from the tarragon sprigs and add to the bowl; discard the stems. Toss to combine. Pour the vinaigrette over the top and toss to combine. Taste and adjust the seasoning.

Place 3 of the reserved lettuce leaves, overlapping the bottoms slightly to form a lettuce cup, in the center of each of 8 chilled luncheon plates. Place a scoop of lobster salad in each nest and garnish with the remaining beans and tomatoes.

YIELD: 8 SERVINGS

PER SERVING

199 CALORIES
4 G. TOTAL FAT
1 G. SATURATED FAT
5 MG. CHOLESTEROL

GREEN AND WHITE BEAN SALAD
(Salade Panachée d'Haricots Verts et Blancs)

The unusual vinaigrette really brings this low-fat, no-cholesterol side dish to the elegant table. Verjuice, the juice of unripened grapes, can be purchased at most specialty food stores.

12	ounces dry Great Northern beans
2	whole cloves
1	medium onion
1	medium carrot, quartered
1	rib celery, halved crosswise
1	bay leaf
1	pound haricots verts or small green beans, trimmed

Salt
½ cup verjuice or ¼ cup white wine vinegar
½ cup White Chicken Stock (page 37)
1½ teaspoons Dijon mustard
Freshly ground black pepper
2 tablespoons olive oil
1 teaspoon chopped fresh tarragon
1 teaspoon chopped cilantro
1 large red bell pepper, roasted, peeled, seeded, and
diced

Place the dry beans in a large bowl and add cold water to cover by about 3″. Allow to soak for at least 4 hours, changing the water several times. Rinse the beans with cold water; remove and discard any broken or discolored beans. Transfer the beans to a large saucepan.

Stick the cloves into the onion and add to the beans. Add the carrots, celery, and bay leaf. Add cold water to cover by 3″. Bring to a boil over high heat. Reduce the heat to medium and simmer for 1 hour, or until the beans are tender. Drain well; discard the cooking liquid and vegetables. Transfer the beans to a large bowl.

Place the haricots verts or green beans in a medium saucepan and add cold water to cover by about 1″. Add a pinch of salt. Bring to a boil over high heat. Cook for 5 minutes, or until the beans are crisp-tender. Drain well. To stop the cooking, immediately plunge the beans into a bowl of ice water. Drain well and pat dry. Add to the bowl and toss well.

In a small bowl, combine the verjuice, stock, and mustard. Whisk well. Season with the salt and black pepper. Whisk in the oil. Stir in the tarragon and cilantro.

Pour ½ cup of the vinaigrette over the beans; reserve the remainder for another use. Toss to coat well. Taste and adjust the seasoning. Place on a platter. Garnish with the red peppers. Serve at room temperature.

YIELD: 8 SERVINGS

PER SERVING
176 CALORIES
2 G. TOTAL FAT
0.4 G. SATURATED FAT
0 MG. CHOLESTEROL

ROASTED PHEASANT WITH CABBAGE AND CHESTNUTS

ROASTED PHEASANT WITH CABBAGE AND CHESTNUTS
(*Faisan Rôti aux Choux et Marrons*)

*Pheasant is somewhat low in fat, so it is a perfect addition to the health-con-
scious diet. However, since it is a bit expensive, it is usually saved for special-
occasion dining.*

32	fresh chestnuts
⅓	cup water
1½	cups sliced celery
1	teaspoon plus 1 tablespoon butter
2	pheasants (3 pounds each), trimmed of all fat and excess skin
	Salt and freshly ground black pepper
1	teaspoon olive oil
2	shallots, sliced
1½	cups Brown Chicken Stock (page 36) or Brown Veal Stock (page 34)
2	tablespoons brandy
1	head cabbage, cored and shredded

Preheat the oven to 350°F.

Using a paring knife, cut an X into the flat side of the chestnut shells. Place the nuts, in a single layer, in a baking dish. Add the water, ½ cup of the celery, and 1 teaspoon of the butter. Place in the oven until the butter melts. Stir to mix well, then roast for 35 minutes, or until the chestnuts are tender when pierced with a knife. Remove from the oven and cover with a clean kitchen towel. Let stand for 10 minutes. Peel the chestnuts and set aside. Discard the celery.

Raise the oven temperature to 450°F.

Wash the pheasants, inside and out, with cold running water. Pat dry. Generously season, inside and out, with the salt and pepper. Reserve the pheasant necks.

Warm the oil in a large nonstick sauté pan over high heat. Add the pheasants, one at a time if necessary, breast side down. Cook for 4 minutes, or until well-colored. Turn and cook each side until well-colored. Transfer the browned pheasants, breast side up, to a large roasting pan.

Roast for 15 minutes. Add the shallots, pheasant necks, and the remaining 1 cup celery. Reduce the oven temperature to 375°F. Roast for 45 minutes, or until an instant-read thermometer inserted in the center of a breast registers 170°F.

(continued)

Carefully transfer the pheasants to a warm platter. Lightly cover with foil and keep warm.

Drain the liquid from the roasting pan through a fine sieve into a medium bowl; discard the vegetables and necks. Remove and discard the fat from the liquid in the bowl.

Place the roasting pan over high heat and add the stock and brandy. Bring to a boil and deglaze the pan, stirring constantly with a wooden spoon to remove all of the browned bits from the bottom. Reduce the heat to medium and simmer for 5 minutes. Using a fine sieve, strain the sauce into a clean saucepan. Taste and adjust the seasoning.

Just before the pheasants are done, bring a large pot of water to a boil. Add a pinch of salt. Add the cabbage. Cover and cook for 4 minutes. Drain well and shake off excess water. Return the cabbage to the pot. Add the remaining 1 tablespoon butter. Season with the salt and pepper. Toss to combine.

Remove the skin from the pheasants. Slice each breast, on the bias, into 4 pieces. Separate the drumsticks from the thighs on each bird.

Mound equal portions of the cabbage in the center of each of 8 warm dinner plates. Place 2 slices of pheasant breast and a drumstick or a thigh in the cabbage. Arrange 4 chestnuts on each plate. Drizzle the sauce over all. Or, place the cabbage on a large serving platter. Top with the pheasants and carve at the table. Remove and discard the skin before serving. Serve the sauce on the side.

YIELD: 8 SERVINGS

PER SERVING

472 CALORIES
12 G. TOTAL FAT
4 G. SATURATED FAT
156 MG. CHOLESTEROL

YULE LOG
(*Bûche de Noël*)

This traditional French Christmas cake is not only healthy but also quite versatile as it can be made with a variety of fillings. For a simpler presentation, forgo the meringue and dust the filled roll with confectioners' sugar.

7	large egg whites
1½	cups granulated sugar
4	large egg yolks
1½	cups plus 2 tablespoons sifted all-purpose flour
1	tablespoon confectioners' sugar
	Vanilla Pastry Cream (page 56)
1	teaspoon pure vanilla extract

Preheat the oven to 400°F.

Line a jelly-roll pan with parchment paper.

In a medium bowl, combine 4 of the egg whites and 3 tablespoons of the granulated sugar. Beat with an electric mixer on medium speed until soft peaks form. Gradually beat in ¼ cup of the remaining granulated sugar and beat on high speed until the whites are stiff and shiny.

In a large bowl, combine the egg yolks and 1 tablespoon of the remaining granulated sugar. Beat with the mixer on high speed until the mixture is very pale and airy. Using a rubber spatula, fold the beaten whites into the yolks. When well-blended, carefully fold in the flour until well-mixed.

Spoon the batter into the prepared pan and evenly spread it using the spatula. Bake for 9 minutes, or until lightly browned and set in the center. Remove from the oven and place on a wire rack. Let stand for 5 minutes. Do not turn the oven off.

Dust a large piece of parchment paper with the confectioners' sugar. While the cake is still warm, carefully turn it onto the paper. Evenly spread the pastry cream over the surface of the cake.

Using both hands, carefully roll the cake lengthwise into a tight log. Carefully lift up the parchment paper and transfer the cake to a heatproof serving platter or a clean baking sheet; remove the paper.

In a large clean bowl, combine the remaining 3 egg whites with ¼ cup of the remaining granulated sugar. Using clean beaters, beat on medium speed until soft peaks form. Gradually beat in the remaining ¾ cup granulated sugar and beat on high speed until the whites are stiff and shiny. Beat in the vanilla.

Transfer half of the meringue mixture to a pastry bag fitted with a large star tip. Press on the bag to form meringue strips lengthwise over the top and sides of the log to completely cover the cake. Form vertical strips on each end to totally cover the log.

Remove the star tip from the pastry bag and replace it with a large round tip. Place the remaining meringue in the bag and create decorative mushrooms on the meringue-covered log: Quickly press the bag once to form a short stem; then squeeze quickly to form a round cap on top of the stem. Scatter these mushrooms on and around the log.

Bake for 4 minutes, or until the log is evenly browned. Remove from the oven and allow to stand in a dry area for at least 15 minutes.

When ready to serve, cut crosswise into 1″ slices.

Chef's Note: You can make a chocolate sponge cake by replacing about 3 tablespoons of the flour with cocoa powder. You can make chocolate pastry cream by making the adjustments to the Vanilla Pastry Cream suggested on page 56.

YIELD: **16** SERVINGS

PER SERVING

294 CALORIES
5 G. TOTAL FAT
2 G. SATURATED FAT
144 MG. CHOLESTEROL

A Winter Night by the Fire

Phyllo-Wrapped Brie

White Bean Brandade

Endive Salad

Duck Pot-au-Feu with Winter Vegetables

Pear Cake

PER SERVING
1,176 CALORIES

38 G. TOTAL FAT (29% OF CALORIES)

11 G. SATURATED FAT

168 MG. CHOLESTEROL

Phyllo-Wrapped Brie
(*Fromage de Brie aux Feuilles Légères*)

This easy-to-do and very pretty appetizer is a wonderful indulgence. Pears or grapes can also be served along with or in place of the apples.

2	tablespoons warm water
1	tablespoon unsalted butter, melted
2	sheets phyllo dough
1	round (4 ounces) Brie cheese
	Coarsely ground black pepper
2	large apples, peeled, cored, and thickly sliced

Preheat the oven to 450°F.

In a small bowl, combine the water and butter. Whisk well to blend. Place 1 sheet of phyllo on a nonstick baking sheet; keep the remaining sheet covered with a damp paper towel. Using a pastry brush, lightly coat the phyllo with some of the butter mixture, making sure to cover the dough completely, especially the edges. Top with the remaining phyllo sheet and brush with the butter mixture. Fold the sheets in half crosswise.

Place the Brie in the center of the folded phyllo. Generously season with the pepper. Neatly fold the phyllo up and over the Brie to enclose it. Brush the edges with the remaining butter mixture and press them closed to tightly seal the packet. Turn the Brie over so that the seam side is facing down and the top is smooth.

Bake for 7 minutes, or until the phyllo is crisp and the cheese is soft. Transfer to an attractive serving plate. Surround the Brie with the apple slices. Serve warm.

YIELD: 8 SERVINGS

PER SERVING

285 CALORIES
8 G. TOTAL FAT
4 G. SATURATED FAT
18 MG. CHOLESTEROL

WHITE BEAN BRANDADE
(*Brandade d'Haricots Blancs*)

Traditionally, a brandade might be flavored with pressed dried tuna roe. Here, we use a few anchovies to add dimension to the mellow white bean puree. Brandade can also be served as an accompaniment to roasts.

1⅓	cups dry white beans
4	whole cloves
1	medium onion
3	cloves garlic
1	medium carrot, halved
3	anchovy fillets, well-drained
	Juice of ½ lemon
¼	cup olive oil
⅓	cup 2% reduced-fat milk
	Salt and freshly ground black pepper
1	large baguette, thinly sliced and toasted

Place the beans in a large bowl and add cold water to cover by about 3". Allow to soak for at least 4 hours, changing the water several times. Rinse the beans with cold water; remove and discard any broken or discolored beans.

Transfer the beans to a large saucepan. Add cold water to cover by about 3". Stick the cloves into the onion and add to the saucepan. Add the garlic and carrots. Bring to a boil over high heat. Reduce the heat to medium and simmer for 1½ hours, or until the beans are very soft. Drain through a fine sieve; discard the cooking liquid and the vegetables.

(continued)

295

Place the beans in a food processor fitted with the metal blade. Add the anchovies and lemon juice. Process briefly. Slowly add the oil, pulsing to incorporate it. Add just enough of the milk to soften the puree without making it pourable. Season with the salt and pepper.

Transfer to a bowl. Place the bowl on a tray and surround it with the toasts. Serve warm.

YIELD: 8 SERVINGS

PER SERVING

181 CALORIES
7 G. TOTAL FAT
1 G. SATURATED FAT
2 MG. CHOLESTEROL

ENDIVE SALAD
(*Salade d'Endives*)

This is a light salad to precede the rich pot-au-feu. If you can't find endive, use any tart green.

½   cup low-fat plain yogurt
2   tablespoons 1% low-fat milk
1   tablespoon Dijon mustard
1   tablespoon minced fresh dill
1   tablespoon minced shallots
    Salt and freshly ground black pepper
8   large Belgian endives, well-washed and cut into
        eighths

In a small bowl, combine the yogurt, milk, and mustard. Whisk well. Stir in the dill and shallots. Season with the salt and pepper.

Place 1 whole endive on each of 8 chilled salad plates. Drizzle with the dressing.

YIELD: 8 SERVINGS

PER SERVING

19 CALORIES
0.3 G. TOTAL FAT
0 G. SATURATED FAT
0 MG. CHOLESTEROL

DUCK POT-AU-FEU WITH WINTER VEGETABLES
(*Pot au Feu de Canard aux Légumes d'Hiver*)

Healthy and satisfying, pot-au-feu is a perfect winter's meal. If you are not a fan of duck, you can replace it with chicken or turkey.

2	ducklings (3½ pound each), trimmed of all fat and skin
4	medium carrots, cut on the bias into ½″ slices
4	ribs celery, peeled and cut into 2″ pieces
	Salt
4	medium turnips, peeled and quartered
	Freshly ground black pepper
4	large all-purpose potatoes, peeled and quartered
¾	cup nonfat sour cream
2	tablespoons Dijon mustard
2	teaspoons freshly grated horseradish
2	cornichons (French sour gherkins), minced

Wash the ducklings, inside and out, with cold running water. Pat dry.

Place in a large pot and add cold water to cover by about 3″. Bring to a boil over high heat. Reduce the heat to medium and simmer for 15 minutes, frequently skimming off any fat that rises to the top.

Add the carrots and celery. Season with the salt. Simmer for 45 minutes. Add the turnips and simmer for 12 minutes. Taste and adjust the seasoning with salt and pepper.

Place the potatoes in a large saucepan and add cold water to cover by about 1″. Add a pinch of salt. Bring to a boil over high heat. Reduce the heat to medium and cook for 20 minutes, or until tender when pierced with a fork. Drain well and keep warm.

In a small bowl, combine the sour cream and mustard. Whisk well. Fold in the horseradish and cornichons. Transfer to a small serving bowl.

Remove the ducks from the broth and place them on a plate to cool slightly. Keep the broth and vegetables warm.

Using a boning knife, carefully remove the breasts from the ducks; slice each breast in half on the bias. Remove the legs and separate the thighs from the drumsticks. Carefully debone the thighs. Place the pieces in a soup tureen. Add the cooking broth and vegetables.

(continued)

297

DUCK POT-AU-FEU WITH WINTER VEGETABLES (PAGE 297)

Place the tureen on the table and ladle into individual shallow soup bowls. Pass the horseradish mixture to be used as a condiment.

YIELD: 8 SERVINGS

PER SERVING

373 CALORIES
7 G. TOTAL FAT
2 G. SATURATED FAT
102 MG. CHOLESTEROL

PEAR CAKE
(*Gâteau aux Poires*)

This cake can also be made with apples. If desired, serve it with nonfat vanilla frozen yogurt.

2	teaspoons unsalted butter
1	tablespoon plus 1½ cups all-purpose flour
1½	teaspoons baking powder
½	teaspoon salt
3	medium pears, peeled, cored, and cubed
¼	cup granulated sugar
½	teaspoon ground cinnamon
2	large eggs
1	teaspoon pure vanilla extract
	Grated zest of ½ lemon
	Juice of 1 lemon
½	cup canola oil
3	tablespoons confectioners' sugar

Preheat the oven to 350°F.

Using your fingers, lightly coat a 6-cup Bundt pan with the butter. Dust with 1 tablespoon of the flour.

Place the remaining 1½ cups flour in a sifter. Add the baking powder and salt. Sift into a medium bowl.

In another medium bowl, combine the pears, granulated sugar, and cinnamon. Toss to combine.

In the large bowl, combine the eggs, vanilla, lemon zest, and lemon juice. Beat with an electric mixer on medium speed until well-combined. Beat in the oil. Fold in the flour mixture. Fold in the pear mixture until well-combined.

Transfer to the prepared pan. Bake for 1 hour, or until a cake tester inserted in the center comes out clean. Transfer to a wire rack to cool.

Invert onto a cake plate and dust with the confectioners' sugar. Cut into slices.

YIELD: 10 SERVINGS

PER SERVING

318 CALORIES
16 G. TOTAL FAT
4 G. SATURATED FAT
46 MG. CHOLESTEROL

INDEX

G